Cambridge Imperial and Post-Colonial Studies Series

The Cambridge Imperial and Post-Colonial Studies series is a collection of studies on empires in world history and on the societies and cultures which emerged from colonialism. It includes both transnational, comparative and connective studies, and studies which address where particular regions or nations participate in global phenomena. While in the past the series focused on the British Empire and Commonwealth, in its current incarnation there is no imperial system, period of human history or part of the world which lies outside of its compass. While we particularly welcome the first monographs of young researchers, we also seek major studies by more senior scholars, and welcome collections of essays with a strong thematic focus. The series includes work on politics, economics, culture, literature, science, art, medicine, and war. Our aim is to collect the most exciting new scholarship on world history with an imperial theme.

More information about this series at
http://www.palgrave.com/gp/series/13937

Ellen R. Feingold

Colonial Justice and Decolonization in the High Court of Tanzania, 1920–1971

palgrave
macmillan

Ellen R. Feingold
Georgetown University
Washington, DC, USA

Cambridge Imperial and Post-Colonial Studies Series
ISBN 978-3-319-69690-4 ISBN 978-3-319-69691-1 (eBook)
https://doi.org/10.1007/978-3-319-69691-1

Library of Congress Control Number: 2017959100

Cover illustration: Photo courtesy of Alexander K. Dewar

Printed on acid-free paper

This Palgrave Macmillan imprint is published by Springer Nature
The registered company is Springer International Publishing AG
The registered company address is: Gewerbestrasse 11, 6330 Cham, Switzerland

For my husband, Alexander K. Dewar, and our daughter, Hannah Pearl,
with an abiding love.
And
In honour of the memory of Dr Jan-Georg Deutsch—rigorous scholar,
imaginative teacher, devoted mentor, and very dear friend.

Acknowledgements

I should like to express my deepest gratitude to those who have supported me in this research project. First and foremost, I am grateful to Dr Jan-Georg Deutsch, who was a devoted and inspiring mentor to me for ten years before his passing in 2016. He helped guide this project from the beginning, and his steadfast support and enthusiasm for this book helped propel it to completion. I will always be indebted to him for training me and generously sharing his creativity and time.

I also thank five other Oxford historians: Prof. Judith Brown, Prof. John Darwin, Prof. Avner Offer, Dr Karl Gerth, and Prof. Antony Kirk-Greene for their advice at various stages of my research. Prof. Kirk-Greene's wonderful encouragement and his essential advice to place a notice in *The Overseas Pensioner* to locate former members of the colonial administration and judiciary in Tanganyika proved to be more fruitful than either of us imagined. It opened up lines of enquiry and provided evidence that I would have found inaccessible, and it made this project much richer than it otherwise would have been. I am also grateful to the Overseas Service Pensioners' Association for placing my notice in their journal, which allowed me to meet so many of its members.

The most satisfying element of this research was interviewing and corresponding with the men and women whose recollections are cited in the chapters and listed in the bibliography. Their generosity with their memories, time, contacts, and personal papers was humbling and invaluable to this project. Beyond sharing their own personal narratives, they helped to shed light on the roles of their long-deceased colleagues, friends, and family members who left behind few records, but have been examined in this book as a result of interviewees' willingness to share their memories with me. Sadly, some of those interviewed for this project have become ill and passed away since I interviewed them, in some cases within months of the interview. I hope that the publication of this book will allow them to take their places in the history of the legal system of Tanzania.

I received help from many people during my fieldwork in Tanzania in 2008. I am grateful to the United Republic of Tanzania for permitting me to carry out my research. I thank Dr Chris Maina Peter for advising me during my fieldwork, as well as other members of the Tanganyika Law Society and Law Reform Commission who offered me advice. I am also grateful to Ilvin Mugeta and Ken LuePhang for their assistance during my time in Dar es Salaam.

I am very grateful to the following bodies at the University of Oxford for their financial assistance: the John Roberts Fund (supported by Merton College and the History Faculty); the Beit Fund; the History Faculty's Arnold, Bryce and Read Funds; the Colin Matthew Fund; the Merton College Research Grant Fund. I would also like to thank the International Seminar on Decolonization in Washington, DC, for giving me the opportunity to conduct research at the National Archives and Library of Congress, and the seminar leaders Prof. W. Roger Louis, Prof. Philippa Levine, Prof. Dane Kennedy, Prof. Jason Parker, Prof. Marilyn Young, and seminarians for their supportive feedback on my work at a crucial stage in the project. Furthermore, I am thankful to the staff at the libraries and archives I visited in Tanzania, the UK, and the USA for their assistance; and to Merton College for providing a vibrant intellectual home during my time at Oxford.

I was remarkably fortunate to find a welcoming community of scholars and colleagues at Georgetown University in Washington, DC, who kindly included me in the African Studies Program in the School of Foreign Service. I am deeply grateful to Prof. Scott Taylor, Prof. Lahra Smith, and Prof. Kathryn de Luna for their openheartedness and friendship. The completion of this book would not have been possible without their support.

I thank the whole team at Palgrave Macmillan, and especially my editors, Molly Beck and Oliver Dyer, for their hard work on behalf of this book, as well as the series editors, Prof. Richard Drayton and Prof. Saul Dubow, for selecting it for their series. I am also grateful to the two anonymous peer reviewers for their thoughtful feedback.

Many colleagues and friends gave me helpful advice on this project. I warmly thank Dr Sarah Stockwell, Dr Leigh Gardner, Dr Yonina Murciano-Goroff, Dr Margret Frenz, Dr Michelle Osborn, and Dr Sarah Weicksel. Similarly, I say *asante sana* to Dr Festo Mkenda for his friendship and guidance.

With love and appreciation, I thank my parents Susan Feingold and Russell Feingold, my stepfather and stepmother, Chester Dussault and Christine Ferdinand, and my sister and brother-in-law, Jessica Feingold Lieberson and Jeffery Feingold Lieberson, for providing continuous encouragement throughout my academic career and especially during my years at Oxford. I also want to honour the memory of my inspiring grandmothers, Pearl Levine and Sylvia Feingold, and grandfathers, Herbert Levine and Leon Feingold, whose love of the law was contagious.

Finally, I thank my husband, Alexander Dewar, for his unwavering confidence in me and this project. No words can convey the depth of my gratitude to him for his true partnership in our life together and for helping me see this book through to completion.

Contents

1 Introduction 1

Part I The High Court of Tanganyika Under British Rule, 1920–1958 23

2 Building a Judiciary for the Empire: The Development of the Colonial Legal Service 25

3 The Marginalisation of the High Court Under Indirect Rule, 1920–1944 53

4 The Resurgence and Expansion of Tanganyika's Judiciary, 1945–1958 87

Part II Decolonising the High Court of Tanganyika, 1959–1971 133

5 Restructuring Colonial Justice, Empowering the High Court, 1959–1964 135

6 Colonial Judges in a Fading Empire, 1961–1965 165

7 Foreign Judges and the Emergence of a Tanzanian Judiciary, 1964–1971 201

8 Conclusion 237

Bibliography 245

Index 267

Abbreviations and Conventions

Abbreviations

ARJ	Annual Report of the Judiciary of Tanganyika/Tanzania
CO	Colonial Office
COL	Colonial Office List
DO	Dominions Office
HO	Home Office
ICS	Indian Civil Service
LCO	Lord Chancellor's Office
LSE	London School of Economics and Political Science Archive, London
MCA	Magistrates' Courts Act of 1963
NACP	National Archives of the United States of America, College Park, MD
RG	Record Group
RHL	Bodleian Library of Commonwealth and African Studies at Rhodes House, Oxford
s/o	'Son of', used in court documents to identify African parties in court
TANU	Tanganyika African National Union
TNA	Tanzania National Archives, Dar es Salaam
TNA (UK)	The National Archives of the United Kingdom, Kew
TSL	Tanganyika Staff List

1 T.L.R. (R)	Tanganyika, *Law Reports of the Cases Determined by the High Court of Tanganyika and on Appeal for Eastern Africa: 1921–1952*, Vol. 1 (revised), (Dar es Salaam, 1955).
2 T.L.R. (R)	Tanganyika, *Law Reports of the Cases Determined by the High Court of Tanganyika and on Appeal for Eastern Africa and the Privy Council: 1953–1957*, Vol. 2 (revised), (Dar es Salaam, 1959).

Conventions

All abbreviations from the above list are given after the first full use in the text or endnotes, other than the two volumes of the revised Tanganyika Law Reports (T.L.R.), which are abbreviated throughout.

Citations of the published Annual Report of the Judiciary of Tanganyika/ Tanzania, Colonial Office List, and Tanganyika/Tanzania Staff List are cited with the abbreviated title (after first use) and the year. For example, the Tanganyika Staff List for the year 1959 is cited as TSL 1959.

Appointment and retirement data were generated from published Tanganyika/ Tanzania Staff Lists, Colonial Office Lists, and Annual Reports of the Judiciary of Tanganyika/Tanzania, unless otherwise noted.

Individuals' names in the text are given with the first name, middle initial, and last names at first use where possible (when first names are unverified first initial is given instead) and cited by the surname only thereafter. Names of interviewees and the holders of private collections in the endnotes and bibliography are given with first and last name only and are listed in full at each use. Names in the endnotes from primary sources are given in the standard form (initials for first and middle names and full surname). Where a name is unknown in archival documents, it is listed as unknown. In the case of unknown names in documents from within the Colonial Office, [CO] is used in the citation to indicate that the author was an employee within the Colonial Office.

List of Figures

Fig. 1.1	Justice Philip Biron's grave in Kinondoni Cemetery	2
Fig. 1.2	Close-up of headstone of Justice Philip Biron's grave in Kinondoni Cemetery	2
Fig. 2.1	Chart showing legal appointments as a percentage of all appointments by the Colonial Office, 1919–1944	31
Fig. 2.2	Chart showing the number of legal appointments by the Colonial Office, 1919–1944	44
Fig. 4.1	The High Court of Tanzania	116
Fig. 4.2	The mural at the High Court of Tanzania	117
Fig. 4.3	Left panel of the mural at the High Court of Tanzania	118
Fig. 4.4	Right panel of the mural at the High Court of Tanzania	119
Fig. 6.1	The building that housed the Dar es Salaam Club during colonial rule and became the home of the Court of Appeal of Tanzania in 1979	177
Fig. 6.2	A portrait of Justice Philip Biron hanging in the High Court of Tanzania	186
Fig. 7.1	A portrait of Chief Justice Philip Telford Georges hanging in the High Court of Tanzania	210
Fig. 7.2	Chart showing categories of judges on the High Court Bench, 1961–1971	223

All photos by A.K. Dewar and E.R. Feingold, Dar es Salaam, December 2008. Photos of the High Court of Tanzania and Court of Appeal of Tanzania taken and reprinted with the permission of the photographers and the Court of Appeal of Tanzania.

CHAPTER 1

Introduction

In January 1982, members of Tanzania's Bar and Bench gathered in Dar es Salaam's leafy Kinondoni cemetery. Under the shade of two large trees, against the back wall of the cemetery, they witnessed the burial of a man who was the last of his kind in Tanzania (see Figs. 1.1 and 1.2).[1] To some of the mourners, the deceased man was a mentor, personal friend, and custodian of the common law system. To others, he was a relic, a remnant of a bygone era. He was Tanzania's last colonial judge.

Justice Philip Biron died in Dar es Salaam almost exactly 20 years after Tanzania gained independence from Great Britain in December 1961. When Biron first arrived in Tanganyika in 1949 British colonial rule in East Africa appeared to be deeply entrenched. Under the employ of the Colonial Legal Service, Biron started his career as a Resident Magistrate, responsible for administering colonial justice according to the British law in Tanganyika.[2] In the decade that followed, he was promoted through the ranks of the colonial judiciary and, in 1961, as Tanganyika transitioned from colony to nation, Biron became a judge of the High Court. For the 20 years that followed, until his death on 31 December 1981, Biron remained on the High Court Bench, forging personal and professional relationships based on his commitment to the new nation that allowed him to outlast every other former member of the British colonial government.

E.R. Feingold, *Colonial Justice and Decolonization in the High Court of Tanzania, 1920–1971*, Cambridge Imperial and Post-Colonial Studies Series, https://doi.org/10.1007/978-3-319-69691-1_1

Fig. 1.1 Justice Philip Biron's grave in Kinondoni Cemetery (Photo by A.K. Dewar and E.R. Feingold, Dar es Salaam, December 2008)

Fig. 1.2 Close-up of headstone of Justice Philip Biron's grave in Kinondoni Cemetery (Photo by A.K. Dewar and E.R. Feingold, Dar es Salaam, December 2008)

During his more than 30-year career in Tanganyika Biron witnessed the growth and decline of the colonial state as an agent of one of the most durable colonial institutions: the High Court of Tanganyika (later the High Court of Tanzania).[3] This Court was one of a multitude of common law courts established by the British in the process of imperial expansion.[4] Among the colonial state institutions the British introduced to their colonies, colonial high courts have been some of the most enduring. These high courts have not only remained intact since the transfer of political power from Great Britain to national governments, but often still sit atop national justice systems, adjudicating some of the most high-profile and controversial cases. The prevalence of common law courts in the British Empire and the survival of these institutions after independence speaks to their utility to colonial authorities and post-independence governments, yet they have been largely overlooked in studies of colonial rule and decolonisation. As the first study of its kind, this book tells the story of the development and decolonisation of a British colonial high court in Africa.

Two central questions drove this study. First, what was the role of colonial high courts and their judges in British colonial rule? Second, why did colonial high courts survive the end of British rule and how did post-independence governments transform them into national institutions? To explore these broad questions, this book traces the history of a single colonial high court, the High Court of Tanganyika, from its establishment in 1920 to the end of its institutional process of decolonisation in 1971.

The High Court of Tanganyika is representative of many of the colonial high courts across the British Empire in terms of its structure, the characteristics of its judges, and the procedures they followed. The British set up the High Court of Tanganyika during the early stages of British rule of the territory, after gaining authority over Tanganyika from Germany under a League of Nations mandate following the end of the World War I. Great Britain took over administration of Tanganyika through a political agreement, rather than through settlement or direct conquest, and the High Court was among a group of colonial state institutions the British established in the early 1920s to formally initiate British rule. This book examines the High Court of Tanganyika's development alongside the establishment and growth of the colonial state and indirect rule system, as well as in relation to the political changes that preceded and followed Tanganyika's national independence in 1961.

The High Court of Tanganyika is a new lens through which to examine the formation of colonial state structures and the process of decolonisation.

This book weaves together the rich history of this institution with a study of its judges, both as a cohort and as individuals, to explore the intersection of imperial policies, national politics, and individual initiative. This approach draws on and contributes to the study of British colonial legal systems, colonial administration and professions, and the process of decolonisation.

Colonial Legal Systems of the British Empire

As Great Britain expanded its empire, it introduced the common law system to new places and peoples around the world. This 'global process' of spreading the common law tradition became a defining feature of British imperialism and remains a legacy of the British Empire.[5] The diffusion of the common law system was not an accidental by-product of empire-building, but rather a crucial instrument of imperial expansion and governance. It served as both a vehicle of imperial ideology and an ideological justification for imperialism;[6] it was 'proof' that imperial expansion was not only about the occupation of land and extraction of resources, but rather was driven by a so-called 'civilising mission' that involved the extension of 'British legal traditions': the rule of law and equity before the law.[7] Common law was also a tool—and sometimes a forceful weapon[8]—of colonial governance that allowed the British to influence the social, political, and economic structures and relationships in their colonies.[9] As the common law system spread across the Americas, Asia, and Africa, it also helped to connect 'disparate parts' of the Empire and provided a common ground for the exchange of policy and staff.[10] Of course, the common law tradition did not fill a legal void in the places to which it travelled, but rather competed with and eventually dominated pre-existing (though not static) 'customary' legal traditions and systems.[11]

Since the decline of colonial rule in the mid-twentieth century, the field of colonial legal history has grown significantly with diverse local, national, and, more recently, global studies.[12] These studies have shown the great variation in and disputes over laws, legal practices, and control of legal institutions within and across modern empires. From this work, it is increasingly evident that the study of colonial law is riddled with paradoxes. For example, Martin Chanock's study of law under British rule in Malawi and Zambia shows that while it was a tool of colonial domination and social and economic transformation, it was also a means through which colonial subjects could resist and reshape colonial rule.[13] Martin

Weiner's study of interracial homicide trials in the British Empire reveals the contradiction between the principles behind the common law system and its application in the colonies. He asserts that while the use of common law was held up as evidence of British liberalism and used as a justification for British expansion, in practice colonial officials used the law to reinforce racial inequality.[14] Underpinning both of these arguments, however, is not a paradox, but the current guiding principle in the field, which is that colonial law was a place of engagement between colonial authorities, settlers, and colonial subjects, and that all three groups sought to use the law to define their relationships to one another.[15] This engagement often took place within the framework of colonial legal institutions that both shaped legal disputes and were shaped by them.

Colonial court systems were a hallmark of British colonial rule in the twentieth century. A crucial machinery of 'formal' colonial states, the courts enforced colonial laws on issues central to the colonial project, such as land, labour, and taxation.[16] British colonial court systems were hierarchical with colonial high courts at the top, subordinate courts in the middle, and Native or customary courts at the bottom.[17] As part of the British policy of indirect rule in Africa, colonial court systems were bifurcated by race. Cases involving Europeans were heard in the common law courts. While cases involving Africans that were not of interest to colonial authorities or related to serious crimes—such as disputes over dowries or child custody—were heard before African authorities and decided according to assertions of custom, with varying provisions for appeal to the highest courts across the colonies.[18]

This hierarchical system, with colonial high courts at the top and customary courts at the bottom, reflects the shift Lauren Benton describes from the 'truly plural legal orders' of early modern empires to the hierarchical and dominant colonial legal systems of modern empires, such as the British Empire.[19] As the British set up new colonial states in Africa in the early twentieth century, the colonial court systems they introduced replicated or reflected the colonial legal hierarchies that had been negotiated or tested elsewhere in the Empire, leaving less room for 'jurisdictional politics' to shape colonial legal structures.[20] The result was markedly uniform systems of colonial legal hierarchy with similar, recognisable institutions of colonial legal authority across a geographically and culturally diverse population.[21]

Notwithstanding the large number of British colonial high courts in Africa and across the British Empire, they have rarely been the subject of careful study.[22] Research has largely focused instead on the courts below and above them in the colonial legal hierarchy. Among the lower-level courts, customary courts have received the most scholarly attention.[23] This is unsurprising given that they heard the largest number of cases and were the courts with which Africans would have interacted. Though far fewer in number, studies of the subordinate common law courts have provided valuable insights into the internal tensions of the indirect rule system between the colonial executive and judiciary over the extension of magisterial powers to administrative officers.[24] Above the colonial high courts were two layers of 'imperial justice', namely the courts of appeal for West and East Africa and the Judicial Committee of the Privy Council.[25] Bonny Ibhawoh's recent book on these imperial courts argues that they were key places where 'colonial legal modernity' was fashioned through the hearing of appeals from colonial high courts.[26] This study focuses on the colonial high courts that sat between the courts of and for Africans and the imperial courts in order to demonstrate the central roles of colonial high courts in the operation and legitimisation of British colonial rule, as well as their impact on it.

British Colonial Judges and the Colonial Legal Service

The British colonial judges that staffed colonial high courts played vital roles in the establishment and maintenance of British rule both inside and outside the courtroom. They adjudicated the most significant civil cases, providing a venue for the resolution of commercial disputes and thereby facilitating the growth of commerce. They also heard serious criminal cases and served as the literal 'cutting edge of colonialism', handing down the most severe penalties, including the death penalty.[27] Beyond deciding cases, colonial judges were agents of the common law tradition and colonial authorities used them as evidence of Britain's proclaimed commitment to 'civilise' colonial subjects through the rule of law. Colonial judges also offered a form of legal leadership and acted both as educators for administrators in their magisterial duties and as a check on them through the reviewing and revising of the decisions of lower courts and hearing of appeals. In short, colonial judges not only represented British judicial ideals, but actually affected a wide range of individuals' lives and livelihoods, directly and indirectly.

Despite their significant and varied roles in colonial rule, there has been little research on twentieth-century colonial judges compared with the substantial body of literature on their administrative counterparts.[28,29] This may be in part because colonial judges have been seen as a category of colonial administrator in studies of colonial professions and administration. For example, to find information on colonial judges in Lewis Gann and Peter Duignan's fundamental work on colonial authorities in British Africa, one must look in the chapter entitled 'The District Officer' under the subheading 'The Judges' and the section is less than seven pages long.[30] Moreover, compared with administrative officers, relatively few judges wrote memoirs of their experiences, leaving little evidence of their personal perspectives on their work and motivations for joining the colonial judiciary.[31]

This book aims to write colonial judges back into the history of colonial administration, alongside and in relation to other colonial professions, to demonstrate that colonial judges were distinct from administrators but still central to the colonial project. To that end this book examines the formation and development of the Colonial Legal Service—the body tasked with staffing colonial benches across much of the Empire in the twentieth century. The Colonial Office established the Colonial Legal Service in 1933 as a separate branch of the Colonial Service in order to standardise policies on recruitment, preparation, compensation, retirement, and more, across the colonial Empire.[32] This change freed colonial legal officers from territory-specific policies and made the Colonial Legal Service more flexible, enabling the Colonial Office to transfer legal officers and judges to any colony that needed them.[33] However, the new rules also detached legal officers from the specific colonies where they served, disconnecting them from the environments and circumstances in which colonial subjects and settlers lived.

Colonial Legal Service policies produced a particular type of judge, one who neither fit into the British legal community nor was wholly integrated into life in the colonies. The result was a judiciary for the Empire, a network of judges who connected the colonies to one another as they moved around and linked the metropole to the 'periphery', without being grounded in either place.[34] Donning powdery white wigs and heavy red or black robes, colonial judges appeared to be better suited to work in the Inns of Court in London than in the tropical climates of many colonial capitals. Despite their appearance, however, they were not an extension of the British Bar. They were specially moulded by the Colonial Legal Service to serve the dual—and at times conflicting—roles as agents of both common law tradition and Empire.

Critical to our understanding of the Colonial Legal Service is how the policies governing the lives and work of colonial judges affected the administration of justice in the colonies. This book uses the High Court of Tanganyika and its judges to connect the history of the Colonial Legal Service to the indirect rule system and to explore the interplay between colonial policy and colonial practice. It examines the roles and positions of colonial judges within the colonial state from the earliest stages of British rule through the decade following national independence. Connecting policies to practices over a 50-year period crucially demonstrates that the role and position of the judiciary shifted over time in relation to changing philosophies of colonial governance as well as to circumstances in the metropole, Tanganyika, and across the British Empire.

Colonial High Courts and Decolonisation

Since most colonial high courts survived the end of British rule with few obvious changes, they can appear relatively unaffected by the process of decolonisation. Indeed, many national high courts continue to operate in the stately courthouses built by colonial governments in the early and mid-twentieth century, some still decorated with symbols of British authority. Yet colonial high courts were not only impacted by the end of colonial rule, but also played a role in the process of decolonisation.

The roles of colonial high courts in the twilight of British rule varied; in some places they supported the colonial governments' actions and policies aimed at destroying independence movements, while in others they worked to limit colonial violence.[35] For example, David Anderson argues that in Kenya the colonial high court was a crucial tool in the government's attempts to crush the Mau Mau rebellion, noting that British judges handed down the death penalty to 1090 individuals accused of crimes against the colonial state.[36] Conversely, in Nyasaland (Malawi) a British judge was employed to critically investigate the way in which the colonial government, especially the police, had responded to protest in the colony.[37] Yet little is known about the role of courts in colonies that had relatively peaceful transitions of power, such as Tanganyika.

Even less is known about how colonial courts, as institutions, decolonised. Since the decline of the British Empire, scholarship on decolonisation has primarily focused on 'high politics' and global dynamics, exploring the question of why the Empire ended.[38] In recent years, new research has begun to shift towards the question of how institutions and individuals in the colonies and Great Britain influenced the process of decolonisation, strategised in relation to it, and were affected by it.[39] That shift has highlighted the limitations of using the moment of constitutional independence or 'transfer of power' as a definition of decolonisation. This book argues that decolonisation, as it relates to colonial states, can be more fruitfully defined and described as a process in which state institutions broke away from colonial structures and systems, and were increasingly shaped by national and local forces rather than imperial policies and practices.[40] The decolonisation of state institutions was connected to the transfer of political power, but often began subtly before the actual date of independence and continued incrementally for many years after the collapse of colonial political structures.

There are two key factors in the decolonisation of colonial courts: structure and personnel. The structure of colonial court systems and colonial state governments largely determined the degree of independence of colonial high courts from colonial administrations as well as their relationships to colonial subjects. Tracing how the position of a court changed relative to these structures in the decades preceding and following independence highlights the specific features that supported the maintenance of British colonial rule and were targeted by post-colonial governments for change. In Tanganyika the decolonisation of the High Court involved restructuring the national court system to give the High Court jurisdiction over all citizens—a jurisdiction it lost in the early stages of indirect rule—and separating officers with administrative functions from magisterial work. The post-colonial government also used the national constitution to remove remnants of colonial executive oversight of the Court, making it the principal institution of a more independent judiciary.

Personnel, both in terms of background and training, is another key factor in the process of institutional decolonisation. Africanisation, the replacement of colonial officials with local African officials, is often regarded as evidence of decolonisation of an institution in Africa. In the decolonisation of colonial high courts, Africanisation was an important aspect of national ownership of the judicial system, but the process was elongated and more complicated than in the administrative and policing sectors because of the professional training required of judges in a common law system. Moreover, the decolonisation of a Bench was not only a matter of who was employed, but also the extent to which colonial ideologies relating to race dictated eligibility to serve in the judiciary. Thus colonial and post-colonial racial categorisations inside and outside the courtroom are a central theme in this book. In Tanganyika, Africanisation of the Bench took place over the course of a decade and relied on the participation and leadership of colonial judges and of foreign judges from former British colonies with training in the common law system. It also involved British and foreign law professors, who trained many of East Africa's first African barristers.[41]

In its examination of Court personnel, this book highlights the importance of analysing the roles of individuals in the transition of state institutions. The end of the Empire created an opportunity for individuals to have a greater influence on institutions than they could when they were linked to wider imperial structures and networks. During British rule Colonial Legal Service policies and colonial state structures left little room for individual colonial judges to have a significant impact on the development and structural position of colonial high courts. In the early 1960s, however, when British imperial structures began to dissolve, colonial state institutions were released from colonial state systems, but were not yet completely integrated into and operated by post-colonial states. This process of institutional decolonisation allowed individual judges to exert greater influence over the courts and their own career trajectories. They began to operate as independent actors, rather than agents of Empire. One significant outcome of this process in Tanganyika was that, in the decade following independence, British, African, and foreign judges sat together on the Bench for the first time. This book provides the first account of how this diverse group of judges helped transform the High Court into a national institution, while forging personal and professional relationships that were underpinned by their shared commitment to the survival of the High Court and common law system after the end of British rule.

In tracing the development and decolonisation of the High Court of Tanganyika, this book argues that the High Court's symbolic and practical roles in the colonial state, and its position relative to the administration, reinforced administrative authority over Africans. Africans were prevented from accessing the High Court and participating in the administration of justice outside the Native Courts. After the end of British rule, Tanganyika's post-colonial government decolonised the High Court by modifying its relationship to the executive and lower courts in order to increase its independence and Africans' access to it, and by appointing Africans to its

Bench to replace the colonial judiciary. In short, the decolonisation of the High Court involved disentangling it from colonial state structures and imperial systems that were built upon racial inequality and administrative dominance, while enhancing the independence of the judiciary and the application of British judicial principles and ideals.

The High Court of Tanganyika: Method and Sources

Histories of courts are often written through the analysis of large numbers of cases or landmark decisions. Jay Gordon asserts that 'The legal mind is content to trace the development of laws and institutions and to describe the changes that have taken place. The historian, however, must start where the lawyer leaves off, and search for reasons that brought about such changes and the effects these changes themselves had'.[42] While a traditional legal approach to the history of the High Court of Tanganyika would provide an important perspective on the work of the Court, this history instead focuses on court structures, relationships, and personnel—and the political and social forces shaping them—utilising a limited number of strategically selected cases and key changes to the law to trace the Court's development. The themes of judicial independence, the separation of powers, and the rule of law guide this book's analysis of the Court and its role in the colonial and post-colonial states over a 50-year period. This approach amplifies the value of this study beyond its specific findings in Tanganyika. Tanganyika certainly had many distinctive features—its status as a League of Nations mandate territory, comparatively small expatriate and settler populations, and peaceful transfer of political power—but this book's central questions and approach are applicable to other British colonial high courts. Moreover, the High Court of Tanganyika's core features, such as the profile of its judges and the nature of the cases it heard, present similarities to other colonial high courts, enabling this case study to shed light on key aspects of British colonial justice beyond Tanganyika's borders.

While this is the first history of the High Court of Tanganyika as an institution, this work builds on two studies of Tanganyika's courts. First, Morris and Read's *Indirect Rule and the Search for Justice* examines the framework of indirect rule in Tanganyika, the development of the territory's laws, and the structure of the colonial court system.[43] Their study provided a crucial foundation for this book's analysis of the functions of the High Court and its judges in the context of indirect rule, particularly before World War II. On the other end of this study's chronological boundaries, Jennifer Widner's *Building the Rule of Law: Francis Nyalali and the Road to Judicial Independence in Africa* explores challenges to the rule of law and independence of the judiciary in sub-Saharan Africa in the 1980s and 1990s through a biography of Tanzania's second African Chief Justice, Francis Nyalali, who took office in 1977.[44] This study is chronologically situated between these two works and offers an alternative perspective on the role of the High Court in the search for justice under British rule and the establishment of judicial independence in the post-colonial state.

This study relies on a combination of largely untapped documentary and oral sources. Public and private archives in Tanzania and the United Kingdom provide essential evidence of the changing role and position of the Court in the colonial and post-colonial states, and of the activities of its judges. This archival material also sheds light on how Colonial Office policies shaped the colonial judiciary and affected its relationship to the colonial administration and colonial subjects. State department files written by American diplomats and informants held at the National Archives of the United States offer an external perspective on the political changes affecting the Court in the 1960s and the foreign judges who arrived to serve in the magistracy and on the High Court Bench. Traditional legal sources, including case files, ordinances, and constitutions also provide primary evidence of changing legal structures and practices during British rule and in the decade following independence.

Oral history interviews were another crucial source for this study. They offered a rare and wholly unique look inside the High Court and the dynamics between judges—a perspective that documentary sources do not provide. Fifty individuals in Tanzania and the United Kingdom shared their memories of their work and lives in Tanganyika, including a former colonial judge (and family members of deceased judges), colonial magistrates, colonial administrative officers, the first Tanganyikan African judges and advocates (including two former Chief Justices), Asian advocates working in Tanganyika before and after independence, a foreign judge, a court interpreter, the first two Attorneys General after independence, and staff and students from the Faculty of Law in Dar es Salaam in the 1960s.[45,46] In particular, testimonies from the colonial, Asian, and African judges (and their family members) who served on the Bench in the 1960s provided unparalleled insights into the process of decolonising the Bench.[47] They also offered a unique perspective on how colonial judges framed their continuity and authority in the Court, especially after national independence.

The interviewees' largely collegial and even reverential tones towards one another—and especially towards some of the deceased colonial and foreign judges—should be understood through the lens of a shared legal culture and profession as well as a belief in a collective mission to preserve the common law tradition. Though the law was a powerful tool of British colonial authority in Africa, many interviewees framed the common law and its agents as separate from the colonial administrative project and regarded it as holding greater legitimacy than other colonial legacies. The aim of this book is not to endorse this point of view, but rather to emphasise that the positive and somewhat 'time-transcendent' narrative about the common law expressed by interviewees enabled them to separate colonial judges and the Court from other aspects of British colonial rule, thereby regarding both as compatible with the independent nation and participants in the process of decolonisation.[48]

Chapter Structure

This book is organised chronologically and divided into two parts. Part I comprises Chaps. 2, 3, and 4, which examine the High Court of Tanganyika during British rule, from 1920 until 1958. Part II comprises Chaps. 5, 6, and 7, which examine the process of the decolonisation of the High Court of Tanganyika between 1959 and 1971.

Chapter 2 explores the development of the Colonial Legal Service and its policies on recruitment, training, appointments and promotion structures, lifestyle in the colonies, dismissal, and retirement. It argues that the Colonial Office's efforts to build a judiciary for the colonial Empire detached colonial legal officers from the specific colonies in which they served and shaped the nature and practice of colonial justice in ways that affected both the judges and the judged. The chapter also confronts widespread stereotypes of colonial judges as second-rate barristers who could not succeed at the English Bar by offering a nuanced assessment of the range of backgrounds of barristers who joined the Colonial Legal Service and the variety of factors motivating them to serve on the Bench.

The third chapter examines the High Court of Tanganyika during the period between the beginning of British rule in 1920 and the start of World War II. It argues that in the late 1920s, as the system of indirect rule became more deeply entrenched and standardised in Tanganyika, colonial judges and professional magistrates were increasingly marginalised in the sphere of colonial justice by the administration. The primary mechanism of this was the Native Courts Ordinance of 1929, which removed Native Courts from the jurisdiction of the High Court and allowed the administration to prevent Africans from accessing the High Court. This reduced the roles of judicial authorities while enhancing the judicial powers of administrative officers. Though severely limited in their role in the administration of justice after 1929, the chapter asserts that colonial judges were nonetheless essential to British rule in Tanganyika because they served both symbolic and practical functions, which facilitated the development of the territory and the maintenance of British rule.

Chapter 4 begins after the conclusion of World War II and argues that in the context of the Colonial Office's efforts towards reconstruction and development in the colonies, and the colonial administration's movement away from some of its indirect rule policies, colonial judges began to regain some of the ground they had lost in 1929. Changes to the judiciary and structure of the court systems inside and outside of Tanganyika between 1945 and 1958 enhanced the jurisdiction and stature of Tanganyika's colonial judiciary. The size and geographic reach of the professional judiciary in Tanganyika expanded and the government took the first steps towards integrating the dual court systems, giving colonial judges a role in deciding, though not complete jurisdiction over, appeals from Native Courts. It concludes by asserting that, as the movement for independence in Tanganyika developed in the late 1950s, the administration turned to the judiciary for help in containing political activity and, as independence approached, used the High Court and its judges in an attempt to reframe the legacy of British colonial rule of the territory.

Chapter 5 explores how Tanganyika's first (1961) and second (1962) constitutions gave the judiciary a greater degree of independence from the executive than it had had during colonial rule and severed the ties between Tanganyika and Great Britain. Once the constitutional framework was in place the government worked to unify the colonial court systems and, between 1962 and 1964, replaced the lower courts with a new system of magistrates' courts, all under the jurisdiction of the High Court. The chapter illustrates how the unification of the dual court systems gave Africans the access to the High Court they were denied during British rule and restored the jurisdiction the High Court lost in 1929. It argues that the unification enhanced the status of the Court in the country and empowered its judges by giving them supervision over an entirely professionalised magistracy and removing all judicial powers from administrative officers.

Though the structure of the colonial court systems was overhauled from 1962, the colonial High Court Bench remained almost entirely intact during the structural decolonisation of the colonial courts. Between 1962 and 1964 many sectors of the government were partly or fully 'Africanised', but the post-colonial government was committed to maintaining professional legal standards for the judiciary, regarding these standards as essential for a democratic state. Thus the dearth of Tanganyikan Africans with legal qualifications prevented the government from placing any Africans on the Bench during this period. Chapter 6 argues, paradoxically, that colonial judges remaining on the Bench was an important part of the process of decolonisation because it allowed the government to maintain the standards set out in the constitution for appointments to the Bench and gave it time to train African citizens to become judges. The chapter also investigates the motivations of colonial judges and magistrates for staying on the Bench and how they framed the choices they made during the twilight of the British Empire.

As colonial judges departed in the mid-1960s the government replaced them with a combination of local and foreign judges. Though the government's goal was to see Tanganyikan Africans join the Bench and magistracy, there were still too few with legal training to fill the open seats. Rather than appoint local Asian advocates to the Bench, President Julius Nyerere appointed foreign judges from West Africa and the West Indies to the magistracy and High Court Bench to serve temporarily. Chapter 7 argues that these foreign judges served as a stepping stone between a colonial Bench and a local one. It also explores the position of foreign judges in the new nation and their responses to early executive encroachment on the independence of the judiciary. The chapter discusses the first Africans to join the Bench, including the first Tanganyikan African judges who earned their legal qualifications abroad and those Africans trained at the new Faculty of Law in Dar es Salaam established in 1961. By 1971 Africans accounted for the majority of High Court judges and the government appointed the first Tanganyikan African Chief Justice. As the structural changes in the early and mid-1960s were also complete by that time, the conclusion of the decolonisation of the Bench in 1971 also marked the end of the process of decolonising the High Court as an institution.

Justice Biron served on the Bench throughout the decolonisation of the High Court of Tanganyika. Like the Court, Biron slowly became more identified with the nation than the Empire that had originally brought him to East Africa. His personal transition from British colonial judge to Tanzanian judge both facilitated the Court's decolonisation and mirrored it. To some, Biron's burial in Dar es Salaam in 1982 broke the final tie between the High Court of Tanzania and Great Britain. To others, however, it marked the death of the first post-colonial High Court judge.

Notes

1. R.J. Muya, interview with author, Dar es Salaam, 17 December 2008.
2. An outline of the offices Biron held is available in: *Who Was Who, 1981–1990: A Companion to Who's Who Containing the Biographies of Those Who Died During the Decade 1981–1990* (London, 1991), p. 66.
3. The term High Court of Tanganyika is used throughout this book to refer to the court prior to the merger of Tanganyika with the island nation of Zanzibar in 1964 that resulted in the creation of Tanzania. The term High Court of Tanzania will be used to refer to the court after the union of the two nations. Even after union, the legal systems of Tanganyika and Zanzibar remained separate and the focus in this book is on the High Court of the mainland. The only notable impact of the union on the High Court of the mainland was that it gained jurisdiction over cases relating to the union itself, of which there were no instances during the 1960s.
4. *Black's Law Dictionary* defines common law as, 'a body of law derived from judicial decisions, rather than statues or constitutions'. The legal systems introduced by the British into their territories were based on common law tradition as well as its procedures, structures, and judicial authorities. In practice, British colonial legal systems combined English common law with local case law, territorial legislation, and statutes. This type of legal system is distinct from the civil law tradition, which relies on codified bodies of law and was introduced by other European imperial powers to their colonies. A.B. Garner and H.C. Black, *Black's Law Dictionary*, 9th edn (St. Paul, 2009), p. 313.
5. S. Engle Merry, 'From Law and Colonialism to Law and Globalization', *Law and Social Inquiry*, 28 (2003), p. 570; M.J. Weiner, *An Empire on Trial: Race, Murder, and Justice Under British Rule* (Cambridge, 2009), p. 5.
6. J. Fisch, 'Law as a Means and as an End: Some Remarks on the Function of European and Non-European Law in the Process of European Expansion' in W.J. Mommsen and J.A. De Moor (eds.), *European Expansion and Law: The Encounter of European and Indigenous Law in 19th- and 20th-Century Africa and Asia* (Oxford, 1992), p. 15.
7. Weiner, *An Empire on Trial*, p. 1.

8. Comaroff uses another term, lawfare, to describe how colonial authorities used the law in 'the effort to conquer and control indigenous peoples by the coercive use of legal means'. J. Comaroff, 'Colonialism, Culture, and the Law: A Foreword', *Law & Social Inquiry*, 26 (2001), pp. 305–314.
9. W.J. Mommsen, 'Introduction' in W.J. Mommsen and J.A. De Moor (eds.), *European Expansion and Law: The Encounter of European and Indigenous Law in 19th- and 20th-Century Africa and Asia* (Oxford, 1992), p. 2.
10. L.A. Benton, *Law and Colonial Cultures: Legal Regimes in World History, 1400–1900* (Cambridge, 2002), p. 3.
11. Inverted commas around the words 'customary' and 'traditional' in relation to African history and culture are included at first use to problematise assumptions about African tradition and custom under colonial rule, but are removed after first use for readability.
12. A recent volume edited by Shaunnagh Dorsett and John McLaren aims to encourage comparative and transnational approaches to imperial legal history and is one of the first works to draw together geographically and chronologically diverse studies on key themes in the field. See: S. Dorsett and J. McLaren (eds.), *Legal Histories of the British Empire* (Oxford, 2014).
13. M. Chanock, *Law, Custom, and Social Order: The Colonial Experience in Malawi and Zambia* (Cambridge, 1985), p. 4; Engle Merry, 'From Law and Colonialism to Law and Globalization', p. 578.
14. Weiner, *An Empire on Trial*, p. 1.
15. K. Mann and R. Roberts, *Law in Colonial Africa* (London, 1991), p. 3.
16. Robinson and Gallagher's notion of the 'formal' Empire is used here to differentiate between colonies where colonial administrators were present versus 'informal' territories under the economic and/or political influence of an imperial power, but without direct administration or the establishment of a legal system with legal officers. J. Gallagher and R. Robinson, 'The Imperialism of Free Trade', *The Economic History Review*, 6 (1953), pp. 1, 5–7. The analysis in this book is confined to the formal British Empire. The terms colonies and territories are used to refer broadly to the range of British 'dependencies' in the twentieth century, including crown colonies, mandated territories, and protectorates. Dominions are referred to separately and as such.
17. Another term often used for superior courts in British colonies was Supreme Court, while High Court was often used in protectorates, but there was no practical difference in status or function. High Court is used preferentially throughout this book to refer to the superior court in a British colonial legal system. J.H. Jearey, 'The Structure, Composition and Jurisdiction of Courts and Authorities Enforcing the Criminal Law in British African Territories', *The International and Comparative Law Quarterly*, 9 (1960), p. 397.

18. In Tanganyika, cases initiated in Native Courts could be appealed to the High Court until the Native Courts Ordinance of 1929 severed their relationship to the common law court system and placed their jurisdiction under the Governor and administrative service. The significance of this shift for the administration of justice in Tanganyika and operation of the colonial administration is explored in Chap. 3.
19. L. Benton, 'Colonial Law and Culture Difference: Jurisdictional Politics and the Formation of the Colonial State', *Comparative Studies in Society and History*, 41 (1999), p. 564; Benton, *Law and Colonial Cultures*, p. 28.
20. Benton defines jurisdictional politics as: 'conflicts over the preservation, creation, nature, and extent of different legal forums and authorities'. Benton, *Law and Colonial Cultures*, p. 10.
21. Benton, 'Colonial Law', pp. 563, 588.
22. One notable exception is a recent book by Abhinav Chandrachud on the history of the High Court of Bombay. A. Chandrachud, *An Independent, Colonial Judiciary: A History of the Bombay High Court during the British Raj, 1861–1947* (New Delhi, 2015). For an overview of the high courts in British colonies in Africa, see: Jearey, 'The Structure, Composition and Jurisdiction', pp. 397–401. The study that provides the most focused analysis on a colonial high court in Africa is Adewoye's work on the judicial system in Southern Nigeria from 1854 to 1954, which has a chapter on the Supreme Court of Nigeria. The chapter primarily examines judgments made by the Court and the focus of the book overall is on the operation of the judicial system rather than on the roles of colonial judges and development of the Supreme Court as an institution. O. Adewoye, *The Judicial System in Southern Nigeria, 1854–1954: Law and Justice in a Dependency* (London, 1977), pp. 253–278.
23. For an overview of the variety of Native Courts systems in Africa, see: Jearey, 'The Structure, Composition and Jurisdiction', pp. 409–414.
24. See, for example, H.F. Morris, 'English Law in East Africa: A Hardy Plant in an Alien Soil' in H.F. Morris and J.S. Read, *Indirect Rule and the Search for Justice: Essays in East African Legal History* (Oxford, 1972), p. 104; Y.P. Ghai and P. McAuslan, *Public Law and Political Change in Kenya: A Study of the Legal Framework of Government from Colonial Times to the Present* (Nairobi, 1970), pp. 138–147.
25. B. Ibhawoh, *Imperial Justice: Africans in Empire's Court* (New York, 2013), p. 6. On the Privy Council, see also D.B. Swinfen, *Imperial Appeal: The Debate on the Appeal to the Privy Council, 1833–1986* (Manchester, 1987).
26. Ibhawoh, *Imperial Justice*, p. 4.
27. The phrase 'cutting edge of colonialism' is used by Chanock to describe the law, but is extended here to emphasise the severity of punishments handed down by colonial judges. Chanock, *Law, Custom, and Social Order*, p. 4.

28. A notable development in this field is a recent dissertation and three articles by Paul Swanepoel. His research on the judges of Kenya and Tanganyika was conducted concurrently with this study and takes a different approach to analysing colonial judges. Swanepoel examines specific court cases and the biographies of individual judges to analyse their personal perspectives and judicial preferences. See P. Swanepoel, 'Indifferent Justice? A History of the Judges of Kenya and Tanganyika, 1897–1963', Ph.D. thesis (University of Edinburgh, 2010); P. Swanepeol, 'Kenya's Colonial Judges: The Advocates' Perspective', *Journal of Asian and African Studies*, 50 (2015), pp. 41–57; P. Swanepoel, 'Transient Justice: Colonial Judges on Circuit in Interwar Tanganyika', *Stichproben: Vienna Journal of African Studies*, 24 (2013), pp. 65–91; P. Swanepeol, 'Judicial Choice during the Mau Mau Rebellion in Kenya, 1952–1960', *Fundamina*, 18 (2012), pp. 145–161.
29. For example, on recruitment and training of administrative officers, see: R. Heussler, *Yesterday's Rulers: The Making of the British Colonial Service* (Syracuse, 1963). For studies of governors as a group of officials, see: L.H. Gann and P. Duignan, *African Proconsuls: European Governors in Africa* (London, 1978); A.H.M. Kirk-Greene, 'Scholastic Attainment and Scholarly Achievement in Britain's Imperial Civil Services: The Case of the African Governors', *Oxford Review of Education*, 7 (1981), pp. 11–22. For a study of junior officers, see: A.H.M. Kirk-Greene, *Symbol of Authority: The British District Officer in Africa* (London, 2006).
30. L.H. Gann and P. Duignan, *The Rulers of British Africa, 1870–1914* (London, 1978), pp. 233–239.
31. For a list of memoirs by former administrative officers, see: T. Barringer, *Administering Empire: An Annotated Checklist of Personal Memoirs and Related Studies* (London, 2004). There are very few memoirs written by colonial judges. The best examples are: G.G. Alexander, *From the Middle Temple to the South Seas*, 1st edn (London, 1927); G.G. Alexander, *Tanganyika Memories: A Judge in the Red Kanzu* (London, 1936).
32. The Colonial Service provided officers to British colonies in the West Indies, Mediterranean, Middle East, Atlantic and South Atlantic, Africa, Far East, Southeast Asia, Pacific, and Central America.
33. The phrase colonial legal officer refers to all officials working in a legal capacity, including but not limited to judges, attorneys general, court registrars, and solicitors general. The phrase is used to denote the larger community of officers with legal qualifications in a territory. Though the focus of this book is on colonial judges, as appointments to colonial benches were made from within the community of legal officers and all legal officials were subject to the same employment procedures and conditions, they are included in this study where their roles intersected with the work of the high courts.

34. On networks and Empire, see: A. Lester, *Imperial Networks: Creating Identities in Nineteenth Century South Africa and Britain* (London, 2001); A. Lester, 'Imperial Circuits and Networks: Geographies of the British Empire', *History Compass*, 4 (2006) pp. 124–141.
35. For a comparative study of the responses of colonial governments to disorder in colonies in the mid-twentieth century, see R.F. Holland, *Emergencies and Disorder in the European Empires after 1945* (London, 1994).
36. D. Anderson, *Histories of the Hanged: Britain's Dirty War in Kenya and the End of Empire* (London, 2005), pp. 6–7.
37. W.B. Simpson, 'The Devlin Commission (1959): Colonialism, Emergencies, and the Rule of Law', *Oxford Journal of Legal Studies*, 22 (2002), p. 17.
38. On 'high politics' see: S. Stockwell, 'Ends of Empire' in S.E. Stockwell (ed.), *The British Empire: Themes and Perspectives* (Malden, 2008), p. 269. For a discussion of the historiographical debate on the causes of decolonisation of the British Empire, see J. Darwin, *The End of the British Empire: The Historical Debate* (Oxford, 1991), especially pp. 1–9; J. Darwin, 'Decolonization and the End of Empire' in R.W. Winks (ed.), *Oxford History of the British Empire* (5 vols., Oxford, 1999), v, pp. 544–555; Stockwell, 'Ends of Empire', pp. 277–282.
39. Of the organisations and institutions within Great Britain affected by the process of decolonisation, political parties have received most attention in the literature, see, for example, P. Murphy, *Party Politics and Decolonization: The Conservative Party and British Colonial Policy in Tropical Africa, 1951–1964* (Oxford, 1995). Another budding body of literature looks at how religious organisations in Great Britain responded to decolonisation, for example, see: S.E. Stockwell, '"Splendidly Leading the Way"?: Archbishop Fisher and Decolonisation in British Colonial Africa' in R. Holland and S.E. Stockwell (eds.), *Ambiguities of Empire: Essays in Honour of Andrew Porter* (New York, 2009), pp. 199–218. On businesses in the colonies and decolonisation, see: S.E. Stockwell, *The Business of Decolonization: British Business Strategies in the Gold Coast* (Oxford, 2000); L.J. Butler, *Copper Empire: Mining and the Colonial State in Northern Rhodesia, c. 1930–64* (Basingstoke, 2007), pp. 255–299. On churches and missionaries in the colonies and decolonisation, see B. Stanley and A.M. Low, *Missions, Nationalism, and the End of Empire* (Grand Rapids, 2003); D. Maxwell, 'Decolonisation' in N. Etherington (ed.), *Missions and Empire, the Oxford History of the British Empire Companion Series* (Oxford, 2005), pp. 285–306. On decolonisation and administrative services, see: A.H.M. Kirk-Greene, *Britain's Imperial Administrators, 1858–1966* (Basingstoke, 2000), pp. 263–273; D.C. Potter, *India's Political Administrators: From ICS to IAS*, 1st Indian edn (Delhi, 1996). And on

the police, see D. Anderson and D. Killingray, *Policing and Decolonisation: Politics, Nationalism and the Police, 1917–65* (Manchester, 1992); G. Sinclair, *At the End of the Line: Colonial Policing and the Imperial Endgame 1945–1980* (Manchester, 2006).

40. Sarah Stockwell offers a similar definition of the process of state building at the end of Empire, arguing that decolonisation involved 'disentangling colonial institutions from the British imperial system' and that this process should be conceptualised as 'institutional devolution and transition' rather than the 'decolonization of the colonial state'. S. Stockwell, 'Exporting Britishness: Decolonization in Africa, the British State, and its Clients' in M.B. Jeronimo and A.C. Pinto (eds.), *The Ends of European Colonial Empires: Cases and Comparisons* (London, 2015), p. 148.
41. On the development of the legal profession in Tanganyika, see: F. Twaib, *The Legal Profession in Tanzania* (Bayreuth, 1997). Twaib's work is focused on Tanzania's private legal profession and does not examine the judiciary.
42. J. Gordon, 'African Law and the Historian', *The Journal of African History*, 8 (1967), p. 338.
43. H.F. Morris and J.S. Read, *Indirect Rule and the Search for Justice: Essays in East African Legal History* (Oxford, 1972). In addition, numerous other works provide overviews of the development of Tanganyika's legal system and the position of the High Court relative to the lower courts. Those that were of the most assistance to this study other than Morris and Read's book include: P. Moffett, 'Native Courts in Tanganyika: A History of the Development of Native Courts from German Times', *Journal of African Administration*, 4 (1952); A.N. Allott, 'The Development of the East African Legal Systems During the Colonial Period' in D.A. Low and A. Smith (eds.), *History of East Africa* (3 vols., Oxford, 1976), iii, pp. 348–382; J.L. Mwalusanya, *The Judiciary in Tanzania* (Dar es Salaam, 1988); Court of Appeal of Tanzania, *The History of the Administration of Justice in Tanzania* (Dar es Salaam, 2004), pp. 28–48.
44. J.A. Widner, *Building the Rule of Law: Francis Nyalali and the Road to Judicial Independence in Africa*, 1st edn (New York, 2001).
45. A list of the individuals interviewed can be found in the bibliography. Some interviewees gave multiple interviews and all interviews were conducted in person, except where otherwise noted. One former Chief Justice is Barnabas Samatta, the other is Augustino Ramadhani, who was Chief Justice at the time of interview and has since retired. Augustino Ramadhani, interview with author, Dar es Salaam, 12 November 2008; Barnabas Samatta, interview with author, Dar es Salaam, 3 December 2008.
46. The term Asian is used in this book to refer to people whose heritage is from countries that are now India and Pakistan.

47. All of the surviving judges from the 1960s were interviewed, including: Louis Makame, interview with author, Dar es Salaam, 19 December 2008; Harold Platt, interview with author, Graz, 30 January 2010; Harold Platt, interview with author, Graz, 31 January 2010; David Williams, interview with author, London, 17 March 2010; Ulric Cross, interview with author, by telephone from Port of Spain, 28 February 2010; Ulric Cross, interview with author, London, 17 August 2010. Family members of deceased judges from the 1960s interviewed and corresponded with for this research included the widow of Justice Eric Law, the children of Justice Abdulla Mustafa, and the son and widow of Chief Justice Saidi: Patricia Law, interview with author, Canterbury, 14 May 2009; Daniel Augustino Saidi (with Elizabeth Kilasara [Saidi]), Dar es Salaam, 18 December 2008; Fawzia Mustafa, correspondence with author, 4 September 2009; Kemal Mustafa, correspondence with author, 15 October 2009.
48. This idea generates from Lee Cabatingan's description of the Caribbean Court of Justice has having a 'time-transcendent' narrative that helps legitimise the young institution. L. Cabatingan, 'Time and Transcendence: Narrating Higher Authority at the CCJ', *Law and Society Review*, 50 (2016), p. 674.

PART I

The High Court of Tanganyika Under British Rule, 1920–1958

CHAPTER 2

Building a Judiciary for the Empire: The Development of the Colonial Legal Service

The creation of the Colonial Legal Service in 1933 and the training of its cadre of colonial judges was a vital part of British colonial state building in the early twentieth century. Following the rapid increase in the number of Britain's formal colonies and subsequent need for a supply of legal officers trained in the common law tradition to staff colonial courts, the development of the Colonial Legal Service marked a significant departure from the piecemeal approach to staffing British colonial courts in the nineteenth century.

The organisation of legal officers serving in British territories into a separate, specialised branch of the Colonial Service allowed the Colonial Office to standardise the policies governing their appointments and employment. This standardisation enabled the Colonial Office to respond to growing staffing crises in colonial courts by transferring legal officers from one colony to the next to fill vacancies, without obstruction from colonial administrations or judges themselves. This approach was not only pragmatic, but was also a reflection of British thinking about the nature and function of a twentieth-century British colony. Colonial administrations relied on a range of institutions replicated from colony to colony, with different types of officers with specialised training.[1] Among them, legal officers with training in the common law tradition were a key part of the framework of the modern British colonial state.

E.R. Feingold, *Colonial Justice and Decolonization in the High Court of Tanzania, 1920–1971*, Cambridge Imperial and Post-Colonial Studies Series, https://doi.org/10.1007/978-3-319-69691-1_2

Colonial Legal Service policies on the training and employment of colonial magistrates and judges differed substantially from those of the Colonial Administrative Service. This chapter traces the development of the Colonial Legal Service and provides an original account of the policies governing the recruitment and employment of legal officers, including an examination of the preparation for their work, promotion structures, lifestyles in the colonies, and retirement. By comparing these policies with those of the Colonial Administrative Service, it is evident that the need for colonial legal officers to be geographically flexible played a key role in shaping the Colonial Legal Service. The differences between the policies of the two services became a source of tension and intense debate within territorial administrations and the Colonial Office during the interwar period. The Colonial Office's efforts to build a judiciary for the Empire was at odds with administrative perspectives on the importance of local knowledge in the administration of colonial justice.

Colonial Legal Service policies contributed to a pre-existing negative reputation of colonial legal officers from the nineteenth and early twentieth centuries, who were accused of being divorced from local conditions, aloof, and second rate. This chapter examines and confronts the stereotypes surrounding colonial judges and offers an alternative perspective on their identities and work. Yet the purpose of this analysis is not to rehabilitate the reputation of colonial judges but to demonstrate how the creation of the Colonial Legal Service and the application of its policies had a tangible impact on the administration of justice in British colonies. Colonial Legal Service policies detached legal officers as a cohort from the specific colonial environments in which they served and the British legal community more broadly. As a result, colonial judges could dispense justice anywhere in the Empire, but belonged nowhere, or at least were neither as at home in Britain as British lawyers nor in the colonies as colonial administrators. Thus colonial judges became a kind of global judiciary—a judiciary for the Empire—that facilitated the logistics of imperial administration, but limited judges' roles and engagement with the places and people they judged.

Approaches to Staffing British Colonial Benches

Judicial structures in Britain's early colonies were diverse. Many did not have a centralised judicial system nor professional colonial legal officers in residence. For instance, in eighteenth-century Newfoundland, Justices of the Peace were stationed in various locations throughout the territory, but sent individuals accused of serious crimes and felonies directly to Great Britain for trial.[2] As the British Empire expanded and transformed in the nineteenth century, however, centralised territorial court systems became the model in Britain's colonies. These centralised systems included high courts, which were staffed by political officers or legal professionals either from the territory or Colonial Office or a combination of both.[3] Barristers in the metropole and in colonies with a well-developed local Bar typically became candidates for appointment to the colonial bench through the patronage and endorsement of an influential person, such as a senior barrister or judge.[4] Thus, the make-up of colonial benches was influenced by individuals and local circumstances, as was the administration of justice. John McLaren, in his recent book on the nineteenth-century British colonial judiciary, argues 'how justice and law were administered across the Empire varied considerably, depending on the level of attention of the imperial government, the stability or otherwise of political, economic, and social conditions, and the extent to which there was an existing or developed legal infrastructure ready and able to take on the challenges'.[5]

By the early twentieth century colonial authorities began to take a more active role in defining and redefining who could serve on colonial courts in terms of professional qualifications, citizenship status, and race. The British broadly utilised two approaches to staffing their high-level colonial courts during the twentieth century.[6] The first model involved combining professional jurists with civil servants drawn from both Britain and the colony and enrolled in the same service. This was the method that developed in India after the Indian Civil Service (ICS) began formally administering it in the mid-nineteenth century. The ICS employed British and Indian civil staff, both of whom would serve as magistrates during their time in the civil service and could be promoted in the judicial sphere without professional legal training.[7] These civil servants, regardless of race, could eventually serve on one of the regional High Courts located in Calcutta, Madras, Bombay, Allahabad, Patna, and Lahore.[8] Rules were specific about the proportional mix of these groups, though. One third of a High Court Bench had to be comprised of professional barristers of the United Kingdom, a further third by the judicial segment of the ICS, and the final third could be drawn from either group or directly from the Indian Bar.[9] This combination of High Court judges was intended to harness both the legal expertise of British barristers and the 'intimate knowledge of the customs, habits and laws of India possessed by Judges belonging to the Civil Service'.[10] Such a mixing of professional lawyers with civil servants on one bench, combined with the policy of allowing British barristers to work alongside Indian and British civil officers, was unusual in the British Empire.

Most British colonies operated in line with the second staffing model, in which the Colonial Office selected and deployed professional English, Irish, and Scottish barristers (and in some cases solicitors) to specific high-level colonial courts.[11] Administrative officers without legal training served as low-level magistrates, but were usually not promoted to the level of judge, as civil servants were in India. Judges who were a part of the Colonial Service—the colonial judges—were a distinct group from administrative officers, even before the creation of the Colonial Legal Service in 1933.

The Colonial Service did not usually employ colonial subjects as colonial judges. This exclusion was rarely a point of debate, however, as most colonial subjects in the territories where this model was in use would not have had access to the legal education necessary to be qualified to apply for judicial positions in the Colonial Service. In the colonies under the jurisdiction of the Colonial Office and where there was a Bar with local barristers, they were integrated into the system in varying degrees, although not often elevated to the highest courts and typically restricted from entering the Native Courts as legal representation for other colonial subjects.

Prior to the rapid expansion of the British Empire into Africa, the phrase Colonial Service did not refer to an organised staffing body, but rather described the practice of the Colonial Office helping to provide staff to the colonies. Antony Kirk-Greene's extensive research on the Colonial Service shows that it developed with, and as a result of, British imperial engagement in Africa, although it served all of Britain's colonies that did not have their own services like India did.[12] As Great Britain institutionalised its new colonial states in the early twentieth century, the Colonial Service not only grew in size, but also transformed into a single entity.

The words Colonial Service often conjure up images of the Colonial Administrative Service. Young district officers and regal colonial governors were important 'symbols of authority' on the ground.[13] Their prominence in the operation and image of the colonial state easily obscures the role of colonial judges and magistrates, who are often seen as a relatively small subgroup of administrators with legal training.

One perceived similarity between colonial legal officers and administrative officers that allows them to be more easily grouped together in larger analyses is their socio-economic background. There is a common perception that colonial judges were a part of the same social class as other senior colonial administrators. Hailing from aristocratic and upper middle-class households in, or originally from, the urban centres in Great Britain, these families often had a commitment to and at times investment in the Empire.[14] Daniel Duman, however, has challenged the stereotype that colonial barristers and judges were all part of the social elite and painted a more nuanced picture, arguing that many of the men in the colonial Bar and on the Bench, while not socio-economically disadvantaged, were more likely to be part of the middle or upper-middle class, such as sons of colonial civil servants and merchants.[15] His analysis of colonial chief justices in the nineteenth century shows that less than 30% were 'the sons of landowners or of members of the gentlemanly professions'.[16] On the whole, colonial barristers and judges were usually 'less privileged' than their 'counterparts who practiced in England'.[17] Nevertheless, a large proportion of colonial officers in the twentieth century, including legal officers, were educated at elite public schools and attended either Oxford or Cambridge, which were producing nearly half of all appointees to the Colonial Service by the late 1920s.[18] Colonial legal officers certainly mixed with the elite layers of society, even if they were not from the top.

Any differences in background between legal officers and administrators, however, are relatively insignificant when compared with the differences in the policies of the Colonial Legal Service and the Colonial Administrative Service. A close study of the development of these policies reveals the distinctions between judges and administrators that impacted the administration of justice and the people in the colonies where these legal officers served.

Recruitment and Appointments

In the 1920s Colonial Service appointments to legal posts were under the auspices of the Legal Adviser and Major Ralph D. Furse, the so-called 'Father of the modern Colonial Service'.[19] Though Furse primarily oversaw appointments of administrative officers, he was a leading force in establishing the character of the Colonial Service as a whole between 1910 and 1948.[20] Furse liaised with the Legal Adviser in selecting candidates for legal posts in the colonies, which were filled on an as-needed basis. This incremental approach reflected the way in which legal systems were established in Britain's new territories: they were built to be minimalist and responsive to territorial needs. Legal establishments were costly and of low priority relative to administrative priorities, especially in the early years of new territorial governments. The Colonial Office generally regarded administrators as capable of dealing with most legal matters that arose in the colonies. Therefore, the Colonial Office sent out legal officers as colonial governments expressed a need rather than prescribing an ideal number of officers in relation to population, territory size, or crime rates. Terms of employment of legal officers, including salaries and emoluments, were set by territorial governments.

One result of this decentralised and incremental system was that there was a tremendous range of experiences and grievances among legal officers. Some postings involved a good quality of life and substantial financial rewards, while others were undesirable and poorly paid. Moreover, some officers resisted transfer between territories because they were aware that while they were a part of the Colonial Service in theory, in practice the terms of their employment and pensions were governed by the territory for which they worked. Therefore, transfer to a new territory might be accompanied by the penalty of losing one's previous pensionable years of service, which remained linked to the territory where a judge had served, not to the length of their service to the British Empire.[21]

In recruiting new legal officers Colonial Office staff had a very specific idea about the type of men they wanted to hire. Candidates for legal postings applied on their own initiative to the Colonial Office and were expected to be less than 40 years of age, have been called to the Bar in England, Ireland, or Scotland, and to have had at least four years of practical experience prior to appointment.[22] Appointments were initially restricted to members of the Bars in the United Kingdom and Ireland, although the Colonial Service did receive and consider some applications from qualified barristers in the Dominions.[23] In some cases administrative officers with experience in the territories but without legal qualifications were considered for legal posts. Colonial Office staff vetted candidates with a paper application and interview, but they did not sit for exams like those required for the more elite ICS.[24] Candidates who met the requirements and were deemed desirable in terms of personality, social standing, and qualifications had their names 'noted' on 'the list', which was a record of acceptable applicants kept by the Colonial Office and consulted only when lower-level vacancies arose.[25] Vacancies of senior postings were almost exclusively filled through internal promotion. This passive method of recruitment of junior officers was intentional, as the Legal Adviser in the 1920s, J.S. Risley, believed that any large-scale advertisement might lead to a 'glut' of 'unsuitable' applicants for a very small number of openings.[26] In the 1920s appointments of legal officers accounted for less than 5% of the total appointments to the Colonial Service (see Fig. 2.1). This self-selecting system made quality control difficult for the Colonial Office, which essentially chose to hire from the applicants they received rather than proactively recruiting attractive candidates.

It was not until in the mid-1930s when, much to the disappointment of the Colonial Office, 'the list ... failed' in the face of increasing demand for legal officers, requiring the Colonial Office to rethink its recruitment method.[27] The Legal Adviser faced mounting criticism from within the Colonial Office and from outside about the poor quality of the officers receiving appointments. Accusations that legal officers were drunks, underachievers, and misfits were rife.[28] In 1933 one officer described 'the list' as the 'old out-of-date principle of "seeing what turns up"' and advocated for the Colonial Office to begin to proactively recruit barristers so they would have more choice and a better chance of attracting higher quality applicants.[29] In response to these concerns, and in the face of an increased demand for legal officers from the colonies, the new Legal Adviser, Henry G. Bushe, worked to establish a Joint Committee for the

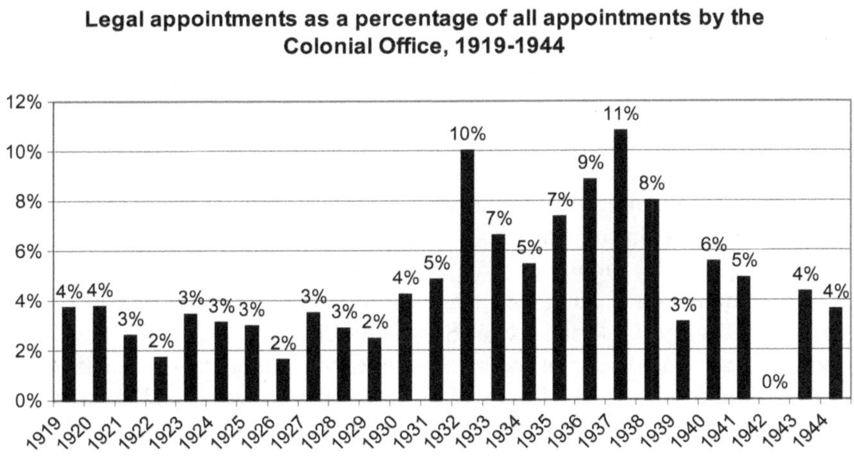

Fig. 2.1 Chart showing legal appointments as a percentage of all appointments by the Colonial Office, 1919–1944 (Data from: Furse, *Aucuparius*, p. 315 (Appendix 1))

Inns of Court in London, which was intended to help identify possible recruits and provide an initial layer of vetting. The Lord Advocate of Scotland and the Lord Chief Justice of Northern Ireland, who wanted to ensure that their candidates were not overshadowed by candidates from the Inns, established their own advisory committees to draw the attention of the Colonial Office to their barristers.[30]

These efforts to expand the recruitment of legal officers were consistent with Empire-wide efforts to unify employees of territorial governments appointed by the Colonial Office under the umbrella of the Colonial Service, and to develop branches within the Colonial Service. One of the branches that resulted was the Colonial Legal Service. The Colonial Office intended the unification scheme to standardise conditions of employment, including salaries and pensions, within each branch.[31] In 1933 the Secretary of State for the Colonies wrote to the colonial governments served by the Colonial Service announcing the creation of the Colonial Legal Service and requesting that they amend their Orders-in-Council and local statutes to remove any stipulations relating to legal or judicial appointments.[32] Officers of the Colonial Legal Service were now all part of a single service under the guidance of the Secretary of State for the Colonies as well as employees of the territorial governments they served.

The policies governing the unification of the Colonial Legal Service had significant implications for the careers of legal officers and those responsible for appointing them. First, the unification allowed the Colonial Office to standardise compensation and employment conditions.[33] Starting in 1933, new legal officers were unable to resist transfer, which became compulsory, making it easier for the Colonial Office to move them between colonial territories. The intention was to use transfer as a means of filling higher-ranking vacancies with the highest quality barristers in the Colonial Service, improving the quality of men in senior posts and hiring new recruits to fill the lower positions. Therefore, senior posts would no longer remain vacant due to shortages in legal staff and the best officers in the whole of the Colonial Legal Service could be selected for any open position, not only those officers conveniently available in the territory or region. The result of this change was that legal officers moved much more frequently than they had before the establishment of the Colonial Legal Service.[34]

The second significant implication of the creation of the Colonial Legal Service was that it gave the Colonial Office greater control over the officers it appointed relative to territorial administrators. The unification of standards of employment prevented territorial governments from imposing their own local requirements and standards on legal officers, which some in the Colonial Office believed distracted legal officers from their primary role and focus: the law. The intended consequence of the increased transfer and the removal of local requirements was that legal officers were less tied and connected to the territories in which they worked.

Even with the unification of the legal service and the expanded recruitment efforts of the 1930s, by the end of the decade there was still concern within the Colonial Office that it could not keep up with the demand for legal officers in the colonies and that the quality of legal officers in the Colonial Legal Service was not improving. Correspondence within the Colonial Office and between officers and older members of the Bar shows that officials did not believe the Joint Committee of the Inns of Court was, in fact, encouraging desirable applicants to join the Colonial Legal Service. The Colonial Office heard rumours that barristers with a potential for success in Great Britain were actually discouraged from joining the Service.[35] Under immense pressure, the Colonial Office was forced to take steps it had rejected in the 1920s. It began to accept applications from Dominions barristers in Canada, Australia, and New Zealand and aggressively publicised careers in the legal service at the Scottish and Irish Bars through articles in law journals.[36] It is not only the decision to open up the service and publicise careers in the Colonial Legal Service that reveals discontent with the number and quality of applicants, it was also reflected in what the Colonial Legal Service said in its own advertisements: 'The Colonial Legal Service is not a place for refuge for those who, for one reason or another, have fallen short in practice at the Bar.'[37] This was the reputation, it seems, that the Colonial Legal Service had garnered by the late 1930s.[38]

Motivations for Joining: Advancement and Adventure

While the Colonial Legal Service had a reputation of being populated with poor-quality barristers, this was not necessarily an accurate assessment of all colonial legal officers. There were a number of motivations for barristers to join the Colonial Legal Service, and a closer look at young barristers' prospects for a career at the Bar in Britain and at the backgrounds of colonial legal officials helps explain why some good quality lawyers joined the service. This also shows that the picture usually painted of the Colonial Legal Service was oversimplified. Indeed, for some, the decision to join was a smart calculation and one based on personal fulfilment and prestige, rather than professional esteem in Great Britain.

After the end of World War I the Bar in England was 'overcrowded' and competitive.[39] It was difficult for young barristers to begin their careers without 'connections' with well-established barristers.[40] For these young men a career in the Colonial Legal Service is likely to have been a second choice, but one with greater potential for reward in terms of compensation, promotion, and social status than they could hope for with a career at the Bar. Though starting salaries did not 'compare favourably to a successful private practice' they were a respectable starting point for junior officers.[41] Moreover, legal officers received many emoluments on top of their base salary, which often included free housing, free passage to the appointment, and immunity from local income tax, among other benefits, making the positions more lucrative financially than they might have seemed at first.[42] A well-connected and successful barrister would have earned more than a colonial legal officer, and may have had the potential to make it to the British Bench at an advanced age. Nevertheless, going into the Colonial Legal Service was a wise career move for young barristers who knew that due to their lack of social connectedness they would have a limited chance of making it to the top of the English Bar, despite their legal acumen.

For many, joining the Colonial Legal Service was not only a professional calculation, it was also a personal one. Some of the barristers who chose to go into the Colonial Service came from families with a tradition of living in British territories abroad and serving the Empire. Some had had colonial childhoods, and might have related more to the lifestyle in a British colony than in Great Britain, only returning to Great Britain for schooling.[43] For instance, Justice Eric J.E. Law was the third generation of lawyers born in Burma and, like his father, he became a colonial judge, eventually serving in East Africa.[44] For men like Justice Law, going into the Colonial Service represented a natural next step rather than a rejection of a career at the British Bar. Other legal officers were attracted to the idea of leaving post-war Great Britain for adventure, freedom, and a taste of personal power and prestige they could not hope to experience at home.[45] This desire to move away from life in the metropole contributed to the stereotype that colonial legal officials were social outcasts. While some colonial judges were, even by the admission of the Colonial Office, of an unsatisfactory quality, many colonial legal officers made personal calculations when deciding to join the service and had a range of abilities and motivations for leaving the English Bar behind.

Preparation and Requirements

When a barrister joined the Colonial Legal Service his preparation was markedly different from his administrative colleagues in the Colonial Administrative Service. The divergence in preparation reveals how the Colonial Office perceived the roles and responsibilities of a legal officer relative to other officers. While neither new administrators nor legal officers were required to have any practical experience in British colonies, or any extensive knowledge of the place where they would serve, they had markedly different experiences before departing for their posts. By the early 1930s newly hired administrators were attending academic courses, called the Colonial Administrative Service course, at Oxford and Cambridge.[46] These courses were aimed at preparing them for their service through a wide range of academic subjects from anthropology to the natural environment. Conversely, new legal appointees did not attend any preparatory courses. The Legal Adviser viewed their years of practical experience at the Bar as sufficient preparation for their initial low-level appointments as magistrates or crown counsel and believed that junior officers would learn any other relevant skills through their experience on the ground.[47] Though additional knowledge of the colonies was a valued attribute of a recruit, the Legal Adviser of the 1930s, Bushe, rejected the notion that experience in the colonies could be a substitute for professional legal training, and attributed the 'less good' reputation of the Colonial Legal Service in the 1930s to the 'incursion into it of a number of people from the administration'.[48] Unlike administrators, new legal officers were sent to their appointments as soon as possible and given little information about the place in which they would serve or the people they would encounter.

One significant difference between administrators who did coursework and legal officers who did not was that administrators gained language skills and were required to continue to improve their proficiency once in their appointed territory. Before the unification of the Colonial Legal Service, some territories had their own regulations requiring legal officers to learn the local language, with the same types of exams prescribed for administrative officers. For instance, in Tanganyika legal officers were required to take the Lower Swahili exam after their first year of service and the Higher Swahili exam to earn a higher salary as a magistrate, which was usually completed after a number of years in the territory.[49] Comparatively, administrative officers generally began learning the relevant language in their preparatory academic training programmes and had substantially less time to complete their advanced exams once they took up their posts.

Thus, among legal officers there was no consistent level of language qualification and they typically conducted their work in English. Some had basic local language skills, with their proficiency based on how long they had served in a territory and whether they had begun their career as junior officers (therefore making them subject to language requirements), or were frequently transferred between territories before becoming High Court judges (who were not expected to gain new language skills). The bifurcated colonial legal systems in territories under indirect rule also meant that most legal officers had little contact with the local population; a large portion of the cases they heard were between members of the expatriate population. In cases involving non-English speakers, most judges accepted their limitations in terms of language skills and readily employed translators. One judge argued that this measure worked to increase the quality of the justice dispensed because, 'A little learning [of a language] is a dangerous thing', and could lead to misunderstandings in the courtroom.[50] Therefore judges relied on interpretation of the local language into English, or at times from a local dialect or language to a regional *lingua franca* and then into English, as was often the case in East Africa with Kiswahili.

At the time of unification of the Colonial Legal Service, language requirements were a source of dispute within the Colonial Office and between the Colonial Office and territorial governments, some of whom already had language requirements in place for legal officers. As the Secretary of State for the Colonies had the power to require territories to remove those requirements, it was up to the Colonial Office to determine whether language skills were necessary for the duties of a colonial legal officer. Legal Adviser Bushe strongly opposed language requirements arguing that they were onerous and 'inconsistent' with one of the main goals of the Colonial Legal Service, which was to create a service with easy and compulsory transfer of the most qualified men from one territory to another.[51] He argued that, for the work carried out by legal officers, language skills were an unnecessary barrier and complained that if language requirements were put in place in all territories, a judge might learn Kiswahili in East Africa, Greek in Cyprus, and Arabic in Palestine throughout the course of his career as he was transferred and promoted from one territory to the next. He proclaimed in an internal note to his colleagues, 'Let us fill the legal posts with good lawyers, not with linguists.'[52]

The question of language skills, however, was not just one of practicality. It reflected differing ideologies regarding how the administration of justice should be carried out in a colony and what knowledge was necessary to do so 'justly'. Bushe took the view that their legal skills were sufficient to apply the common law anywhere. The views of administrators generally differed though. Many believed that the appropriate application of the law required local knowledge, and that without language skills legal officers would not be aware of local conditions or be able to interact with the non-expatriates, consequently impairing their ability to administer justice. The question of language requirements was just one issue among a range of differences over the administration of justice to Africans that developed between administrators and judges in the 1920s and 1930s. What is particularly relevant for this discussion of the employment conditions of colonial legal officers is that language requirements similar to those of administrative officers were initially in place in numerous territories before the founding of the Colonial Legal Service and that the unification of the service was a step towards diminishing the local attachments of legal officials and developing a more universal colonial legal character that could be employed and applied anywhere.

Though the employment requirements for legal officers were, to a large extent, dictated by the Colonial Office, during any significant change in policy or debate over socially or politically sensitive issues there was often a flurry of correspondence, often initiated by the Legal Adviser, to representatives of the colonial governments (both in the administrative and judicial spheres). Officials in the colonies were vocal and resisted top-down policy changes, often citing the conditions in their own territory as warranting an exception to whatever change the Colonial Office was attempting to initiate. One example of this process of negotiation that is particularly relevant to analysing colonial judges has to do with the race of legal officials. It has already been noted that the model in use at this time was for barristers from the metropole (and some Dominions territories) to be sent out to serve in the colonies and it was understood by those in the Colonial Office and colonial governments that these barristers would be white.[53] Though Colonial Office policies did not explicitly exclude non-white applicants to the Colonial Service or other overseas services, few applied for and succeeded in receiving appointments. Colonial subjects in their home territories who were not white were integrated into the territorial government in varying degrees. In some areas of the Empire, however, like the West Indies, there were mixed-race barristers who met the qualifications required for joining the Colonial Legal Service and were interested in being sent to other territories to work. When the Colonial Office faced a shortage of legal officials for open posts in East Africa it considered appointing men 'with a slight touch of colour' from the West Indies.[54] Ambivalent about how these appointments would be received, a Colonial Office official wrote to the Governors of Kenya, Uganda, and Tanganyika to enquire whether they would be comfortable with the appointments. The Governors of Kenya and Tanganyika aggressively discouraged these appointments.[55] They replied that they were concerned about how the European population would react and described the expatriates in the territories as 'not level-headed' and even 'cruel', expressing concern that 'mixed-race' judicial officers and their wives would be socially ostracised from the rest of the Colonial Service and expatriate community.[56] The Governors' reactions persuaded the Colonial Office and it did not ultimately offer these men appointments in the Colonial Legal Service in East Africa.

This decision of the Colonial Office to defer to the preferences and opinions of the colonial authorities on the ground illustrates that settlers and expatriates played a role in shaping the profile of the judges who would serve in *their* courts. It was imperative for them that a colonial judge not only have the legal expertise to understand and apply British law but also the ability to blend into white colonial society. The selection of legal officers was a topic of debate about the necessary characteristics of colonial legal authorities. It was the context in which rhetoric about colonial justice and its 'civilising' qualities had to be transformed into officers on the ground, and therefore brought out the practical questions of what justice could and should look like in the colonial context.

Promotion, Tenure, Dismissal, and Retirement

The recruitment, appointment, and preparation processes under discussion thus far have been in reference to junior officers entering their first appointments as magistrates or crown counsel. This is because, as noted above, appointments to senior positions, such as a territorial High Court bench, were almost exclusively made from within the Service. H.F. Morris and James Read argue that the Colonial Legal Service provided a 'specific career structure' for its staff.[57] This career path only applied, though, to men at the beginning of their careers. There are three reasons why the Colonial Legal Service saw itself and wanted to be seen as offering a career rather than simply a job opportunity to career-less young barristers. First, although the Colonial Office wanted good quality barristers for the Colonial Legal Service, it would have been difficult if not impossible to attract applications from successful barristers already advanced in their careers, namely because the Colonial Legal Service could not compete with their incomes or prestige within British society.[58] Therefore, drawing in barristers before they had established themselves and had a high initial salary was the only affordable and feasible approach. While this argument is compelling, it assumes that the Colonial Office would have actually wanted to hire advanced, older barristers had they sought employment. The second rationale for their approach, and perhaps one that offers more insight into the reasoning underpinning Colonial Legal Service policies, is that the Colonial Office wanted to hire junior officers so they could train them to be legal officials of the British Empire rather than British barristers. The Colonial Office recognised that this required many years of experience and acculturation to colonial life. When the Legal Adviser was struggling to find good quality staff for high-level postings in the 1930s, Bushe adamantly resisted the idea of considering recruiting directly from the older Bar arguing that the move

> would be contrary to all our traditions, and I do not think it would be satisfactory. To take a man of 45 to 50 years of age and send him to the Colonies for the first time, is taking a serious risk. We have recognised this for a generation, and we have recognised that if we did that, we should leave all the junior legal officers in the air so far as promotion is concerned.[59]

The ambiguous 'risk' Bushe feared could refer simply to the difficulty a middle-aged person might have adjusting to a new lifestyle or climate. However, an alternative reading of his words points to a concern that older, confident barristers, without a long-term commitment to the Empire or a career that depended on it, might not adhere to colonial policy, or might disrupt colonial life by challenging colonial laws or society, and would do so from a position of authority within the colonial government.

Bushe's concern about the idea of hiring older barristers speaks not only to the desire to acculturate legal officers to colonial law and life before putting them in senior postings, but also highlights the third rationale for promotion from within, which is the necessity of having openings at the top. While it might seem that these young barristers were lucky to have the corner on senior appointments, the trade-off was that they would normally need to relinquish any plans to return to the British Bar. Once a barrister joined the Colonial Legal Service, he jeopardised his chances of developing a legal career in Britain, both due to the tarnished reputation of the Colonial Legal Service and because he would not develop the relationships within the legal community that were crucial for success. In return, men who joined the service and stayed in it could be almost guaranteed promotion, and at a faster rate than in other branches of the Colonial Service.[60] The career prospects and a 'very constant and substantial flow of promotion from the junior to the senior legal and judicial posts' were necessary incentives to draw in higher quality barristers.[61] Hiring from outside the Colonial Legal Service would have removed this crucial benefit of joining and made it harder to recruit good barristers for junior posts in the future. The Colonial Office had to balance a demand for better quality senior officers in the short term with the long-term concerns over the state of the Colonial Legal Service and how those officers would fare and behave on the ground.

Once a barrister began a career with the Colonial Legal Service, he could expect to start with an appointment in Africa, Malaya, or the West Indies and then be transferred anywhere served by the Colonial Service.[62] Legal officers, on average, moved more often than those in the administrative service.[63] Though some of these transfers were from the same post in one territory to another, transfer often also meant promotion. As the Colonial Office had intended, after unification of the Colonial Legal Service it could select candidates from anywhere it served. While the Colonial Office regarded it as efficient and preferable to choose officers from within the same region for promotion in a nearby territory, because they could rely on and benefit from their previous experience, it was not uncommon for officers to transfer from Asia to Africa to move a relatively small step up from magistrate to senior magistrate. The implications of this were that judicial officers were regularly less acquainted with the circumstances in the territory in which they were working than the rest of the junior and mid-level Colonial Service officers from other sectors. In some cases, however, senior judges outlasted senior administrators and spent their entire careers in one region with long periods in each territory, seeing numerous governors come and go during their tenure on the Bench.[64] Even those who had lived in the region where they served for long periods of time could not shake the criticism that they were divorced from local conditions due to their lifestyles in the colonies.

Colonial judges were not required to retire from the Colonial Legal Service until the age of 62 and often had their service extended until they were 65, unless ill health prevented them from carrying out their duties or they engaged in misconduct.[65] Thus colonial judges were often the oldest colonial officials in a territory as administrators were required to retire by the age of 55.[66] The rationale for the increased age of retirement was that legal officers had to have four years of practical experience, which made them enter the Service later than administrative officers.[67] Therefore colonial judges would have had a smaller pension if required to retire at 55, which might have deterred young barristers considering a career as a colonial legal officer. In Tanganyika the average age of entry of a legal officer was 32, while the average age of entry for administrative officers was a decade younger, at 22.[68] The age differential between the judiciary and administrators was significant because the advanced age of judges both added to their authority and the biases against them. Some administrators alleged that judges' advanced ages made them less useful and gave them too much power in relation to younger officers.

Despite these criticisms, colonial judges were relatively secure in their tenure. Though their appointments and promotions were initiated by the Colonial Office and territorial governments, once in office they enjoyed some protections, which, for the most part, prevented dismissal, except in cases involving misconduct or ill health.[69] They technically held office at the pleasure of the Crown, but since 1870 the Secretary of State for the Colonies claimed he would refer possible dismissals of judges serving in the Empire to the Judicial Committee of the Privy Council (hereafter the Privy Council).[70] While High Court judges had some promise of security, the same assurances were not provided for junior judicial officers. Their fates were mainly determined by the highest officers within the territories in which they served.[71] Though the Secretary of State for the Colonies made assurances that cases of dismissal would go to the Privy Council, some judges believed that their independence was threatened by the provision allowing the Crown to dismiss them, so they therefore regularly sought clarification on the rules relating to their tenure and dismissal. This reflects not only a concern over job security in the most straightforward sense, but also the belief of colonial judges that they should be as truly independent from the executive as judges were in Great Britain. Colonial judges wanted confirmation that if they challenged administrators' actions or colonial policies in the courtroom, that they would not be risking their livelihood with the Colonial Service. This debate is revisited in Chap. 4, when a dismissal of a colonial judge set off an extensive and highly publicised row over the conditions of employment. What is relevant for the discussion here is that colonial judges were stuck between idealised British notions of judicial independence and the realities of colonial administrations, which did not reflect these principles. Colonial judges both saw themselves and wished to be seen as having the same independence as judges in Britain, but simultaneously were a crucial part of the machinery enforcing colonial law and keeping order in the colonies.

Lifestyle in the Colonies

Even though some senior judges had lived and worked in specific territories for long periods of time, their lifestyles in and outside the colonies contributed to their reputation of being divorced from local conditions. Colonial judges typically lived in the capital city, where the colonial government and high courts were based. Junior legal officers were based at stations throughout the territory, similar to junior administrators, but High Court judges led a lifestyle similar to that of the Governor. They were provided with comfortable housing, often in the form of a bungalow outside town.[72] They had servants who prepared their food and cleaned for them, luxuries they may not have had at home in Great Britain. Judges with families had nannies or servants who cared for their children. The High Court Bench was prominent in formal ceremonies and when judges left the capital city on circuit, they were typically celebrated by a Guard of Honour of African soldiers and local colonial officials at their destination.

Since judges were based in the territorial metropolis, they were rarely seen by most people living in the territory. Though judges went on circuit, they only stayed long enough to hear the serious cases under their jurisdiction that had accumulated since the last visit of the Court. The impact of this system was that colonial judges seldom interacted with non-Europeans, and when they did it was because they were hearing cases involving them, or being served by them. No matter how long they spent in a territory, judges often remained unaware of the conditions and traditions playing a role in the cases they heard. The lifestyle of colonial judges contributed to their reputation as aloof and uninterested in the circumstances of the people they judged.

For some judges, their service in the colonies was an effective means of moving up the social ladder. The Chief Justice was ranked second in the territorial hierarchy after the Governor and was generally referred to as 'His Honour'.[73] Not only were the lifestyles of colonial judges comfortable in the colonies, but their status in London would drastically change over their careers. They may have been looked down upon by the Bar, but they nonetheless would ascend to high society upon return to London. When a colonial judge came to London on leave to 'refresh himself with things English' he could expect to be invited to elite social events and even included in parties for British judges in Britain, such as His Majesty's Dinner for Judges.[74] Many of the colonial chief justices and those with extended service in high courts were knighted, a sign that they had reached a very high social status, on a par with that of a colonial governor.[75] Colonial judges remained a part of British society, no matter how long they spent in the colonies, but at the same time were sandwiched in between the British legal elite, with whom they socialised but to whom they did not belong, and the colonial cadre, of which they were a part but at times were alienated from.

Conclusion: 'The Bad Old Irish J's'?

The unification and expansion of the Colonial Legal Service was aimed at meeting a mounting need for legal officers in developing colonial administrations, standardising the service throughout the Empire, and increasing the quality of the men they appointed. By 1938 these efforts were showing some returns in raw numbers, as nearly twice as many legal officers were appointed than in 1928. Yet all these labours were cut short by World War II as appointments decreased substantially after 1939 (shown in Fig. 2.2).

Nonetheless, the period between 1920 and 1939 had been the formative phase for the Colonial Legal Service. The creation of a cadre of colonial judges who could travel across the Empire from post to post reflects the Colonial Office's perspective on the staffing needs of twentieth-century colonial states. It also demonstrates its belief in the transferability of the common law and the essential—though limited—role of the colonial courts in the colonies. The new employment policies for legal officers had a permanent impact on the roles and functions of the colonial judiciary, as well as on how it was viewed and utilised by those inside and outside the Colonial Office. Colonial judges were not integrated into the British legal community nor into colonial society—and were restricted both socially

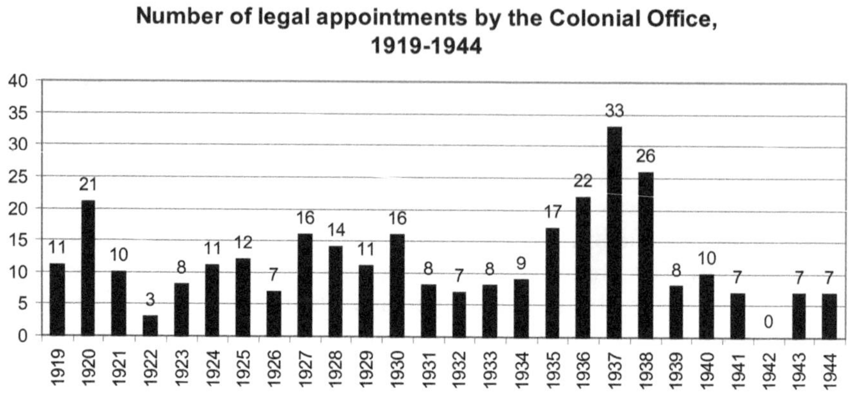

Fig. 2.2 Chart showing the number of legal appointments by the Colonial Office, 1919–1944 (Data from: Furse, *Aucuparius*, p. 315 (Appendix 1))

and politically by their profession. In unifying colonial legal offices into a single service, the Colonial Office not only established the framework to create a judiciary for the Empire, it also shaped the nature and practice of colonial justice in ways that would fundamentally affect both its judges and the people they judged.

The impact of Colonial Legal Service policies on colonised people is explored in the following chapters, but here one final question remains: were the stereotypes of colonial judges a realistic reflection? The reputation of these colonial judges was partially summed up by one colonial administrator who served in the 1950s and recalled that one of his senior colleagues at the time referred to earlier generations of colonial judges as 'the Bad Old Irish J's'—the J in the phrase stands for judge.[76] Elements of this label reflect actual Colonial Office policies and recruitment demographics. Colonial judges were 'old', in the sense that they were allowed to serve at an older age than any other member of the Colonial Service, and were substantially more advanced in age than many of their most aggressive critics, some of whom were administrative officers newly out of school. It is also true that the Colonial Legal Service admitted Irish barristers and that many elected to join the Colonial Legal Service; but not all colonial legal officers were Irish and, in the case of Tanganyika, only three of the ten legal and judicial officers in 1936 were members of the Irish Bar.[77]

The notion that colonial judges were 'bad' may reflect not only a judgement of the professional abilities of judges, but also their characters and behaviour. Archival evidence supports the view that the Inns of Court did not send their best students to the Colonial Legal Service before World War II, and that some barristers were attracted to the Colonial Legal Service because they did not have a good chance of succeeding in the English legal community. There are also indications that some colonial judges did not behave in accordance with social and professional standards of the time. However, these generalisations oversimplify the range of motivations that propelled barristers of personal and professional merit to join the Colonial Legal Service, not the least of which was an attachment to or desire for a colonial lifestyle with all its benefits.

If the belief that colonial judges were 'bad' reflects the view that they had a destructive effect on the administration of colonial justice, however, then questions of personality and policy must be answered separately. On the characters of colonial judges, the existing evidence shows that while some took considerable advantage of their freedom in their personal lives and in the courtroom, others used their positions to curb the excesses of the colonial administration and expatriates and to provide an outlet for colonial subjects to resist colonial injustices. For example, Bridget Brereton argues that Justice John Gorrie, a nineteenth-century colonial judge, challenged colonial elites and as a result was deeply admired by colonial subjects.[78] Gann and Duignan assert that colonial laws 'allowed vast scope for differences of application or even for the personal idiosyncrasies of individual judges'.[79] The administration of justice was certainly shaped by how individual judges behaved on the Bench and how they interacted with the people they judged, but it was also deeply affected by the jurisdictional limitations and policies that circumscribed their work. In the following chapters, the High Court of Tanganyika provides fertile ground for exploring how the policies of the Colonial Legal Service influenced the administration of justice in a British colony in Africa.

Notes

1. On specialised colonial careers, see: C. Andersen, *British Engineers and Africa, 1875–1914* (London, 2011); A. Crozier, *Practising Colonial Medicine: The Colonial Medical Service in British East Africa* (London, 2007); J.M. Hodge, *Triumph of the Expert: Agrarian Doctrines of Development and the Legacies of British Colonialism* (Athens, 2007).
2. J. Dupont, *The Common Law Abroad: Constitutional and Legal Legacy of the British Empire* (Littleton, 2000), p. 51.

3. On staffing colonial benches in the nineteenth century, see: D. Duman, *The English and Colonial Bars in the Nineteenth Century* (London, 1983), pp. 121–142; J. McLaren, *Dewigged, Bothered, and Bewildered: British Colonial Judges on Trial, 1800–1900* (Toronto, 2011), especially pp. 49–52.
4. McLaren, *Dewigged*, pp. 49–50.
5. Ibid., p. 37.
6. This analysis does not include the Dominions, namely Canada, Australia, New Zealand, and South Africa, which had previously received some judges from Great Britain, but by the early twentieth century were viewed as self-governing by Great Britain and therefore 'did not concern the Colonial Office from a staffing point of view'. R. Heussler, *Yesterday's Rulers: The Making of the British Colonial Service* (Syracuse, 1963), p. 1. There are a growing number of studies examining the origins of national judiciaries in dominion territories. For example, see: M. Chanock, *The Making of South African Legal Culture, 1902–1936: Fear, Favour and Prejudice* (Cambridge, 2001), pp. 221–240.
7. ICS district officers were called collectors and magisterial work was one duty among many that the administration expected a collector to carry out. On the duties of collectors, see: D.C. Potter, *India's Political Administrators: From ICS to IAS*, 1st Indian edn (Delhi, 1996), p. 35. Though Indians were employed as judicial officers in the ICS, they accounted for less than 11% of the total number of judicial officers in 1929. This changed rapidly in the 1930s, however, and by 1939 Indians accounted for 44% of the total number of judicial officers. P. Mason, *The Men Who Ruled India* (2 vols., London, 1963), ii, pp. 364–365.
8. S. Schmitthener, 'A Sketch of the Development of the Legal Profession in India', *Law and Society Review*, 3 (1969), p. 357.
9. C. Ilbert, *The Government of India: Being a Digest of the Statute Law Relating Thereto*, 2nd edn (Oxford, 1907), pp. 237–238; Schmitthener, 'A Sketch', pp. 355–356.
10. L.S.S. O'Malley, *The Indian Civil Service, 1601–1930*, 2nd edn (London, 1965), p. 161.
11. One exception is Sudan, which had its own service called the Sudan Political Service. It recruited officers directly for service in Sudan and was not under the auspices of the Colonial Office or India Office. On the Sudan Political Service, see: A.H.M. Kirk-Greene, *Britain's Imperial Administrators, 1858–1966* (Basingstoke, 2000), pp. 164–201.
12. A.H.M. Kirk-Greene, *On Crown Service: A History of HM Colonial and Overseas Civil Service, 1837–1997* (London, 1999), pp. 11–13.
13. A.H.M. Kirk-Greene, *Symbol of Authority: The British District Officer in Africa* (London, 2006).

14. L.H. Gann and P. Duignan, *The Rulers of British Africa, 1870–1914* (London, 1978), p. 237; P.J. Cain and A.G. Hopkins, *British Imperialism: Crisis and Deconstruction, 1914–1990* (London, 1993), pp. 209–210.
15. Duman, *The English*, p. 123. Kirk-Greene asserts that there is also merit to the generalisation that the Colonial Administrative Service had a large portion of sons of upper middle-class professional families and that there were few administrators from aristocratic households. Kirk-Greene, *On Crown Service*, p. 95.
16. Duman, *The English*, p. 138.
17. Ibid., p. 125.
18. Kirk-Greene, *On Crown Service*, p. 25, Table 2.4.
19. Ibid., p. 32.
20. Heussler, *Yesterday's Rulers*, p. 14. Furse chronicled his role in designing the Colonial Service recruitment policies and techniques in: R. Furse, *Aucuparius: Recollections of a Recruiting Officer* (London, 1962).
21. Justice Alexander, who served in Fiji prior to transfer to Tanganyika, complains about the terms of service for officers and possible financial penalties of transfer in his memoir: G.G. Alexander, *Tanganyika Memories: A Judge in the Red Kanzu* (London, 1936), p. 11.
22. Colonial Office, *The Colonial Service: Legal Appointments* (London, 1931), p. 6. English and Irish solicitors, Scottish law agents and writers to the Signet could also apply for some positions, but accounted for only a small portion of Colonial Legal Service officers.
23. The National Archives of the United Kingdom at Kew (TNA (UK)), Colonial Office (CO) 877/7/5, F.R.W. Jameson to unknown [CO], 6 July 1931.
24. Gann and Duignan, *Rulers*, p. 204. Kirk-Greene asserts that the Colonial Service was often described as second-rate to the ICS, which typically drew the highest achieving young men earning firsts, while the Colonial Service was 'content with … a sound Second'. Kirk-Greene, *Britain's Imperial Administrators*, p. 164. This view of the Colonial Service as a whole perhaps contributed even further to the low opinion of legal officers in the Colonial Legal Service.
25. TNA (UK), CO 877/10/6, A.F. Newbolt to R.D. Furse and H.G. Bushe, 6 February 1933.
26. TNA (UK), CO 877/1, [file in bound series: 'Legal Vacancies in the Colonial Service'], unknown [CO] to A. Milner, 28 August 1920.
27. TNA (UK), CO 877/10/6, 'The need for means of stimulating recruitment', n.d., p. 1.
28. For example, see: TNA (UK), CO 877/16/17, unknown [CO] to H.G. Bushe, 14 July 1938. This evidence challenges Kirk-Greene's claim that, 'the Colonial Office's recruitment staff was proud of its reputation

that it would rather leave a vacancy unfilled than appoint a misfit or a dud'. Kirk-Greene, *On Crown Service*, p. 98.

29. TNA (UK), CO 877/10/6, A.F. Newbolt to R.D. Furse and H.G. Bushe, 6 February 1933.
30. For Scotland, see: TNA (UK), CO 877/14/10, H.G. Bushe, draft letter to R. Rowe, 18 March 1937. For Northern Ireland, see: TNA (UK), 877/16/18, Private Secretary to the Lord Chief Justice of Northern Ireland W.M. Johnson to R.D. Furse, 11 July 1938.
31. Dupont, *The Common Law*, p. xvii.
32. TNA (UK), CO 850/25/2, P. Cunliffe-Lister, draft circular to Officer Administering the Government of [intended for numerous colonies], 15 July 1933.
33. Gann and Duignan, *Rulers*, p. 208.
34. Dupont, *The Common Law*, p. xvii.
35. TNA (UK), CO 877/13/4, 'Extract from minute on Appointments', n.d.
36. TNA (UK), CO 877/14/9, R.D. Furse, draft letter to D.E. Fouhy, S.M. Wadham, and J.M. Macdonnell, 21 June 1937. This decision to accept barristers from bars in the Dominions was contemporaneous with the Dominion Selection Scheme, which facilitated the establishment of selection boards, initially in Canada, Australia, and New Zealand, to assist with recruiting administrative officers for the Colonial Service. Kirk-Greene, *On Crown Service*, p. 29. H.G. Bushe, 'The Colonial Legal Service', *The Irish Law Times and Solicitor's Journal*, LXX (1936), pp. 231–233.
37. Ibid., p. 233.
38. This reputation of colonial judges was not new, but rather an extension and, perhaps, decline from their already tarnished reputation in Great Britain in the nineteenth century. See: McLaren, *Dewigged.*
39. TNA (UK), CO 822/65/8, H.G. Bushe, draft letter to unknown, [first words: 'The Bar is excessively overcrowded'], n.d.
40. Ibid.
41. C.J. Jeffries, *The Colonial Empire and its Civil Service* (Cambridge, 1938), p. 147.
42. Colonial Office, *The Colonial Service: Legal Appointments*, p. 19.
43. Many officers in the ICS also had experience with and a preference for life in the colonies. Elizabeth Buettner argues that many young men who grew up in India in families serving the ICS took advantage of the benefit of being sent to the UK for schooling and then 'rejoined the colonial community as adults, enjoying much higher social status than if they had not left India—or if they had never returned overseas'. E. Buettner, *Empire Families: Britons and Late Imperial India* (Oxford, 2004), p. 24.
44. Patricia Law, interview with author, Canterbury, 14 May 2009.

45. TNA (UK), CO 822/71/5, P.E. Mitchell to J.H. Thomas, 24 April 1936, p. 1. Gann and Duignan, *Rulers*, pp. 202–203.
46. Kirk-Greene, *On Crown Service*, p. 27. Training courses were first established in 1908 for colonial administrators. They lasted only a few months and were held in the Imperial Institute in London. By the late 1920s year-long courses were being held at Oxford, Cambridge, and later at the London School of Economics and Political Science. On imperial education for colonial officers, see also: C. Prior, *Exporting Empire: Africa, Colonial Officials, and the Construction of the Imperial State, c. 1900–1939* (Manchester, 2013), pp. 35–62.
47. Jeffries, *The Colonial Empire*, p. 143.
48. TNA (UK), CO 822/65/8, H.G. Bushe, draft letter to unknown, [first words: 'The Bar is excessively overcrowded'], n.d.
49. TNA (UK), CO 850/40/6, 'Summary of Replies', n.d., p. 4.
50. Bodleian Library of Commonwealth and African Studies at Rhodes House, Oxford (RHL), MSS. Brit. Emp. s. 307, David Edwards Papers, D. Edwards, 'H.M. Colonial Legal Service, 1900–1960', 23 November 1965, p. 19.
51. TNA (UK), CO 850/40/6, H.G. Bushe to unknown [CO], 16 October 1935.
52. Ibid., p. 3
53. Dupont, *The Common Law*, p. xvii, fn 12.
54. TNA (UK), CO 850/84/8, J. Byrne to G.J.F. Tomlinson, 9 June 1936, p. 1.
55. The Governor of Uganda did not object to the appointments, but did not want 'appointments of this nature confined to Uganda'. TNA (UK), CO 850/84/8, P.E. Mitchell to G.J.F. Tomlinson, 18 June 1936, p. 1.
56. TNA (UK), CO 850/84/8, H. MacMichael to G.J.F. Tomlinson, 4 June 1936. Though the Governors of Kenya and Tanganyika expressed concern over the racism of some of the settlers, they may also have been using the settlers to disguise their own racism and discomfort with mixed-race officials. TNA (UK), CO 850/84/8, J. Byrne to G.J.F. Tomlinson, 9 June 1936, p. 1.
57. J.S. Read, 'The Search for Justice' in H.F. Morris and J.S. Read, *Indirect Rule and the Search for Justice: Essays in East African Legal History* (Oxford, 1972), p. 310. There are, however, examples of transfer between services and some colonial officers left the service after only a short period.
58. TNA (UK), CO 822/65/8, J.H. Thomas, draft letter to the Governors of Kenya, the Uganda Protectorate, the Tanganyika Territory, Nyasaland, Zanzibar, and Northern Rhodesia, 7 January 1936.
59. TNA (UK), CO 822/65/8, H.G. Bushe, draft letter to unknown, [first words: 'The Bar is excessively overcrowded'], n.d.

60. TNA (UK), CO 822/65/8, J.H. Thomas, draft letter to the Governors of Kenya, the Uganda Protectorate, the Tanganyika Territory, Nyasaland, Zanzibar, and Northern Rhodesia, 7 January 1936; Jeffries, *The Colonial Empire*, pp. 145–147.
61. Ibid., p. 145.
62. Ibid.
63. Ibid., pp. 143–145.
64. Read, 'The Search for Justice', p. 310.
65. TNA (UK), CO 850/13/2, L.C.M.S. Amery, circular to the Officer Administering the Government of [sent to numerous colonies], 20 September 1928.
66. TNA (UK), CO 850/209/10, 'Report of a Committee appointed by the Secretary of State for the Colonies: Colonial Legal Service', 16 February 1945, p. 7.
67. Ibid.
68. Tanzania National Archives in Dar es Salaam (TNA), 25586, 'Government Circular No. 39 of 1945: Appointment of Ex-Servicemen to the Colonial Service (Rules Regarding Seniority and Initial Salaries)', 30 November 1945, p. 2.
69. Jeffries, *The Colonial Empire*, pp. 147–148.
70. TNA (UK), CO 850/13/2, Lord Passfield [S.J. Webb], circular to the Officer Administering the Government of [sent to numerous colonies], 26 July 1929, p. 1.
71. Ibid., p. 2.
72. Gann and Duignan, *Rulers*, pp. 236–237.
73. Jeffries, *The Colonial Empire*, p. 147.
74. Gann and Duignan, *Rulers*, pp. 236–237. TNA (UK), CO 850/111/7. This file contains multiple letters discussing the invitation of colonial judges to the dinner.
75. Judges were typically awarded for their service in the colonies or Commonwealth by being made knights of the Most Distinguished Order of Saint Michael and Saint George (abbreviated GCMG, KCMG or DCMG, and CMG) or were awarded the title Knight Bachelor (the title is not of a specific order and is abbreviated Kt), which became more common for judges serving outside the UK in the mid-twentieth century. Jeffries claims that announcements of knighthood of members of the Colonial Legal Service were frequent and Cain and Hopkins describe these honours as 'liberally bestowed' on senior members of the Service. Jeffries, *The Colonial Empire*, p. 147; Cain and Hopkins, *British Imperialism*, pp. 209–210.
76. Mark Thomas, interview with author, Oxford, 29 July 2008.

77. TNA (UK), CO 822/71/5, 'List showing the source of recruitment of the judicial and legal officers now serving in East Africa', n.d., p. 4. It is also possible that administrative bias against the barristers in the Colonial Legal Service partly stemmed from the fact that a number of legal officers were Irish and some British barristers held the attitude that the Dublin Bar was of a lower quality because Ireland was British colony that had only recently achieved independence. Administrators may have also used the idea that all judges were Irish as a way of indicating that they were a secondary and separate group from the administration.
78. B. Brereton, *Law, Justice, and Empire: The Colonial Career of John Gorrie, 1829–1892* (Kingston, 1997). p. xi.
79. Gann and Duignan, *Rulers*, p. 234.

CHAPTER 3

The Marginalisation of the High Court Under Indirect Rule, 1920–1944

British colonial judges first arrived in Tanganyika in 1920, following the conclusion of World War I and the conversion of the territory from a German colony to a League of Nations mandate under British administration. From the early 1890s until World War I Tanganyika had been part of a German protectorate called German East Africa, which also included land that is now part of the states of Rwanda and Burundi. This chapter explores the beginnings of British administration in Tanganyika, the work of its first colonial judges, and the relationship between the High Court of Tanganyika and the lower colonial courts in the territory.

In the early years of British rule the High Court had jurisdiction over the subordinate courts and Native Courts. As the policies and ideologies underpinning the indirect rule system became more entrenched under Governor Donald C. Cameron, however, the judiciary was increasingly marginalised in the sphere of colonial justice. The primary instrument for this was the Native Courts Ordinance of 1929, which removed most cases involving Africans from the jurisdiction of colonial judges and placed them in the hands of administrators. The clashes between the Governor and Chief Justice over this ordinance and other matters relating to the role of colonial judges in the territory illustrate competing ideologies between the judiciary and the administration about the administration of justice for Africans under indirect rule. More broadly, the debate elucidates the

E.R. Feingold, *Colonial Justice and Decolonization in the High Court of Tanzania, 1920–1971*, Cambridge Imperial and Post-Colonial Studies Series, https://doi.org/10.1007/978-3-319-69691-1_3

mechanics of the developing indirect rule system in Tanganyika and the role of the courts in the assertion of colonial authority.

As the colonial administration reached a new pinnacle of authority in 1929, colonial judges correspondingly found their domain more limited. The High Court, however, still remained a crucial part of the colonial state in Tanganyika both functionally and symbolically. An examination of the roles these judges played in the colonial state reveals how they practically facilitated colonial rule and embodied British imperial ideology and rhetoric. However detached from the practicalities of colonial administration some judges believed they were, they were nevertheless an essential part of British colonial rule of Tanganyika.

The Administration of Justice in Tanganyika Before British Rule

When His Majesty's High Court of Tanganyika began operating on 3 January 1921, it marked the beginning of approximately 40 years of the administration of British colonial justice. The British justice system was not, however, the first time colonial courts had been set up in the territory. Germany solidified its claim to this and other regions of Africa following the Berlin Conference of 1884–1885, when European imperial powers agreed that they would be obliged to undertake 'effective occupation' of the regions they claimed, which typically involved the establishment of an administration with justice and penal systems.[1] In accordance with this expectation and to entrench the authority of the territorial administration, German colonial authorities set up a court system in German East Africa in the early twentieth century. Prior to German rule African communities had varied mechanisms for dispute resolution, but there is little archival evidence about these mechanisms and the authorities administering them from which to draw conclusions about the administration of pre-colonial justice.[2]

The German colonial legal system was structured along racial lines. There was an explicit bifurcation between 'natives' and 'non-natives'. 'Non-natives'—defined as Europeans and others regarded as similar due to their skin tone, including, but not limited to, Japanese persons, Parsees, Christian Syrians, and Goanese—were under the jurisdiction of established laws and procedures.[3] District Judges presided over cases involving 'non-natives' in the District Courts in Dar es Salaam, Tanga, Mwanza,

Moshi, and Tabora. Individuals included in this racial category also had the right of appeal from District Courts to the Superior Judge, who was based in Dar es Salaam. Persons classified as 'natives'—Africans, Indians, and Arabs—however, did not have access to the court system or to the laws and legal standards afforded to 'non-natives'.[4] Instead, German administrative officers decided cases involving 'natives' or delegated this responsibility to Akidas. Akidas were typically individuals of African or Arab descent empowered by German colonial authorities to carry out various judicial and executive functions.[5] The mechanism German officers used to adjudicate cases were district councils, called *shauri*.[6] *Shauri* involved both German officers and local African elites and served a variety of functions, including acting as a local court.[7] When *shauri* convened as a court, the administrative officer in charge autocratically adjudicated criminal and civil cases according to German law in relevant criminal matters or 'native' law in civil matters. He also handed down sentences, some of which were carried out immediately following the meeting. The rulings of administrative officers could be appealed, in theory, to the territorial Governor who could choose to refer the cases to the Superior Judge, but Jan-Georg Deutsch asserts that appeals were 'almost impossible' in practice and that the decisions made by administrative officers were, 'the only law that existed' for Africans.[8]

The court system that German colonial authorities had used in German East Africa remained after Germany lost the territory during World War I. By 1916 much of German East Africa was under the military administration of Great Britain. Sir Horace Byatt was initially sent to the territory to serve as the British Civil Administrator and eventually became the territory's first Governor in 1920.[9] Lacking other options, Byatt maintained the foundations of the German colonial system and relied on German methods and structures of rule.[10] The laws in place were a combination of martial law, select German colonial laws, and newly enacted British codes, many of which were transplanted from India.[11]

The Beginning of British Rule in Tanganyika

Following the conclusion of World War I negotiations at the Paris Peace Conference in 1919 resulted in the division of Germany's former colonial territories between the Allied Powers. Britain was granted a League of Nations mandate to take on formal administration of most of German East Africa and the territory was officially renamed The Tanganyika

Territory and referred to as Tanganyika.[12] The official reading of the Order in Council for Tanganyika at Buckingham Palace on 22 July 1920 inaugurated the era of British colonial rule in the territory.[13] Though Tanganyika's position as a League of Nations mandate gave it a separate legal status from Britain's other colonies, it quickly received British imperial institutions and staff, and became 'regarded as a permanent part of the British imperial family, albeit with certain international obligations and restrictions'.[14]

Since Tanganyika's incorporation into the British Empire occurred after it had largely stopped acquiring new territories, the British administration in Tanganyika reflected the lessons colonial authorities had learnt from establishing and maintaining British rule in its earlier colonial experiments. The system of governance and ideology underpinning British rule in Tanganyika was indirect rule, which meant that colonial authorities governed through, so-called traditional authorities and institutions.[15] Indirect rule was an appealing form of administration for colonial authorities because it was cost effective and administratively convenient. This system allowed the British to minimise the number of staff on the ground and relied on a select group of colonial subjects to cooperate with colonial officials and help legitimise the colonial government to other colonial subjects.

While the British had used forms of indirect rule in their earlier colonies, such as in the princely states in India, the version often attributed to Lord Lugard in Nigeria is the model that was extended to Tanganyika.[16] From the inception of formal British rule in Tanganyika, the system of governance was indirect in nature and incorporated African authorities, but it was under Governor Cameron—Tanganyika's second and most famous British colonial governor—that indirect rule as a system and ideology became fully entrenched.[17]

In the late 1920s Cameron introduced a new organisational structure to the territory with an administrative hierarchy that consisted of district officers, who worked under district commissioners in 42 new districts, whose work was in turn supervised and supported by the provincial commissioners of the 11 new provinces. Provincial commissioners were supervised by the Governor and his Secretariat, both based in Dar es Salaam. In all, the administrators were few in number and enjoyed a great deal of autonomy in their daily work. This 'thin white line' of administrators communicated government policies to African authorities, called the Native Authority, who were defined as chiefs, sultans, akidas, jumbe, or headmen 'recognised as such by the Governor'.[18] Native Authorities were expected to implement and enforce colonial polices on behalf of the British. The crux of the indirect rule system was the relationship between Native Authority and District Officer. This relationship also became central to the colonial justice system and helped shape the structure of the colonial court system.

The Structure of the Colonial Court System

Colonial judges of the High Court were the core of the centralised British court system in Tanganyika. The structure was similar to the court systems established in other British dependencies in the twentieth century, especially in West Africa.[19] The laws applied by the courts were primarily territorial ordinances, orders, and proclamations, as well as the common law, doctrines of equity, and statues of general application in force in Great Britain at the time.[20] Many of the colonial codes initially introduced to Tanganyika were essentially copies of those developed for use in India, such as the Criminal Procedure Code, Penal Code, and Indian Evidence Act.[21] The High Court was established under the Tanganyika Order in Council and its relationship to lower courts was developed through the Courts Ordinance of 1920. The most superior court in the appellate system was the High Court, which had 'full jurisdiction, civil and criminal, over all persons and over all matters in the territory'.[22] The High Court also had Admiralty jurisdiction and the power to hear cases involving crimes and disputes that had occurred before the commencement of formal British rule.[23] For this purpose the Special Tribunal was created to dispose of cases pre-dating the British courts, most of which were 'civil claims caused by war conditions'.[24]

Below the High Court were the subordinate courts, which were categorised as First, Second, or Third Class and had designated authorities, jurisdictions, and powers of punishment.[25] First Class courts were presided over by magistrates or district-level political officers;[26] Second Class courts were presided over by experienced political officers; and Third Class subordinate courts were presided over by assistant political officers of little experience.[27] Beneath the British subordinate courts were Native Courts, which were loosely defined as courts of Native Authorities, some of whom held judicial power prior to British rule. Under this system, cases could be appealed from any subordinate or Native Court directly to the High Court.[28] The High Court also had the right to revise sentences that reached a prescribed level of severity. By utilising administrative officers and Native Courts, this structure required few professional legal staff beyond the judges, Registrar of the High Court, Deputy Registrar, a few Crown Counsels, an Attorney General, and a Solicitor General. This basic system was inexpensive for the colonial government.

This court system was, in essence, under the purview of the judges of the High Court, who had full jurisdiction over everyone living in Tanganyika regardless of colonial racial classification. This changed in 1929, however, when a new ordinance removed Native Courts, and therefore most cases involving Africans, from their jurisdiction. This ordinance fundamentally altered the position of the colonial judiciary in relation to the administration and the African population. The administration's motivations for this ordinance, and its implications for both the judiciary and administration, illustrate the development of the indirect rule system in Tanganyika and the role of colonial judges within it. Before analysing the significant impact of the Native Courts Ordinance, it is necessary to first explore the functions of the High Court and the courts beneath it.

The High Court of Tanganyika

The High Court of Tanganyika was both a British establishment and a colonial construct. It was a 'hybrid institution' in that it bore qualities of a traditional British legal institution as well as the modifications effected for the colonial context.[29] The Court began its work in 1921 in Dar es Salaam, the colonial capital, with three colonial judges: a Chief Justice, William M. Carter; and two puisne judges, Gilchrist G. Alexander, and Robert Walker.[30] At that time the High Court occupied the old German courthouse and, while the exterior was a reminder of the German colonial legacy, inside it quickly took on a 'British atmosphere' along with the rest of the territory.[31] Judges wore wigs and red or black gowns like those in use in Britain. The judiciary was very small relative to the administrative cadre. If the colonial administrators were a 'thin white line' throughout the territory, then the judiciary could be most accurately described as a red dot in Dar es Salaam.

After its establishment in 1920 the High Court was focused initially on resolving a backlog of civil disputes, more than half of which fell under the jurisdiction of the Special Tribunal.[32] As civil disputes resulting from the conditions in Tanganyika during and after World War I were resolved by the Court, the number of civil cases decreased and by 1925 the majority of cases heard at the High Court were on criminal matters. These criminal cases increased from the 133 tried in 1925 to 312 a decade later in 1935, which may be evidence of the growing reach of the British system rather than an increase in crime in the territory.[33] The High Court judges' time was occupied by revising and confirming sentences from subordinate courts in both civil and criminal matters and by hearing appeals, most of which related to criminal matters.[34]

While the High Court enjoyed a superior position within the territory, it did not exist in isolation from the larger legal structures in the British Empire. Cases heard by the High Court could be appealed to the Eastern African Court of Appeal, which was established in 1902 for appeals from the East Africa Protectorate, Uganda, and British Central Africa (Nyasaland).[35] By 1921 the Court had increased its jurisdiction, hearing appeals from Kenya, Uganda, Nyasaland, Tanganyika, and Zanzibar.[36] Its Bench was comprised of three judges from the territories under its jurisdiction and these judiciaries were connected to one another through the Court. Typically, the right of appeal was only exercised by defendants in serious criminal cases and in substantial civil disputes between expatriates. When a party did appeal a judgment, the original sentence would not be carried out until after the case was either dismissed or heard by the Court of Appeal, which happened in a minority of cases.[37]

Cases heard by the Eastern African Court of Appeal could be appealed to the Privy Council, which served as a final court of appeal for all territories in the British Empire with established court systems.[38] This meant that in the early twentieth century it had jurisdiction over appeals from 'one quarter of the world population'.[39] The right of appeal to the Eastern African Court of Appeal and Privy Council connected colonial subjects in Tanganyika to the rest of Britain's territories in Africa and across the globe. In principle and theory this linked the courts in Tanganyika to the British court system, but in practice it was rare for appeals to transcend the physical and legal colonial boundaries of Tanganyika and reach the Privy Council.

Within the British colonial court system there was a clear division based on race, which reflected colonial social categories. The existence of two court systems, the Native Courts for Africans and the British courts for non-Africans, meant that most cases involving Africans were not initially heard by the British courts. Moderately serious violations of the law would be heard by administrative officers in their capacity as magistrates in the first instance. Therefore, only very serious cases would be heard in the first instance by the High Court or by a magistrate working with extended jurisdiction of the High Court. Most cases of this nature tried at the High Court involved an African male charged with a crime such as rape, murder, manslaughter, or grave offences against property, such as arson.

Non-Africans, on the other hand, could expect to have both their civil and criminal cases—no matter how minor—heard by a British subordinate court or by the High Court. Unsurprisingly, the civil jurisdiction of professional courts was utilised almost exclusively by the expatriate community. Though Asians comprised less than 1% of the population, civil cases between members of the Asian community accounted for 48% of the total civil cases in 1939.[40] Similarly, while Europeans accounted for less than a tenth of a per cent of the population, civil cases between members of that community account for nearly 8% of the total. In that year 98% of civil cases involved at least one non-African party. While some few Africans did have civil cases tried at the High Court and expatriates were tried for serious violations of criminal law, in general, the High Court only saw Africans when they were accused of committing a serious criminal offence and saw expatriates when they engaged in civil disputes.

In order to conduct trials, colonial judges had to travel around Tanganyika. Travelling courts, also called assizes, were occasionally in use in Britain to allow judges to hold sessions in smaller villages, but the enormous size of Tanganyika combined with its small judiciary required the High Court to hear most of its cases on the circuit.[41] Between 1923 and 1926, on average, less than 15% of criminal cases were heard in Dar es Salaam and more than 85% on circuit.[42]

When serious crimes occurred outside the colonial capital, administrators would apprehend the accused and hold them in prison in the district until either a magistrate working with extended jurisdiction or a High Court judge was available to hear the case. Administrators periodically informed the Court of the pending cases in their districts and at some point thereafter a judge would travel, usually via the railway system, motorised vehicle, or steamer, to multiple towns clearing the backlog of cases from the surrounding district at each stop.[43] The number of cases and logistics of travel dictated when, and to some extent where, the circuits were held, although some standard routes were in use, with the Court often stopping in Mwanza and Moshi. The Central Line Railway, which ran from Dar es Salaam in the east to Kigoma in the west, was one of the primary paths for the High Court circuits.[44] The circuits were the principal means through which colonial judges learnt about the territory in which they worked and the Africans they met in court. Colonial judges seldom interacted directly with Africans during their travels, however. Judges primarily socialised with district and provincial administrators, and other expatriates, while on the circuit and learnt about the local circumstances and members of the local community through them.[45] Colonial judges typically stayed at rest houses and hotels, when available, but also stayed with 'friends' in the expatriate community or administration when hotels were unavailable, and socialised with them.

Though the use of the circuit system gave judges an opportunity to hear cases involving Africans outside Dar es Salaam, it also created challenges for Africans drawn into cases as defendants, litigants, or witnesses. For the accused outside Dar es Salaam, it could be a very long wait in prison before a judge came close enough to his/her location to hear the case, especially in the 1920s when the High Court travelled on circuit fewer than ten times per year and typically for only two to three weeks at a time.[46] The circuit system could also cause suffering for witnesses, as they could be forced to travel long distances to get to the judge's location. At times the colonial government would pay for witness transportation to the location where the Court had convened, and for those involved in cases at a subordinate court. When transportation was not made available for this purpose, however, Africans could be forced to walk long distances, causing the 'hardships' of being away from their homes and families as well as the risk of illness.[47] The practice of transporting Africans to the location of the Court may also have impacted the quality of the justice it dispensed. One provincial commissioner noted that the witnesses who were aware of the privations caused by this travel might be less likely to come forward.[48] Another hypothesised that the whole experience of travelling to the courts and being subject to British procedures in the courtroom might affect the 'reliability' of witnesses.[49] Despite these concerns, the reliance on the circuit system continued and expanded in its geographic reach during British rule in the territory. It was regularised during the 1930s through the organisation of standard circuit routes in 1937.[50] The circuit system was revised and extended further after World War II, when the colonial government began to make colonial judges more available to hear cases in the territory after complaints from the Colonial Office about the overuse of extended jurisdiction by magistrates in serious cases, as well as severe delays in trials. High Court circuits remained the primary means through which colonial judges adjudicated cases involving Africans during British rule and they were a peripatetic symbol of British colonial justice outside the colonial metropole.

Whether working on circuit or in the High Court in Dar es Salaam, the Court relied on the assistance of colonial subjects to carry out its work. British officials employed African 'intermediaries' to bridge 'linguistic and cultural gaps that separated European colonial officials from subject populations'.[51] The professional courts were particularly aided by two categories of intermediaries: assessors, who were intended to fill the 'cultural gap' between colonial judges and Africans by providing local information; and interpreters, who bridged the 'linguistic gap'. Assessors and interpreters were also in use in subordinate courts and assessors could be used in Native Courts. Both assessors and interpreters provided judges and magistrates with a means of accessing information about Africans and local circumstances.

While the English jury system had been introduced into many of Britain's earlier colonial dependencies, including India and much of British West Africa, juries were rarely in use in East and Central Africa and were not used in Tanganyika.[52] Instead the courts relied on one or more assessors to advise the judge or magistrate. Assessors had a variety of loosely defined functions, which included advising a judge on specific topics in question, such as local custom and customary law, and offering an opinion on the guilt or innocence of an accused party.[53] In sum, they had the qualities of both expert witnesses and juries.[54] Assessors were distinct from juries, however, in that they were not asked to reach agreement before giving their opinions and High Court judges were not bound by their findings.[55] Colonial racial and ethnic categorisations organised the assessor system in Tanganyika and the backgrounds of assessors typically matched those of the parties involved in a case.[56] Judges used assessors to query local custom and circumstance. Assessors were usually older, supposedly esteemed, male community members, like chiefs or headmen.[57] Though younger men could technically be chosen as assessors, it was rare for them to be asked. Women were also seldom invited to serve in this capacity.

Colonial authorities' preference for assessors over juries speaks to the role of race in shaping the procedures of colonial courts. The British notion of a 'jury of one's peers' was problematic in a colonial context due to institutionalised racial prejudice in the court system, which relied on race as an organising principle.[58] Some believed that there was a high risk that juries of Europeans would acquit each other for crimes against Africans, or that Africans would acquit each other for crimes against Europeans.[59] Furthermore, the racist and prevalent view in colonial rhetoric that Africans were not intellectually and politically advanced may have affected colonial administrations' decisions about whether Africans were capable of sitting as jurors, as juries' findings on matters of fact would be binding for the judge in most respects.[60] This may have influenced early decisions to reject jury trials and the subsequent trend of employing assessors instead. Since judicial officials in Tanganyika could choose to ignore the opinions of assessors, some judges believed that assessors therefore minimised the risk of racial differences and prejudices dictating the final outcome of cases.[61] This, of course, assumed that judges would not be influenced by their own perceptions of race and its relationship to criminality.

Assessors were more than a compromise from an idealised jury trial system, however. Ibhawoh asserts that assessors served both 'practical' and 'moral' purposes for the colonial regime.[62] They were, 'practical in the sense that European judges often could not understand … the customs of people in the dock, and moral in terms of legitimising "alien" courts in the eyes of Africans'.[63] Assessors remained in use after independence and continued to be regarded as a vital part of the judicial process at the High Court.[64] During colonial rule they offered colonial judges a unique means of connecting to the colonial context while maintaining the freedom to reject the opinions of colonial subjects in favour of their own notions of justice.

Like assessors, interpreters provided the medium for interaction between colonial authorities and subjugated peoples. They played a crucial role in communication within the colonial justice system, in which professional magistrates and judges were ordinarily unskilled in the *lingua franca*. In Tanganyika the language of the British courts was English and few legal authorities had more than a basic proficiency in Kiswahili. Moreover, many Africans did not speak Kiswahili, but spoke a local language. As a result, interpreters were 'essential in judicial work'.[65] Finding qualified interpreters, however, was a problem for the colonial government, as interpretation was required from Kiswahili, Arabic, and local languages into English for the courts. At times two interpreters would be used, first to translate from a local language into Kiswahili and then from Kiswahili to English. In the absence of interpreters, magistrates with basic proficiency would often carry out court proceedings in Kiswahili, but some acknowledged that their own interpretation skills did 'not allow for quick and accurate work'.[66] The issue of language and interpretation was a constant hurdle in the colonial courtroom, leaving room for mistakes and misinterpretations of the evidence. Translation was also a 'malleable' process and one that was 'prone to manipulation' by all players in the courtroom.[67] Even so, court interpreters were an important fixture at the High Court in Tanganyika, so important that it sought to play an active role in selecting and training its own interpreters.[68] The Court needed interpreters in order to communicate British notions of justice and institutional practices to Africans, and also relied on them to relay information from Africans.

The use of assessors and interpreters demonstrates that the colonial High Court was a product of a process of negotiation between British legal traditions and the social, political, and economic realities of colonial life. This can be further illustrated through the impact of the relationships between expatriates on the administration of colonial justice. The colonial courts both resolved conflicts between expatriates and reified what expatriate behaviour was legally acceptable in relation to Africans. Colonial judges played this role, however, as members of the expatriate colonial society, not as outsiders. As part of the colonial elite the colonial judges often personally knew the expatriate parties in cases before them, especially those in Dar es Salaam. Justice Alexander remarked in his memoir that on the same day he would hear a case involving a European, he might see that same person 'on the golf course, or the tennis court, or [be] his fellow guest on that very evening at a dinner party'.[69] This circumstance differed from the typical experience of the British judge in Great Britain, who would not normally have personal knowledge of the parties in the cases he adjudicated and would not anticipate interaction with them afterwards. The relationships between colonial judges and European litigants created potential conflicts of interest, especially in cases where the outcome could cause social conflict in small and tightly knit expatriate communities. The dual role of the colonial judge as both member and mediator of a colonial society illustrates that, while the High Court was in theory a replica of a British court, its location in the colonial context created additional and distinct challenges to the independence of the judiciary from social pressures.

Despite the adaptations for and pressures of the colonial context, the High Court aspired to be a British institution. In the territory it was the primary symbol of British justice and was more similar to British courts than the courts beneath it. Though colonial judges tried to infuse their notions of British judicial practices and principles in the subordinate courts, these courts applied even fewer British legal procedures and often blurred the line between the administration and judiciary.

The Subordinate Courts: Professional Magistrates and District Officers

Tanganyika had two categories of British subordinate courts: those of professional magistrates; and those of administrative officers. Professional magistrates, also known as resident magistrates and stipendiary magistrates, typically had professional legal training, especially after the unification of the Colonial Legal Service, and only carried out magisterial duties. They were few in number—only five served in Tanganyika during the first decade of British rule—and sat directly below the High Court in jurisdiction, serving as First Class courts. These magistrates were effectively acting as High Court judges, especially in the 1920s and 1930s when they were often granted extended jurisdiction in order to prevent delays in cases waiting to be heard by a High Court judge on circuit. Professional magistrates normally had similar backgrounds to colonial judges. Indeed, many went on to become colonial judges, but their lifestyles and work differed in that they usually lived outside Dar es Salaam, had a greater variety of cases within their jurisdiction, and travelled on circuits only within the region in which they were based.

While these professional magistrates were a close extension of the High Court, both in nature and practice, the subordinate courts of administrative officers were markedly different. Under indirect rule the courts of administrative officers processed both civil disputes and crimes. These officers, who were magistrates *ex officio*, combined executive and judicial duties.[70] At the higher levels, provincial and district commissioners convened a court of first instance within their districts for matters that fell under the jurisdiction of Second and First Class courts, at times having the same level of jurisdiction as professional magistrates. Low-level district officers usually held Third Class powers, at times exercising powers higher than their rank. Like professional magistrates, administrators' powers of punishment could be extended in the absence of qualified judicial authorities. The courts of political officers were guided by basic procedures and the presiding officer usually had sole responsibility for recording the events in the courtroom.

This use of administrative officers in a judicial capacity was in conflict with the principle of the separation of powers between the executive and the judiciary. Moreover, the administrative duties of district officers could directly facilitate their role as magistrates, because they could also be called upon to investigate crimes, apprehend the accused, conduct preliminary inquiries, and prosecute cases. This fusion of judicial and executive duties in one person was heavily criticised by the professional judiciary, whose members resisted any intervention in their sphere by non-professionals and were sceptical of this breach of what they held as a treasured British principle.

It was essential for the minimalist indirect rule system that administrative officers processed most violations of the law in their districts, but their more significant role was as the link in the administrative system between the Native Authorities and the British administration. Even though the average administrative officer 'occupied a comparatively lowly position in the colonial hierarchy', he was 'the effective agent of its policy, the man on whom the success or failure of that policy mainly depended'.[71] In the court system specifically, administrative officers played the crucial role of connecting Native Courts to British courts and, after 1929, directly to the administration. Between 1925 and 1929, administrative officers heard appeals from Native Courts in their capacity as magistrates of subordinate courts and their decisions could be appealed directly to the High Court of Tanganyika, the Court of Appeal, and even the Privy Council. District Officers also supervised Native Courts by reviewing the records of decisions and punishments to ensure that their work did not interfere with British notions of 'justice' and 'morality' or directly contradict colonial policy.[72]

The Native Courts

Native Courts were numerous and heard the greatest number of cases—by 1949 there were over 600 Native Courts which heard about 114,000 cases annually—but they held the most limited powers of punishment and the lowest prestige.[73] Native Courts were essentially tribunals administered by African authorities for Africans, according to their perceived local customary law and practices, operating under the auspices of the colonial government. The courts of non-Africans categorised as 'natives', as well as courts functioning according to Shari'a law or Islamic practices under khadis and liwalis were also considered Native Courts.[74] These courts primarily functioned on the coast, but also existed in some inland areas.[75]

The specific placement of the Native Courts in Tanganyika's court system was ill-defined until 1925 when two ordinances established their jurisdiction and created First and Second Class Native Courts.[76] The ordinances also laid out the appeals procedure within the Native Courts system, and defined the relationship between Native Courts and British courts. At this time, cases originating in the Native Courts system could be appealed to the High Court or revised by it.[77] The ordinances also defined both the civil and criminal jurisdiction of the courts.[78] But the types of cases that came before the Native Courts were usually civil disputes over issues such as marriage (including bride-price and dowry), adultery, divorce, custody of children, inheritance, and personal property (frequently about ownership of cattle), or relatively minor criminal violations.[79] The geographic jurisdiction of a particular Native Court effectively corresponded to the administrative jurisdiction of the Native Authority in charge.

Like the High Court, Native Courts were a product of the colonial environment. They functioned according to a specific set of assumptions about Africans and African society.[80] Native Courts across British colonies in Africa were a complex and dynamic combination of British and African ideas about African tradition and custom, influenced and shaped by administrative concerns and preferences. The fundamental idea underpinning the Native Courts system, and indirect rule more broadly, was that all Africans belonged to 'tribes' and that those tribes had traditional authorities in a position to act as the Native Authority, some of whom had pre-existing judicial powers.[81] John Iliffe's seminal assertion that, 'The British wrongly believed that Tanganyikans belong to tribes; Tanganyikans created tribes to function within the colonial framework' offers some insight into how the colonial administrative structures and ideas about Africans reshaped African society through the use of the tribe as an organising principle.[82]

The British expounded the idea that customary law was a pre-existing body of traditional practices in dispute resolution which could be articulated as facts by a tribe's Native Authority and applied in Native Courts. Colonial authorities regarded what Africans asserted as customary to be a continuation of indigenous practices that both supported the Native Courts system and the claim that colonial authorities had maintained African practices. The British Mandate for East Africa and subsequent territorial Order in Council emphasised that the territorial government should consider customary law and practices when resolving disputes between Africans and should attempt to provide 'substantial justice without undue regard to technicalities of procedure'.[83] British legal authorities only intervened in the application of customary law and procedures when it contradicted colonial authority (either orders from administrators or colonial legislation) and when it deemed a practice 'repugnant' to British notions of 'natural justice, equity, or good conscience'.[84] The 'repugnancy clause' derives from the notion that there is a 'natural' law or means of justice that is universal and innate for all human beings. The British regarded their legal traditions as natural law in this sense and some African traditions and laws as unnatural, and therefore repugnant to British ideas of natural justice and morality.

The 'repugnancy clause' was inserted into government ordinances relating to the courts in most British colonies in Africa and allowed colonial judicial authorities, including the High Court, to be 'guided by native law' in their court work when hearing cases involving Africans, but did not spell out exactly how judicial authorities should deal with claims about custom.[85] This clause enabled British colonial authorities to transform anything that Africans asserted as customary, but colonial officials found unacceptable, into a practice that colonial authorities could accept as customary, or to simply ignore it. In practice, the judiciary only invoked the clause in a small number of reported cases, but Read asserts that administrative officers 'no doubt' relied on it often in cases on appeal from Native Courts.[86]

Customary law was a dynamic product of the encounter between colonial authorities and Africans.[87] While colonisers arguably 'invented' or at least influenced and elaborated on customary traditions to draw Africans into the colonial structures and under colonial authority, some Africans also used both law and legal procedures as a 'weapon' or 'resource' within their own communities and against British authority.[88] The development of customary law and the ability of African authorities to articulate and negotiate it were closely linked to the individuals deemed to be Native Authorities. British administrators had substantial control over the selection of Native Authorities and could remove those who were not willing to fall into line with British policies and methods.[89] In communities lacking a centralised authority or perceived tribal identity, the British attempted to establish Native Authorities who held both executive and judicial powers concurrently, much like a District Officer. They were given the opportunity to articulate the customs of their communities and this arguably fortified their personal power. Ultimately, the colonial Native Court became a 'corner-stone' of administrative efforts to rule indirectly.[90] The Native Courts, however, remained under the auspices of the judiciary until Governor Cameron revised the relationship between Native Courts and the judiciary in 1929.

Governor Cameron, Chief Justice Russell, and the Native Courts Ordinance of 1929

When Cameron became Governor of Tanganyika in 1925 he found a loose and somewhat unstructured system of indirect rule. Determined to expand the system, he quickly set about 'restructuring' the Native Authorities.[91] He codified his ideas about effective colonial governance in an ordinance in 1926, which was aimed at expanding the authority and standardising the role of Native Authorities in African communities throughout the territory.[92] Shortly after adopting the ordinance Cameron turned his attention to developing the Native Courts. He wanted them to become an extension of the powers granted to Native Authorities and a means of reinforcing tribal units, which theoretically would be more efficiently governed as a result. This was central to his idea of effective indirect rule. Cameron also reportedly thought, 'that by recognising the juridical rights of a Native Authority he could not only restore old equilibriums, but also force African law into adapting to changing conditions'.[93]

In Cameron's vision the Native Courts would not only serve as platforms for the resolution of disputes between Africans, but would also be institutions through which administrative orders could be implemented and reinforced, since they were to become the 'tribunal for trying cases arising out of orders and rules issued by Native Authorities'.[94] By disconnecting the Native Courts from the British courts, Cameron created a 'self-contained system under administrative supervision'.[95] The mechanism for this was the Native Courts Ordinance, which gave administrators the sole right to hear appeals from Native Courts and prevented judges from interfering in cases under the jurisdiction of the Native Courts. Cameron maintained, despite claims of administrative hegemony from his critics, that his proposed policy was motivated by protecting Africans from the 'alien' British court system and 'legalism' and 'technicalities' of British judges, who he believed would impose British legal principles that would be damaging, confusing, and disruptive to Africans and their traditions.[96] Cameron's position was supported by much of the administration, who regarded the legal procedures championed by judges to be completely inappropriate for Africans and out of step with British goals in the territory.

The Governor's efforts to garner support for his initiative to remove Native Courts from the supervision of the judiciary provoked aggressive opposition from the judges. Though Tanganyika's second Chief Justice,

William A. Russell—referred to by his middle name Alison—had initially supported Cameron's indirect rule policies, he fervently rejected Cameron's attempts to place the Native Courts under administrative control, regarding the proposed change as a 'return to a pioneer stage of administration'.[97] This subject became the central matter—among many—of disagreement between the two men. Their differing opinions over the ordinance are well documented.[98] Yet, in the late 1920s, the fissure between Cameron and Russell over the jurisdiction of the courts grew into a feud, well known in Tanganyika and to the Colonial Office through a seemingly endless series of strongly worded letters from both parties. The non-jurisdictional matters of disagreement in their correspondence, which have been mostly overlooked by historians of indirect rule in Tanganyika, reveal rival ideologies over the role of the professional judiciary under indirect rule and help to shed light on how the ordinance was a part of a larger marginalisation of the judiciary under Cameron. Cameron's view that the judiciary should have a very limited role in Tanganyika and should be secondary to the administration was in direct conflict with Russell's efforts to expand the judiciary and maintain its position as the authority in all legal matters.

In addition to their differences over the supervision of the Native Courts, Cameron and Russell disagreed strongly over the size of the judiciary and the salaries for its members. Cameron believed that only a small colonial judiciary would be needed to process very serious cases in Tanganyika once his policies were in place and therefore resisted any attempts to enhance the size of the judiciary or add to its influence. He even sought to decrease the number of judicial officials in Tanganyika, believing the judiciary to be inefficient, underworked, and a financial drain on the colony.[99] According to Cameron all that the territory needed was a small court able to hear the most serious criminal matters and civil suits between expatriates. Cameron resented, and perhaps feared, Russell's attempts to deal with Africans directly and complained that the Chief Justice's actions were 'outside the sphere of his own duties'.[100] Cameron protested that the High Court judges, 'know nothing of the language, the customs, the modes of life and thought of natives, whereas, on the other hand, the natives know nothing of the High Court and do not understand its intervention between themselves and their Administrative Officer, who in their eyes represents the Governor'.[101]

Russell, on the other hand, sought to maintain the judiciary's oversight of all judicial matters and suggested an increase in the number of judicial officers due to an overwhelming workload for the courts.[102] While there is not sufficient evidence from the period to substantiate claims from either side about work hours of individual judges and magistrates, correspondence on the number of cases waiting to be heard by the courts gives credence to Russell's claim that at least part of the judiciary was not able to keep up with the cases filed in all of the court system. In 1928, advocates complained bitterly to the Registrar of the High Court that there was a backlog of 247 civil cases in one district, which one advocate regarded as 'tantamount to an almost complete cessation of the administration of justice in the District'.[103] Ultimately, debate over the size of the judiciary in the late 1920s did not affect the number of judges and magistrates working in Tanganyika. Nevertheless, the debate about court size illustrates that as Tanganyika moved towards a more rigid application of Cameron's form of indirect rule, senior administrators attempted to minimise the role of the judiciary in the territory and feared its intercession in *their* sphere.

Furthermore, Cameron viewed the work of the judiciary as having a comparatively low value to that of the administration. Cameron's appraisal of the value of the judiciary was evident in another squabble with Russell over the salaries of judges. Cameron rejected raises for the judiciary and 'reduced' Russell's salary to that of the Chief Secretary.[104] This move was both a personal affront to Russell and a political statement that the Chief Justice, who was typically regarded as second only to the Governor in terms of status, should not be ascribed a greater value through his salary than that of a high-level officer.

It seems that despite the significant political and ideological differences between Russell and Cameron, the immovable positions they both occupied stemmed from, or were exacerbated by, the vicious personality conflict between them. Tanganyika was beginning to build a tradition of dueling governors and chief justices as Governor Byatt and Chief Justice Carter, who preceded Cameron and Russell, were also 'known to disagree' and apparently did not have an amicable interpersonal relationship.[105] One might question whether the negotiation of the structure of the early colonial government provoked interpersonal conflicts between the two individuals who acted as heads of their spheres of government.

One possible indication of the personal nature of the conflict between Cameron and Russell is that after Russell's retirement, which was regarded as a protest against Cameron's actions and the Native Courts Ordinance of 1929, Cameron changed his views on the salary and the size of the judiciary.[106] Cameron eventually supported efforts by the new Chief

Justice, Joseph A. Sheridan, to increase the salaries of judges and acknowledged the need for more judicial staff in Tanganyika not long after Russell's departure.[107] Chief Justice Joseph Sheridan worked more easily with the administration than his predecessor and his 'popular personality' seems to have eased his work in the territory and facilitated somewhat improved relations between the judiciary and the administration.[108]

In the end the Colonial Office had to determine whether to allow Cameron's proposal to remove the Native Courts from the jurisdiction of the High Court.[109] Despite protests from the judiciary and Legislative Council in the territory, the Colonial Office sided with Cameron.[110] The result was the Native Courts Ordinance of 1929, which gave the administration absolute power over Native Courts. When the ordinance came into effect, provincial commissioners gained the authority to create or eliminate Native Courts, determine when sessions were held, remove any member of a Native Court, appoint individuals to serve as courts of appeal, exclude individuals from the jurisdiction of a court, revise proceedings, and transfer any case from the courts to the subordinate courts. Additionally, the Governor could make and amend all rules in relation to the courts, setting fees, practices, and procedures at will. The Native Courts were given jurisdiction over Africans in both civil and criminal matters and were expected to carry out proceedings according to customary law, subject to the repugnancy clause. Advocates were barred from entering Native Courts.

It was the ordinance's provision relating to appeals, however, which deeply affected the position of the High Court and split the bifurcated system into two separate court systems in the territory. The ordinance specified that appeals from the Native Courts system would go to the administrative chain of command: first to the District Officer (in his capacity as an administrator, not as a magistrate), then to the Provincial Commissioner, and finally to the Governor.[111] This move disconnected Native Courts from the British appellate system, removing most disputes between Africans from the jurisdiction of the High Court, sidelining judges and isolating them from Africans.[112] It was a definitive victory for the British administration. Challenges to its authority and to that of the Native Authorities were safely under administrative supervision.[113] The ordinance represented the climax of the transformation of indirect rule under Cameron, significantly elevating the power and prestige of the colonial administration and Native Authority over Africans, and endowing Native Courts as stronger agents of the colonial government.

The combined impact of removing most cases from the supervision of the High Court and Cameron's assault on the size of the judiciary was a marginalisation of the judiciary in the sphere of colonial justice. Colonial judges had even more limited interactions with and influence on Africans as a result of the ordinance. At the height of indirect rule in Tanganyika, colonial judges reached their lowest point of prestige and least influence in the administration of justice.

This process in Tanganyika bears some key similarities to the episode of judicial reorganisation in 1914 in Southern Nigeria under Lord Lugard, although one of the driving concerns there was limiting the role of the African lawyer, which was not under debate in Tanganyika at the time because there were not any Africans with legal qualifications.[114] The similarities are not surprising given the years Cameron had spent working in Nigeria following the reorganisation there and prior to becoming Governor of Tanganyika.

Though Tanganyika's colonial judges watched their jurisdiction shrink, they had other functional and symbolic roles in the territory, which were maintained and even expanded after 1929. Colonial judges were both an embodiment of the rhetoric supporting British rule and facilitated the application of indirect rule polices in Tanganyika. Thus the judiciary remained a central part of the development of Tanganyika as a British colony.

The Roles of Colonial Judges in Tanganyika

It is clear that the main role of colonial judges throughout British rule was to adjudicate cases under their jurisdiction. In doing so, they helped to establish British rule in Tanganyika and maintain law and order. Yet their mere presence was also of symbolic importance to British rule in the territory. The rhetoric justifying the presence of British authorities in Tanganyika during the interwar years was not only that of 'protecting' Africans but also 'civilising' them. The 'civilising mission' purported to bring British ideas of civilisation to 'uncivilised' Africans. The colonial law, British courts, and British control over customary courts were at the heart of twentieth-century colonial *civilisation*. Mahmood Mamdani asserts that 'The torchbearers of that civilization were supposed to be the colonial courts. The courts were intended neither just as sites where disputes would be settled nor simply as testimony to effective imperial control; rather, they were to shine as beacons of Western civilization.'[115] The judiciary saw itself and was pointed to in colonial rhetoric as a human embodiment of the law and served as evidence of Britain's proclaimed commitment to 'civilise' the territory, not just rule it.[116] Still, there was a fundamental contradiction between 'civilising' rhetoric encouraging the introduction of British ideas and institutions, and the driving idea behind indirect rule, which was to keep Africans 'native'. In this sense, the judges as *civilisers* were in conflict with indirect rule policies, yet remained a symbol of British rhetoric aimed at legitimising colonial rule, and the Empire more broadly. Moreover, the presence of colonial justice systems, the common law, and colonial judges, may have also helped to project the idea that colonial administrations were 'just' and circumscribed by the law, thereby minimising the more repressive character of colonial rule and making it more acceptable to liberals in the metropole.

Colonial judges also provided practical facilitation of the indirect rule system's reliance on administrators serving as magistrates. Using administrative officers as magistrates minimised the need for professional legal staff, keeping costs down and limiting the interference of trained lawyers in African affairs. Though many judges would have preferred for only professional lawyers to have judicial powers, this was typically recognised as a financial impossibility, and administrators needed guidance and instruction on how to perform magisterial duties.[117] The judiciary facilitated this key element of indirect rule by acting as legal leadership and educators for administrators in their magisterial duties. Colonial judges held ten-day courses for new cadets on the penal code, criminal procedure code, and code of civil procedure, and sent out circulars with instructions to magistrates on how to carry out their duties.[118] Russell personally created a handbook for magistrates to communicate the judicial point of view on how justice should be administered to junior magistrates and officers.[119] His aim was to improve the quality of the work of lay magistrates by providing them with professional guidance. Colonial judges further facilitated the administration of law exams to new administrative officers, who were required to pass a series of them, usually within their first year in the territory.[120] The training of lay magistrates allowed the judiciary and administration to work together. It was also a means through which senior judges would impress on junior administrative officers their ideas about how to administer justice.

While colonial judges aided the work of administrative officers, they also provided a check on their actions through revising magistrates' decisions and hearing appeals. In these ways judges could curb excessive punishments or quash decisions that were out of line with the law in force at the time (barring those cases originating in Native Courts after 1929). The law both fortified and limited the power of the colonial administration as colonial judges could use the law to curb the power of individual administrators who attempted to use the administration of justice as a means of increasing their local authority or personal prestige. Furthermore, the judiciary had a direct line of communication with the Legal Adviser at the Colonial Office and could complain about the activities of the administration without a threat to their tenure in the Colonial Legal Service. Therefore, the judiciary had a means for attempting to resist administrative policy initiatives within the territory, however unsuccessfully at times.

Though the main role of the judiciary was to apply the laws necessary to maintain order as well as limit crime in Tanganyika, the jurisdiction of the professional courts over civil disputes meant that many cases before colonial judges were related to civil transactions and commerce. Colonial judges saw themselves as assisting 'normal methods of trading' and providing 'the security of recourse to the Courts in the giving of credit'.[121] Parts of the community of expatriate traders also apparently regarded professional judges and magistrates as facilitating their civil transactions.[122] This was of particular concern to much of the Asian population, which grew dramatically during the first decade of British rule to more than double its original size.[123] Many members of the Asian community were involved in trade and brought a substantial number of civil cases to the professional courts. The Indian Association even requested the establishment of a permanent court in a location which lacked one, arguing that since the province was,

> rapidly progressing in all its commercial developments, my association feels the necessity of having a permanent Court at this station, to facilitate larger credit transactions in trade, and also because a permanent Resident Magistrate would naturally be able to pay more attention to all Court affairs, than the District Officers, who, although doing excellently, are mostly engaged in administrative work.[124]

In providing a mechanism for the resolution of business disputes and transactions, colonial judges assisted with the development of commerce in the territory and facilitated its economic development in line with imperial economic aims.

Finally, colonial judges in Tanganyika were in a unique position to engage with their counterparts in neighbouring British territories due to their role on the Eastern African Court of Appeal. By virtue of being members of the High Court, judges in Tanganyika were also on the Bench of the Court of Appeal. Thus they travelled to other East African territories to hear cases as well as host judges from the other benches when appeals sessions were held in Tanganyika. In this capacity colonial judges became a link to the rest of Britain's East African territories, and part of attempts to draw the new Tanganyika Territory closer to the more established colonies of Kenya and Uganda. This link supported the Colonial Office's agenda of creating a closer relationship between the three territories and its efforts to standardise the administration of justice across East Africa.

Through these multiple roles, colonial judges were active participants in the colonial rule of Tanganyika. Though they saw themselves as having higher social and moral objectives than the administration, as well as a unique impact on the lives of Africans, in reality they had little contact with Africans, to most of whom the High Court was essentially inaccessible, especially after 1929. Yet the various roles of the High Court beyond adjudicating cases reveal that it was a multi-faceted institution, which facilitated the policies of the colonial government and the work of expatriate communities, while also acting as a check on some of the powers of the low-level colonial administrators. Colonial judges undoubtedly assisted in colonial development of the territory and were a part of larger imperial efforts to connect Tanganyika to neighbouring British colonies and the Empire.

Conclusion

The 1929 Native Courts Ordinance had a significant impact on the administration of justice in Tanganyika. The government's decision to sever the relationship between the Native Courts and the High Court may have had little practical effect on most court cases in the Native Courts, as few had made it to the High Court before 1929, but it reshaped the structure of colonial justice under indirect rule in Tanganyika, as well as the position of the judiciary in the colonial state.

The Native Courts were an effective tool in the elevation of administrative power under Governor Cameron. Removing Africans' right to appeal to the High Court on matters relating to administrative policy and Native Authorities tipped the balance of power between the judiciary and administration, entrenching administrative power over African life and law.[125]

Cameron's policies significantly marginalised the judiciary in the sphere of colonial justice, severely limiting the High Court's jurisdiction. The marginalisation of the judiciary was far from complete, however. In fact, it could not have been so without damaging the colonial state, because indirect rule in Tanganyika relied on a functioning judiciary with British colonial judges for a variety of symbolic and practical purposes.

Though the 'parallel' court systems—the Native Courts system and the British court system—remained in place until after national independence, the appellate system and the relationship between the two systems underwent numerous revisions both before and, more significantly, after World War II. In the decade preceding World War II, the court systems were revised twice by new ordinances, both of which made noteworthy changes, but neither fundamentally altered the position of the High Court, the nature of colonial justice, or the identities of the individuals who were a part of the systems. First, the Courts Ordinance of 1930, which replaced the 1920 ordinance, laid out who in Cameron's new administrative structure would serve as a magistrate and at what level in each district. It also, for the first time, defined the jurisdiction of resident magistrates, making them courts of the First Class.[126] A little over a decade later and during World War II, the Courts Ordinance of 1941 abolished the system of multiple courts of varying levels in a single district and created a single District Court in each administrative district.[127] Magistrates of all three levels could sit at this Court with defined powers of punishment based on individual administrative rank. Any case heard in the District Court could be appealed directly to the High Court, excluding appeals of cases from Native Courts heard by the same officers, but in their administrative capacity.

While the administrative appellate system for cases generated in Native Courts remained in place alongside the changes of the 1930s and early 1940s, there was one important modification to the appeals process for cases in Native Courts in 1940. Though the Governor remained the final word in these appeals, he began to officially convene an appeals board to make recommendations to him on case verdicts.[128] The membership of the appeals board was initially confined to members of the elite administration, including the Attorney General, the Administrative Secretary, and a Provincial Commissioner.[129] Its creation marked the beginning of the transfer of the Governor's powers to those more involved in African administration and justice, and it was a precursor to post-World War II changes that began the slow reintegration of judges into the decision-making process on Native Court cases and the long journey back to the level of appellate authority the Court had before 1929.

Notes

1. M.E. Chamberlain, *The Scramble for Africa*, 3rd edn (Harlow, 2010), p. 54.
2. For a short discussion of pre-colonial institutions and practitioners involved in dispute resolution in Tanganyika, see: F. Twaib, *The Legal Profession in Tanzania* (Bayreuth, 1997), pp. 16–17; Court of Appeal of Tanzania, *The History of the Administration of Justice in Tanzania* (Dar es Salaam, 2004), pp. 1–8.
3. 1 T.L.R. (R), p. v.
4. The term 'native' represents a colonial categorization present in the archival documents. The term is neither condoned nor accepted by its use and will remain in inverted commas throughout, except when it appears in titles of courts or authorities, such as the Native Courts and the Native Authority.
5. On the use of Akidas under German rule see: W.M.H. Hailey and the Royal Institute of International Affairs, *An African Survey: A Study of Problems Arising in Africa South of the Sahara*, 2nd edn (London, 1945), p. 435.
6. The word *shauri* does not uniquely refer to district councils held by German colonial officers. It is a generic word in Kiswahili for council and was used by Germans to refer to other practices and institutions used to facilitate interaction with Africans in German East Africa. See: M. Pesek, 'Cued Speeches: The Emergence of Shauri as Colonial Praxis in German East Africa, 1850–1903', *History in Africa*, 33 (2006), p. 388.
7. J.G. Deutsch, 'Celebrating Power in Everyday Life: The Administration of Law and the Public Sphere in Colonial Tanzania, 1890–1914', *Journal of African Cultural Studies*, 15 (2002), p. 93.
8. Ibid., p. 100. In civil matters 'natives' could appeal directly to the Superior Judge when the value in dispute involved more than 1000 rupees. P. Moffett, 'Native Courts in Tanganyika: A History of the Development of Native Courts from German Times', *Journal of African Administration*, 4 (1952), pp. 17–18.
9. For Byatt's impressions and experiences of Tanganyika after World War I, see: H. Byatt, 'Tanganyika', *Journal of the African Society*, 24 (1924), pp. 1–9.
10. A.F. Madden and J. Darwin, *The Dependent Empire, 1900–1948: Colonies, Protectorates, and Mandates* (London, 1994), p. 781; J. Iliffe, *A Modern History of Tanganyika* (Cambridge, 1979), pp. 318–319.
11. 1 T.L.R. (R), p. vi.
12. Article 22 of the Covenant of the League of Nations established the mandate system.

13. The Order in Council placed Tanganyika under the Foreign Jurisdiction Act 1890, which formally established the Crown's jurisdiction over the territory. H.F. Morris, 'Protection or Annexation? Some Constitutional Anomalies of Colonial Rule' in H.F. Morris and J.S. Read, *Indirect Rule and the Search for Justice: Essays in East African Legal History* (Oxford, 1972), p. 46.
14. M.L. Bates, 'Tanganyika: The Development of a Trust Territory', *International Organization*, IX (1955), p. 42.
15. J. Cell, 'Who Ran the British Empire?' in W.R. Louis (ed.), *More Adventures with Britannia. Personalities, Politics, and Culture in Britain* (Austin, 1998), pp. 306–307.
16. See: F.J.D. Lugard, *The Dual Mandate in British Tropical Africa*, 5th edn (London, 1965); H.A. Gailey, *Sir Donald Cameron, Colonial Governor* (Stanford, 1974), p. xi.
17. H.F. Morris, 'The Framework of Indirect Rule in East Africa' in H.F. Morris and J.S. Read, *Indirect Rule and the Search for Justice: Essays in East African Legal History* (Oxford, 1972), pp. 3–4.
18. A.H.M. Kirk-Greene, 'The Thin White Line: The Size of the British Colonial Service in Africa', *African Affairs*, 79 (1980), pp. 25–44; Native Authority Ordinance 1921, s 2 & 8. The 1921 ordinance was repealed and replaced by the Native Authority Ordinance 1923, which defined Native Authorities in the same way and further outlined the powers of chiefs in relation to the prevention of crime and maintenance of law and order within their communities.
19. On British colonial legal systems in West Africa see: O. Adewoye, *The Judicial System in Southern Nigeria, 1854–1954: Law and Justice in a Dependency* (London, 1977); T.O. Elias, *The Nigerian Legal System* (London, 1963); G.O. Onagoruwa, 'The History of the Judiciary in Commonwealth African Countries with Special Reference to West Africa', Ph.D. thesis (University of London, 1969).
20. E. Cotran, 'Tanzania', in A.N. Allott (ed.), *Judicial and Legal Systems in Africa* (London, 1970), p. 146.
21. H.F. Morris, 'The Reception and Rejection of Indian Law' in H.F. Morris and J.S. Read, *Indirect Rule and the Search for Justice: Essays in East African Legal History* (Oxford, 1972), pp. 110–118.
22. Tanganyika Order in Council *1920*, s 17(1).
23. Ibid., s 18(1).
24. 1 T.L.R. (R), p. vii; Special Tribunal Ordinance 1920. Cases of this nature were usually adjudicated by a colonial judge, but could be handled by resident magistrates or district-level political officers when they involved an amount below a specified threshold.
25. Tanganyika Order in Council 1920, s 22(1).

26. This refers to the German districts in place when the Order in Council and Courts Ordinance became law in 1920. Under Cameron, these districts were replaced by provinces and provincial commissioners became the highest administrative officers on a regional level.
27. Courts Ordinance 1920, s 3(1–3).
28. Ibid., s 22.
29. This is an extension of Brett Shadle's characterisation of customary courts in Kenya as 'hybrid institutions' in: B. Shadle, 'African Court Elders in Nyanza Province, Kenya, ca. 1930–1960: From "Traditional" to "Modern"' in B.N. Lawrance, E.L. Osborn, and R.L. Roberts (eds.), *Intermediaries, Interpreters, and Clerks: African Employees in the Making of Colonial Africa* (Madison, 2006), p. 181.
30. Puisne is a French word that roughly translates to later born and has been used in common law systems, including Tanganyika's during British rule, to refer to the junior status of judges of the High Court relative to the Chief Justice. Alexander's memoir of his experience in Tanganyika is the only work of its kind by a colonial judge of Tanganyika before the late 1950s. G.G. Alexander, *Tanganyika Memories: A Judge in the Red Kanzu* (London, 1936).
31. Ibid., p. 30. Chief Justice Carter requested funds to build a new court building claiming the German building was 'quite unsuitable and inadequate'. TNA, AB.538, W.M. Carter to H.A. Byatt, 22 November 1920, p. 5. Governor Byatt rejected this request arguing that the existing German court building met 'reasonable requirements'. TNA, AB.538, H.A. Byatt to W.M. Carter, 20 December 1920, p. 2. As a result, the first purpose-built British High Court of Tanganyika was not completed until 1958.
32. TNA, AB.461, 'Annual Report of the Legal Department, 1922', n.d.
33. TNA, AB.480, 'Annual Report of the Judicial Department for 1925', n.d.; ARJ 1936, p. 3.
34. The provisions for appeals to the High Court and revision by the High Court were provided for by the Courts Ordinance 1920, s 19 & 22.
35. J.S. Read, 'A Century Plus of Appeal Courts in Tanzania', in C.M. Peter and H.K. Bisimba (eds.), *Law and Justice in Tanzania: Quarter of a Century of the Court of Appeal* (Dar es Salaam, 2007), p. 63.
36. Eastern African Court of Appeal Order in Council 1921. The ability of a party to appeal to the Court of Appeal from Tanganyika was established in 1922 with the Appeals to the Court of Appeal Ordinance 1922. Cases where the High Court exercised its powers of revision to enhance a sentence could also be appealed to the Eastern African Court of Appeal.
37. See, for example: ARJ 1936, p. 7.
38. On African appeals to the Privy Council, see: B. Ibhawoh, *Imperial Justice: Africans in Empire's Court* (New York, 2013).

39. L.J. Blom-Cooper, G. Drewry, and B. Dickson, *The Judicial House of Lords: 1876–2009* (Oxford, 2009), p. 337.
40. Tanganyika Territory, *Census of the Native Population 1931* (Dar es Salaam 1932), p. 10; Tanganyika Territory, *Report on the Non-Native Census 1931* (Dar es Salaam, 1932), p. 10; ARJ 1939, p. 8.
41. On colonial judges on the circuit in Tanganyika, see: P. Swanepeol, 'Transient Justice: Colonial Judges on Circuit in Interwar Tanganyika', *Stichproben: Vienna Journal of African Studies*, 24 (2013), pp. 65–91.
42. Data from unpublished annual reports for the years 1923–1926: TNA, AB.66, 'Annual Report of the Judicial Department for the Year 1923, Tanganyika Territory', n.d; AB.67, 'Legal Department Annual Report for the Year 1924', n.d.; AB. 480, 'Judicial Department Report 1925', n.d.; AB. 497, 'Annual Report for the Judicial Department for the Year 1926', 7 April 1927.
43. TNA, 10201, I.O. Bancroft to J. Scott, 7 December 1927; Acting Registrar of the High Court to L.B. Freeston, 30 September 1943; TNA, 205–78 Vol. II, M.J.R. Coakley to J.S.R. Cole, 20 March 1958.
44. Widner asserts that Chief Justice Carter's trips on the Central Line, which involved handing down many death sentences in capital cases, caused a play on words involving changing Carter's name to *kata*, which is the Kiswahili verb meaning 'to cut up, divide, or bring to an end'. Widner argues this was 'an apt characterisation of Justice Carter's job description'. Widner, *Building*, p. 42. Alternatively, it is possible that the connection sometimes made between the name Carter and the Kiswahili word *kata* may be related to the phrase *kukata rufaa*, which means to appeal or to appeal a decision, as lower decisions could be appealed to High Court judges like Carter during his tenure and Carter's decisions could be appealed to the Eastern African Court of Appeal. Leopold Kalunga, interview with author, Dar es Salaam, 31 October 2008. The phrase *kukata rufaa* is currently in use in Tanzania for appeals. Claims and speculation relating to whether Africans connected Carter's name in any way to the pre-existing Kiswahili word or phrase have not been substantiated, but perhaps reflect an ongoing interest in or concern about the nature of the early High Court circuits in Tanganyika.
45. RHL, MSS. Afr. s. 592, Mark Wilson Papers, Box 8/1, M. Wilson to L.C. Dalton, 'Memorandum', 14 June 1939, p. 1.
46. TNA, AB.480, 'Annual Report of the Judicial Department for 1925', n.d.
47. TNA, 10201, Provincial Commissioner of Iringa to D.J. Jardine, 20 January 1931, p. 1; Provincial Commissioner of the Northern Province to H.C.D.C. Mackenzie-Kennedy, 14 May 1938, p. 1; Provincial Commissioner of the Lake Province to L.B. Freeston, 14 March 1940, p. 2.

48. TNA, 10201, Provincial Commissioner of the Northern Province to H.C.D.C. Mackenzie-Kennedy, 14 May 1938, p. 1.
49. TNA, 10201, Provincial Commissioner of Iringa to D.J. Jardine, 20 January 1931, p. 2.
50. ARJ 1937, pp. 5–6.
51. B.N. Lawrance, E.L. Osborn, and R.L. Roberts, 'African Intermediaries and the "Bargain" of Collaboration' in Lawrance et al. (eds.), *Intermediaries, Interpreters, and Clerks*, p. 4.
52. R. Knox-Mawer, 'The Jury System in British Colonial Africa', *Journal of African Law*, 2 (1958), p. 161; J.H. Jearey, 'Trial by Jury and Trial with the Aid of Assessors in the Superior Courts of British African Territories: I', *Journal of African Law*, 4 (1960), pp. 133–146; J.H. Jearey, 'Trial by Jury and Trial with the Aid of Assessors in the Superior Courts of British African Territories: II', *Journal of African Law*, 5 (1961), pp. 36–47; J.H. Jearey, 'Trial by Jury and Trial with the Aid of Assessors in the Superior Courts of British African Territories: III', *Journal of African Law*, 5 (1961), pp. 82–98.
53. J.S. Read, 'Customary Law under Colonial Rule' in H.F. Morris and J.S. Read, *Indirect Rule and the Search for Justice: Essays in East African Legal History* (Oxford, 1972), p. 188, fn 61; J. Gray, 'Opinions of Assessors in Criminal Trials in East Africa as to Native Custom', *Journal of African Law*, 2 (1958), pp. 5–6.
54. A.N. Allott, 'The Judicial Ascertainment of Customary Law in British Africa', *The Modern Law Review*, 20 (1957), p. 250.
55. Gray, 'Opinions', pp. 5–6.
56. B. Ibhawoh, 'Historical Globalization and Colonial Legal Culture: African Assessors, Customary Law, and Criminal Justice in British Africa', *Journal of Global History*, 4 (2009), p. 434.
57. Ibid.
58. Knox-Mawer, 'The Jury', p. 162.
59. Alexander, *Tanganyika Memories*, pp. 90–91.
60. Y.P. Ghai and P. McAuslan, *Public Law and Political Change in Kenya: A Study of the Legal Framework of Government from Colonial Times to the Present* (Nairobi, 1970), pp. 168–169.
61. Alexander, *Tanganyika Memories*, p. 91.
62. Ibhawoh, 'Historical', p. 435.
63. Ibid. Ibhawoh credits the idea behind his comments quoted here to: L.A.A. Kyando and C.M. Peter, 'Lay people in the administration of criminal justice: The law and practice in Tanzania', *African Journal of International and Comparative Law*, 5 (1993), p. 669.
64. R.W. Moisey, 'The Role of Assessors in the Courts of Tanzania', *East African Law Journal*, 3 (1967), pp. 348–353.

65. Great Britain, *Report of the Commission of Inquiry into the Administration of Justice in Kenya, Uganda and the Tanganyika Territory in Criminal Matters, May, 1933, and Correspondence Arising out of the Report* (London, 1934), p. 45. It was designated Command Paper No. 4623. Henceforth referred to and cited as: The Bushe Report.
66. TNA, 11648, O.L. Bancroft to J. Scott, 10 August 1928, p. 1.
67. Lawrance, Osborn, and Roberts, 'African Intermediaries', p. 15.
68. TNA, 23509, C.J. Tyndale-Biscoe to P.E. Mitchell, 19 December 1934, p. 1.
69. Alexander, *Tanganyika Memories*, p. 189. Justice R.M. Cluer also complained about this type of mingling on the circuit in a memorandum on defects in the administration of justice in Tanganyika in 1943. TNA (UK), CO 691/191/42439, 'Memorandum by Mr. Justice Cluer', 31 December 1943, p. 17.
70. E.K. Lumley, *Forgotten Mandate: A British District Officer in Tanganyika* (London, 1976), p. 60.
71. Ibid., p. 9.
72. M.L. Bates, 'Tanganyika under British Administration, 1920–1955', D.Phil. thesis (University of Oxford, 1958), p. 136.
73. The African Studies Branch, 'A Digest of the Tanganyika Local Courts Ordinance 1951', *Journal of African Administration*, 4 (1952), p. 22.
74. Courts Ordinance 1920, s 3(4).
75. J.N.D. Anderson, *Islamic Law in Africa*, 1st edn (London, 1970), p. 122.
76. Native Courts Proclamation 1925, s 3–6; Native Courts Rules 1925.
77. Native Courts Proclamation 1925, s 11.
78. Ibid., First and Second Schedules.
79. RHL, MSS. Afr. s. 505, M.B. Ronaldson, 'Digest of Appeals, Mbulu District', [1937–1960], January 1961.
80. This is an extension of Chanock's idea that customary law was a product of colonial interactions between colonisers and Africans. M. Chanock, *Law, Custom, and Social Order: The Colonial Experience in Malawi and Zambia* (Cambridge, 1985), p. 4.
81. 'Tribe' is placed in inverted commas to problematise the use of the word in describing African communities—it will henceforth be used without.
82. Iliffe, *A Modern History*, p. 324.
83. Tanganyika Order in Council 1920, s 24.
84. Allott, 'The Judicial Ascertainment', p. 245.
85. Tanganyika Order in Council 1920, s 24.
86. Read, 'Customary Law', p. 177.
87. Chanock, *Law, Custom, and Social Order*, p. 4.

88. T.O. Ranger, 'The Invention of Tradition in Colonial Africa' in E.J. Hobsbawm and T.O. Ranger (eds.), *The Invention of Tradition* (Cambridge, 1983), pp. 211–263; T.O. Ranger, 'The Invention of Tradition Revisited: The Case of Colonial Africa', in T.O. Ranger and O. Vaughan (eds.), *Legitimacy and the State in Twentieth Century Africa. Essays in Honour of A. M. H. Kirk-Greene* (London, 1993), pp. 62–111; Chanock, *Law, Custom, and Social Order*, p. 4; Mann and Roberts, 'Law in Colonial Africa', p. 3.
89. F. Mkenda, 'Building National Unity in Sub-Saharan Africa: The Impact of State Policies on the Chagga Community in Northern Tanzania', D.Phil. thesis (University of Oxford, 2009), p. 185.
90. H.F. Morris, 'Native Courts: A Corner-Stone of Indirect Rule' in H.F. Morris and J.S. Read, *Indirect Rule and the Search for Justice: Essays in East African Legal History* (Oxford, 1972), pp. 131–166.
91. Gailey, *Sir Donald*, p. xi. For Cameron's statement on his policies and ideology, see: D.C. Cameron, *Recent Progress in Tanganyika* (London, 1931); D.C. Cameron and R. Heussler, *My Tanganyika Service and Some Nigeria*, 2nd edn (Washington, D.C., 1982).
92. Native Authority Ordinance 1926; Gailey, *Sir Donald*, p. xi.
93. Gailey, *Sir Donald*, p. 73.
94. Hailey, *An African Survey*, p. 442.
95. Ibid.
96. Gailey, *Sir Donald*, p. 80; H.F. Morris, 'English Law in East Africa: A Hardy Plant in an Alien Soil' in H.F. Morris and J. S. Read, *Indirect Rule and the Search for Justice: Essays in East African Legal History* (Oxford, 1972), p. 84.
97. Chief Justice Russell replaced Chief Justice Carter in 1924 and arrived in Tanganyika close to the beginning of Governor Cameron's tenure in the territory. Russell's words quoted by Austen in: R.A. Austen, 'The Official Mind of Indirect Rule: British Policy in Tanganyika, 1916–1939' in P. Gifford and W.R. Louis (eds.), *Britain and Germany in Africa: Imperial Rivalry and Colonial Rule* (London, 1967), p. 589.
98. See: Moffett, 'Native Courts', pp. 19–21; Bates, *Tanganyika Under British Administration*, pp. 133–134; Austen, 'The Official Mind', p. 589; Gailey, *Sir Donald*, p. 81; Morris, 'Native Courts', pp. 144–147; Madden and Darwin, *The Dependent Empire*, pp. 781–782, especially fn 1; Mkenda, 'Building National Unity', pp. 147–149.
99. TNA (UK), CO 691/91/4, D.C. Cameron to L.C.M.S. Amery, 8 March 1927.
100. TNA (UK), CO 691/91/4, D.C. Cameron to L.C.M.S. Amery, 11 April 1927, pp. 2–3.
101. Ibid., p. 3.

102. TNA (UK), CO 691/91/4, A. Russell to D.C. Cameron, 5 April 1927, pp. 4–5. The data on the number of cases tried in various courts available in the ARJs from the period does not indicate where there were backlogs in the Court and how significant they were.
103. TNA (UK), CO 691/95/1, A.R. Napier Clark to W.A. Wilson, 11 June 1928, pp. 1–2. This reported backlog was apparently due to an increase in criminal cases, which took precedence over civil cases, as well as the presence of only one magistrate with the jurisdiction to dispose of them.
104. TNA (UK), CO 691/95/1, unknown [CO] to W.C. Bottomley, 18 December 1928, p. 5. Though this claim is made in the correspondence, data on salaries indicates that Russell's salary started and remained at 2000 GBP per annum during his time as Chief Justice in Tanganyika. This was the same rate that his predecessor, Carter, had earned in 1924 when Russell took over the post. The Chief Secretary's salary, however, was raised to the same level as the Chief Justice in 1927 (which was an increase of 200 GBP per annum) and since Russell's requests for a raise were denied, he seemingly regarded this relative salary shift as a reduction to his salary. It is also notable that after Russell left, the new Chief Justice, Sheridan, saw his salary rise by 200 GBP per annum after two years of service in Tanganyika and the rest of the High Court Bench also received a raise of 50 GBP per year, an initiative Russell had championed but did not succeed at during his tenure. Salary data from: COL 1924, pp. 426–427; COL 1927, pp. 451–452; COL 1932, pp. 461–462.
105. Bates, *Tanganyika Under British Administration*, p. 65.
106. Austen, 'The Official Mind', p. 589.
107. TNA (UK), CO 691/110/4, unknown [CO] to G.F. Seel, 22 May 1930, p. 1; TNA (UK), CO 691/110/4, 'Salaries of the Judicial Department, Tanganyika', n.d., p. 6.
108. TNA (UK), CO 691/104/3, 'Biographical Information on Sheridan', n.d.
109. Gailey, *Sir Donald*, p. 81.
110. Moffett, 'Native Courts', p. 20; Gailey, *Sir Donald*, p. 81.
111. Native Courts Ordinance 1929, s 33–34.
112. Though the ordinance disconnected the Native Courts from the High Court, some few cases did make it from the Native Courts to the High Court through the provision allowing appeals of cases from the Native Courts system to be transferred to subordinate courts by a District Officer. One example is *Rex* v. *Joshua son of (s/o) Danieli*, (1939) 1 T.L.R. (R), 60–63.
113. The only exception to this was in cases involving a breach of the orders of the Native Authority, which administrators could transfer to the British court system. Neither colonial judges nor Africans could facilitate or initiate the transfer of a case and therefore authority over the Native Courts remained firmly in the hands of administrators.

114. Adewoye, *The Judicial System*, pp. 137–169, 255.
115. M. Mamdani, *Citizen and Subject: Contemporary Africa and the Legacy of Late Colonialism* (Princeton, 1996), p. 109.
116. For example, in a letter to Cameron, Russell emphasised the role of the judiciary in the 'rapid civilization' of the Tanganyika Territory. TNA (UK), CO 691/95/1, A. Russell to D.C. Cameron, 12 June 1928, p. 4.
117. Lumley, *Forgotten Mandate*, p. 60.
118. ARJ 1939, p. 7.
119. A. Russell, *Handbook for Magistrates*, 2nd edn (London, 1928).
120. ARJ 1939, p. 7.
121. Alexander, *Tanganyika Memories*, p. 22.
122. TNA (UK), CO 691/95/1, A.R. Napier Clark to W.A. Wilson, 11 June 1928, pp. 1–2.
123. Tanganyika Territory, *Non-Native Census 1931*, p. 10.
124. TNA (UK), CO 691/91/4, Indian Association of Bukoba to A. Russell, 14 March 1926, p. 1.
125. It is notable that in Cameron's next post as Governor of Nigeria he allowed appeals from the Native Courts to the High Court on some matters and revised some of his views on the role of judges and lawyers in a colony. J.S. Read, 'Patterns of Indirect Rule in East Africa' in H.F. Morris and J.S. Read, *Indirect Rule and the Search for Justice: Essays in East African Legal History* (Oxford, 1972), p. 268; Adewoye, *The Judicial System*, pp. 222–223.
126. The Courts Ordinance 1930, s 3(b).
127. The Courts Ordinance 1941.
128. Native Courts (Appeals) (Amendment) Ordinance 1940.
129. TNA (UK), CO 691/191/42439, 'Internal Report: Relations Between the Judiciary and the Administration', n.d.

CHAPTER 4

The Resurgence and Expansion of Tanganyika's Judiciary, 1945–1958

After the end of World War II British authorities began to assess the impact of the war on colonial administrations, including reduced manpower, scarce resources, and impaired infrastructures. In the years that followed the Colonial Office implemented policies aimed at reasserting, and even bolstering, British colonial rule. These policies and their accompanying rhetoric centred on colonial reconstruction and development and were supported by the Colonial Development and Welfare Act of 1945.[1] Kirk-Greene asserts that the Act 'stood British practice on its head by replacing the hallowed economic policy of colonial self-sufficiency with large sums of grants for development and staff increases within the colonies'. At the time, the prevailing political view in the metropole was that the Empire—or at least parts of it—would be under British rule for many years to come. Though nationalist movements in African colonies were in the early stages of development compared with those in India, Iliffe argues that Africans 'began to demand a voice in post-war planning' because World War II had 'brought greater awareness of external affairs' to the continent and provided a new perspective on their position as colonial subjects.[2]

In Tanganyika the colonial administration proceeded with its post-war development agenda. Changes on the international stage had affected the legal status of the colony, but they had little impact on the way in which the British administered the territory. The founding of the United Nations

E.R. Feingold, *Colonial Justice and Decolonization in the High Court of Tanzania, 1920–1971*, Cambridge Imperial and Post-Colonial Studies Series, https://doi.org/10.1007/978-3-319-69691-1_4

and related dissolution of the League of Nations placed Tanganyika (and all other mandate territories) under the United Nations' Trusteeship Council. The Council had different aims from its forerunner; whereas the mandate system had provided the legal framework for victorious imperial powers to expand their colonial domains after World War I and further entrench colonial rule, the Trusteeship system emphasised development towards self-government.[3] Many regarded the Trusteeship system as a 'liquidator of colonialism', but it did not precipitate any immediate movement for the independence of Tanganyika.[4] Instead, the Colonial Office and government of Tanganyika paid lip service to the priorities of the United Nations while operationalising their colonial development schemes for the territory, including export-oriented agriculture and the reform of local government.[5]

Governor Cameron's version of indirect rule in Tanganyika remained mostly intact throughout World War II, but while it can be understood as a means to an end during the interwar period, Iliffe argues that 'it became an end and not a means' in the post-war period.[6] By the early 1950s administrators began to view the structures underpinning indirect rule as a barrier to the new colonial development policies.[7] The heavy reliance on administrative officers as police officers and magistrates was not producing the results the pre-war administration had envisioned and was subject to renewed scrutiny by the Colonial Office. Yet concerns about the justice system were not new. These criticisms were holdovers from the raging debate of the 1930s, both highlighted and exacerbated in a famous commission of inquiry report known as the Bushe Report. While many of the recommendations in the Bushe Report were not taken up in Tanganyika in the 1930s, after World War II the administration began to implement some of the Bushe Commission's suggestions. This post-war environment created a space for the judiciary to regain some of the ground it had lost under Cameron. Between 1945 and 1958 the judiciary grew in size and geographic reach, took the first steps towards unification and integration of the court systems, and increased its stature inside the territory. Changes to imperial courts outside Tanganyika also increased the prestige of the colonial judiciary in general and enhanced its importance in the maintenance of the colonial state and Empire.

The position of colonial judges in Tanganyika was further affected by debates in the metropole. Judges in London and the colonies reinvigorated a long-standing debate about the independence of the colonial judiciary from the administration, focusing on the process of dismissal of colonial judges.[8] The post-war round of this long-standing debate was sparked by the forced retirement of a judge in the Colony of the Straits Settlements named A.K. a'Beckett Terrell, and had no direct relationship to the functioning of Tanganyika's judiciary. But his dismissal drew attention to the tenuous position of colonial judges throughout the Empire and opened the door for them to challenge it. At this time the Colonial Office was also reviving and revising its efforts to hire better quality barristers and facilitated administrative officers being called to the Bar. As a result of these activities and changes, precipitated by World War II, some of the post-war colonial legal officers in Tanganyika held perspectives and had experiences that differed considerably from those of their predecessors.

This chapter demonstrates that while the post-war era was hardly a renaissance for colonial judges in Tanganyika, it was a period of resurgence and expansion of the judiciary in comparison with the interwar years. This phase of relatively clear skies for the British in Tanganyika after World War II nurtured green shoots in the judiciary, which sprung up through the cracks in the dusty foundations of the indirect rule system.[9] This growth was opportune for the administration as it would, in turn, depend on the newly strengthened judiciary to help it redefine its legacy and legitimise its resistance to the next gathering storm: the movement for national independence.

The Bushe Commission and the Judiciary of Tanganyika

Among the numerous colonial commissions of inquiry sent to Africa, the Bushe Commission remains one of the most famous. Though it had little impact on the administration of colonial justice in Tanganyika during the interwar period, colonial administrators revisited its findings after World War II and its recommendations became an important part of post-war planning in Tanganyika. The Secretary of State for the Colonies tasked the Commission with examining the administration of justice in relation to Africans in Tanganyika, Kenya, and Uganda. It provided a platform for members of the administration, judiciary, and colonial society to air their grievances and offer their opinions on colonial justice.[10] Approximately 86 witnesses from the three territories testified before the Commission. The Bushe Report and associated evidence, published in 1934, are rich sources on colonial courts and procedures, penal practices, and notions of justice in British East Africa.[11] The Commission's report reveals the differing points of view of the administration and judiciary on the causes of deficiencies in the courts, and on proposed remedies.

The Secretary of State for the Colonies appointed the Bushe Commission shortly after the replacement of the Indian Penal and Criminal Procedure Codes in 1930 with new codes.[12] Colonial administrations enacted the new codes to quell concerns within and outside the Colonial Office that the Indian codes had been altered too far from English legal practice in order to take local circumstances into account and were, as a result, unsuitable for use in British colonies in East Africa.[13] Some colonial administrations, however, aggressively criticised the new codes claiming that they were inappropriate for Africans because they implemented procedures and practices which they viewed as unnecessarily technical and therefore an impediment to the administration of justice. The Commission's charge was to examine the administration of the criminal law under the new codes, including the procedures and practices of courts and police, as well as other matters in relation to the administration of justice. The Native Courts, as institutions, were outside the Commission's terms of reference, but it did examine the issue of punishment because it was a concern for the Colonial Office and territorial governments.

Bushe, the Legal Adviser of the Colonial Office at the time, led the Commission, which included the Attorney General of Kenya, a settler living in Kenya, the Secretary for Native Affairs of Tanganyika, the Registrar to the High Court of Uganda, and a Judge of the High Court of Uganda.[14] They went on a two-month journey through the three territories and at the end of the trip all the members reached a general consensus on the Bushe Report's recommendations.[15] Supporters of the Commission's conclusions cited the diverse range of positions and perspectives of its members as evidence that it was unbiased and provided a fair and accurate picture of the situation in East Africa. Yet its detractors argued that it was driven by officials looking to enhance the position of the judiciary in the region. Given that the Chair was the Legal Adviser and that three of the members had legal backgrounds (all of whom eventually became Chief Justices) it is not surprising that the Commission definitively supported many of the viewpoints held by the judiciary.[16] Nor is it surprising that its findings were vigorously rejected by many of the members of the East African administrations and that they aggravated pre-existing tensions between the judiciary and administration in East Africa.

These tensions stemmed from differing views in the administration and the judiciary about who should be involved and who could be most effective in the administration of colonial justice. This topic had been at the heart of the 1920s debate in Tanganyika over the supervision of the Native Courts. By the 1930s, however, the debate shifted focus to the role of administrative officers as magistrates, case delays, and extension of jurisdiction to magistrates for serious cases. By the 1930s there was general consensus that a British court system in Tanganyika was necessary for the territory and that the system was dysfunctional and in need of revision in order to limit the delays and hardships for witnesses.[17] Therefore the discussion centred on how to improve the system within Tanganyika and who would be responsible for administering justice to Africans.

Administrators and judges held 'sharply divided opinions' over who could carry out court work most efficiently and effectively: the judges with their legal training and courtroom skills; or the administrators with their local experience and self-proclaimed knowledge of 'the native'.[18] While some individual members of the Bushe Commission, and many in the colonial judiciary, objected to the use of administrative officers as magistrates in principle, because it violated the principle of the separation of powers, the Commission accepted that 'financial considerations' would not allow for a complete professionalisation of the courts. Instead it opted to make recommendations for how to fix the broken judicial 'machinery', based on the assumption that administrators would continue to have some magisterial duties.[19]

The Commission was primarily concerned with the delays resulting from the small size of the High Courts and, in Tanganyika specifically, its centralisation of the High Court in Dar es Salaam.[20] The Report cited the situation in Lake Province, where individuals accused of crimes might wait, on average, three and a half months for a trial and could be forced to wait as long as seven months. These delays were unjust, especially for those accused of murder and held in remand during that time, and it had an adverse effect on the memories of witnesses.[21] It was also alarmed by the 'excessive jurisdiction' of magistrates and the overuse of extending the jurisdiction of the High Court to lower authorities. The Commission complained that the overuse of administrative officers in a magisterial capacity not only led to rampant misapplication of legal procedure, but also worsened delays because High Court judges were forced to spend a great deal of their time reviewing and revising incorrect procedures and practices in District Courts.

Therefore, the Commission sought to limit the use of magistrates without legal training as much as possible by increasing the number of High Court judges in Tanganyika by two to a total of five, and placing the new judges at Mwanza (Lake Province) and Tanga or the Northern Province to limit the extreme delays experienced in those areas with high caseloads that were far removed from Dar es Salaam.[22] The increased personnel would remove the need for extended jurisdiction from the magistrates in all areas of the territory, except for the more isolated Lindi Province and south of Western Province, which were difficult for the Court to reach.[23] The Commission further suggested that the Court should use the circuit as an opportunity to deal with the appeals, confirmations, and revisions at or near the local station from where they were generated, rather than deal with them in Dar es Salaam, thereby lessening delays due to the difficulty of communication and transportation of documents.[24] The professional magistracy should be expected to deal with a larger percentage of serious cases, committing only capital cases to the High Court and leaving the less serious cases to magistrates to handle within their own jurisdictions.[25] Rather than simplify or revise British procedure in accordance with administrative preferences, the Commission advocated maintaining the procedures under the new codes, but wanted them carried out as much as possible by those with legal training.[26]

Upon publication the Bushe Report garnered significant attention among colonial officials and has been aptly described by Morris as a 'watershed' in East African legal history.[27] The Report was arguably an early sign of a shift from a 'rough and ready'-style colonialism to one which could withstand scrutiny in the metropole, by the League of Nations, and from colonial society.[28] Nevertheless, it had little practical impact in the years immediately following its publication.[29] The governors of Kenya, Uganda, and Tanganyika aggressively rejected the Report's substantial recommendations relating in principle to the overuse of administrators in a legal capacity.[30] Though the territorial governments and Secretary of State for the Colonies did accept many of the smaller and more limited recommendations, few were carried out.[31] Financial limitations, logistical challenges, and the outbreak of World War II are potential explanations for why the recommendations that were accepted before World War II were either only partially implemented or did not come to fruition in the 1930s.[32]

Yet the rejection of the major recommendations can be understood differently. It is clear that the acceptance of all the Bushe recommendations by territorial governments would have had profound consequences for indirect rule. Had they been implemented they would have diminished the role of administrators in court work and cast doubt on the legitimacy of the system in place, creating upheaval in the territorial government, which was still progressing in the implementation of Cameron's renovations from the 1920s. This is perhaps the most useful explanation for why the Report provoked such an aggressive response inside and outside East Africa. As one editorialist put it, 'the report has been described as contrary to the whole spirit of indirect rule'.[33] Indirect rule relied on both judges and administrators, but it privileged and prioritised the administrators, reinforcing and counting on their personal power and influence. To change the administration of justice in the way the Bushe Commission envisioned would have fundamentally altered the nature of indirect rule in Tanganyika, which neither colonial administrators nor the Secretary of State were prepared to do in the 1930s.[34]

The Report and its recommendations were limited to East Africa, but it reverberated across the continent because it cast doubt on the legitimacy of non-legal judicial authorities in British territories in Africa. Furse, the head of recruitment at the Colonial Office, reported after a visit to the Sudan that 'nothing has created such apprehension in the Sudan Service as the Bushe Report'.[35] The Sudan Political Service, which was separate from the Colonial Service, relied on administrative officers to carry out magisterial duties, including conducting full trials in isolated stations, where one officer could be judge, jury, and counsel for the defence.[36] Administrators were required to pass a law exam before they could earn an increase in salary, but, as in Tanganyika, were often very inexperienced in the administration of justice in the early stages of their service.[37] Moreover, the Sudan Political Service staffed its judiciary more like the Indian Civil Service than the Colonial Service in that it chose judges from the administration to join professional judges on the Bench.[38] The limited number of professional magistrates and judges in the territory created a worrying contrast between the administration of justice in East Africa, already under intense criticism, and that in Sudan. Furse reported that the findings of the Commission had provoked high-level administrators in the Sudan to consider a scheme to choose experienced administrative officers from their service and send them to London to obtain legal training, be called to the Bar, and then return to the Sudan as provincial judges of the territory with increased salaries.[39] The Commission's conclusions did not go unnoticed in London either, where it sparked debate in papers and journals as well as within the Colonial Office.[40] The Report, therefore, had a greater significance than its impact on East Africa alone and its overall effect cannot be measured by the few changes on the ground in the three territories in the 1930s.[41]

Concerns over the administration of justice in British colonies, and indeed most matters under the purview of the Colonial Office, were dwarfed by the outbreak of World War II in Europe. The issues raised by the Report were brushed aside in the face of wartime exigency. Still, they were not forgotten by the Colonial Office or those in the government of Tanganyika. After the conclusion of war efforts, officials in London and Dar es Salaam began to reference the Report as their focus shifted to post-war reconstruction and development. Moreover, the legacy of the Bushe Commission was not only its recommendations, but also the 'harmed' relations between the administration and judiciary, which persisted in East Africa during World War II.[42] The Governor of Tanganyika bemoaned the situation in a letter to the Colonial Office in 1944:

> There is quite a long history of sporadic bickerings, interspersed by periods of definitely strained relations between the Judiciary and Administration in this Territory, and this has resulted in an attitude on the part of the Administrative branch generally, and indeed, of some other sections of opinion, towards the High Court which is tinged with resentment and impatience, while the attitude of the High Court Judges on the other hand often shows signs of extreme irritability with, and lack of consideration towards the administrative branch. This is an unsatisfactory state of things, and I think every possible step should be taken to try and remedy it when opportunity offers.[43]

The administration decided to urge the Colonial Office to replace individuals in the judiciary that it blamed for the 'discord'.[44] Justice R.M. Cluer, who was especially outspoken and regarded by the administration as adversarial to its policies, was the first to be transferred and joined the Bench in Jamaica.[45]

With such deeply rooted animosity, however, the Governor feared that the dispute between the administration and the judiciary had become 'almost tradition'.[46] When the territory needed a new Chief Justice to replace Ambrose Henry Webb, the Governor requested the appointment of someone from outside of Tanganyika who might help renew positive relations with the administration. As a result, Justice Mark Wilson, who was a long-standing member of Tanganyika's judiciary and regarded by the Governor himself as qualified for the post, was passed over for the appointment.[47] Instead, in 1945, George G. Paul, known as Graham Paul, was brought in from Sierra Leone where he had already served as Chief Justice. The method of replacing individuals without a memory of pre-war and wartime tensions in the territory was an attempt by the government to wipe the slate clean. This infusion of new judges seems to have produced the desired effect, as the Attorney General reported improved relations between the administration and judiciary in the early 1950s.[48] This new rapport helped to pave the way for the modifications to the judicial system in the decade that followed.[49]

A Growing Bench

Following World War II, the Colonial Office's emphasis on reconstruction and development led to the adoption of new policies and mechanisms of colonial rule, which led to a number of innovations to the judiciary, including an increase in the number of judges on the Bench in Tanganyika. Some of these new policies were discordant with the interwar approach of governing through 'traditional structures' and 'the man on the spot' and therefore necessitated a greater number of officials with a post-war perspective to carry them out. The post-war rhetoric of development as the key to the durability of the Empire influenced the cohort of administrators that went to work in East Africa after the end of World War II. Many of this new generation considered their predecessors' paternalistic and minimalist approach 'out of fashion' and 'anachronistic'.[50] These men did not relish their role in the courts as it would seem their forerunners had. Instead, some found court work 'irksome' and regarded it as a 'real burden' given their mounting administrative duties under the new government policies.[51] The increase in the size and geographic reach of the judiciary was therefore intended to improve efficiency and decrease the role of administrators as magistrates, 'so as to allow them to give more of their time to their administrative duties'.[52] To this end, the government expanded the size of the professional judiciary, enhanced the judicial infrastructure, and facilitated the extended use of the circuit.

The post-war augmentation of the High Court roughly followed recommendations of the Bushe Commission and the government pursued the increase of the number of judicial staff 'as fast as funds and staff permitted'.[53] By 1953 the Court had six judges—double its size from 1933. The professional magistracy also grew dramatically, tripling in size by 1953 and more than quadrupling by 1959.[54] Among this new cohort the government began to designate senior resident magistrates, who were experienced and likely candidates for promotion to a High Court Bench.[55]

The government and Court set the target that 80% of court work in the territory would be carried out by resident magistrates, leaving 20% to be handled by administrative officers under their magisterial powers.[56] Though the total number of magistrates grew, placement and distribution across the provinces remained a problem. Some regions still did not have regular access to a resident magistrate or had too few magistrates to substantially reduce the legal burden on administrators. For example, there was only one resident magistrate for the whole of the large Central Province, even after the infusion of more magistrates to the territory in 1953. The Provincial Commissioner complained that the Resident Magistrate covered only 30% of the criminal court work and doubted that the magistracy had been expanded enough and distributed in such a way that the government would reach the 80% target.[57] Thus administrative officers continued to perform magisterial duties in areas without resident magistrates. In areas where resident magistrates had been posted, administrative officers often still carried out magisterial duties when the magistrate went away on circuit or leave, and when the post was vacant due to a shortage of candidates suitable for the Colonial Legal Service.

The model of stationing resident magistrates in areas with a large caseload was, for some, a blueprint of what could be done with the High Court Bench. There were multiple proposals which referenced the Bushe Commission's recommendation of decentralising the Court by placing High Court judges in locations outside Dar es Salaam. This became a topic of significant debate because of the political implications of such a change, beyond the logistical and financial considerations. Supporters believed that the move would improve efficiency and access to the Court, as well as have a positive effect on relations between the administration and judiciary.[58] Detractors, however, feared that it would be costly, create difficulty when a resident judge was on leave or ill, and would be 'a detriment to the judicial community' as it would cut judges off from their 'brother judges'.[59] There was also the concern that it would lower the status of judges and could draw them into local politics in the towns where they would be based.[60] Whether judges would remain based in Dar es Salaam was therefore not only a question of logistics, but also about the nature of the post-war judiciary. Would they remain a somewhat isolated and tightly knit Bench in Dar es Salaam, or would the Court be restructured in a way that mirrored and meshed with the administrative provincial system?

In 1949 the government decided that it would establish a smaller, second High Court in Mwanza—a station with some of the worst delays that was already receiving the Court circuit four or five times per year.[61] The administration opted to build a courthouse and related accommodation suitable for one judge, and treated it as 'high priority' over and above administrative building schemes and accommodation of 'unhoused staff'.[62] Despite significant delays due to the limited availability of cement, the Mwanza High Court opened in August 1951.[63] The establishment of this satellite court was a precursor for post-independence changes that would further decentralise the High Court through establishing additional courts and registries in the territory and posting more judges to them. Moreover, the government reconsidered pre-war appeals for a new High Court building in Dar es Salaam, which had been shelved with the outbreak of war, and approved a plan for a new High Court building in 1953.[64] In the post-war milieu of accelerated reconstruction and development the fact that the government prioritised strengthening the judicial infrastructure illustrates its new attitude towards the utility and role of the judiciary. The administration had begun to see the judiciary as an asset.[65]

Even with the expansion of the Bench and improvement in court buildings, the High Court and District Courts had difficulty keeping up with the growing caseload in the mid-1950s. By 1954 the number of criminal offences in District Courts had more than tripled since 1945.[66] They reached an all-time high in 1958 of five times the 1945 figure.[67] The total number of cases filed at the High Court had also increased substantially, more than tripling over the same period. The reason for the increasing caseload at the courts is not clear from the existing records. There may have been a real increase in the number of offences, but a more likely explanation for the larger figure is that more cases were coming before the courts due to the growth of the colonial administration and presence of its officers throughout the territory, as well as a growing awareness of the colonial state functions by Africans. The number of cases in court may reflect the changing ability of the colonial authorities to prosecute cases or a 'selective use of the legal system' and belief by more Africans that it was advantageous to utilise the formal system.[68]

To cope with the increased workload, the expanded High Court Bench amplified its circuits by making them more frequent and visiting more towns. The number of High Court circuits increased from an average of ten per year in the 1920s to 16 circuits in 1958.[69] That year the court visited 20 different towns at a frequency of one to six times, totalling 41 sessions. This was made possible in part by improved transportation infrastructure in the territory, including the increased use of aeroplanes.[70]

Though the circuit had been, at times, uncomfortable for judges during the interwar years, it became appealing in the post-World War II era. The government provided funds to make travel more desirable and functional. One High Court judge recalled that life on the circuit was so good it was, 'truly the life of a plutocrat', allowing him a 'taste' of that lifestyle.[71] The old Central Line route, made famous by Chief Justice Carter in the 1920s, became 'popular' among judges who enjoyed the luxurious train cars and travel conditions.[72]

After World War II, Tanganyika's British court system progressed in the direction the Bushe Commission had advocated for, increasing the size of the magistracy and High Court, starting to permanently place judges in locations outside Dar es Salaam, and decreasing the role of administrative officers as magistrates. While these changes were a break with the interwar period, they can be best described, as they were by a judge at the time, as 'evolutionary rather than revolutionary'.[73] The government continued to rely on administrative officers to undertake magisterial duties within and, at times, beyond their powers of punishment, and the High Court remained mostly centralised in Dar es Salaam for the duration of British rule.

Towards Structural and Racial Integration of the Courts and Bench

Post-war changes not only expanded the High Court, but also cleared the way for unification of the racially divided court systems during the process of decolonisation. The 'parallel' court systems and their division by the 1929 Native Courts Ordinance came under increasing attack after World War II. The division of the Native Courts system from the British court system on the basis of race and the lack of 'nexus' between the two became a target for politically active Africans, who cited it as a glaring example of how the British did not live up to their professed legal, social, and political ideals in their colonies.[74] Justice Wilson also complained that the Native Courts were 'losing touch with the ordinary people who use[d] them' and feared that the courts would be unsatisfactory to the African soldiers who had 'seen something of the world and will find it difficult to entrust settlement of their differences to what has been, perhaps somewhat unkindly, described as an illiterate and ignorant body of old men—the present administrators of justice in the Native Courts'.[75]

With these criticisms mounting, and pressure from the Colonial Office for the colonies in Africa to reassess their policies relating to Native Courts, the territorial government of Tanganyika considered various proposals on how to revise the Native Courts system in the post-war era. By 1951 the government settled on a new ordinance that replaced the Native Courts with Local Courts.[76] This change set the course in the 'direction of the incorporation of the native (or customary) courts in the general judicial system of the territory', although at this point the Local Courts were still separated from the British Courts and continued to exclude legal professionals and judges, except at the highest level of appeal.[77] The arguments behind this restyling of the Native Courts, however, mark an early milestone in the movement away from the racial divisions underpinning colonial justice in Tanganyika.

The Local Courts were essentially a mirror image of the Native Courts. The new ordinance had minimal impact on the practical workings of the courts and amounted to little more than 'a change in terminology'.[78] The courts maintained much of the same civil and criminal jurisdiction over the same people, but the categorisation of this group of people was changed from 'native' to 'African'.[79] The Local Courts gained jurisdiction in civil or criminal matters over some people not categorised as Africans, including Arabs, Somalis, Comorians, Baluchis, and Malagasis, but only with their permission.[80] Like the Native Courts, local authorities were allowed to apply customary law, subject to the repugnancy clause.[81] Though the name of the new courts, Local Courts, was an initial step towards jurisdiction based on a geographic 'local' area, as opposed to racial or tribal identity or status, in essence the same people who had been under the jurisdiction of the Native Courts were under the jurisdiction of the Local Courts.[82]

Administrators also maintained their supervisory powers over the Local Courts.[83] Provincial commissioners had the ability to establish and dissolve Local Courts, dismiss members, define the jurisdiction of a given court, and revise decisions.[84] All significant punishments handed down by a Local Court were subject to approval by the district commissioner.[85] Though the provincial commissioner was no longer a level of appeal under the new ordinance, appeals could only reach the highest level—the new

Central Court of Appeal—with his permission and only after a case was first heard by the Local Court of Appeal and second by the district commissioner.[86] Administrative officers also had the power to transfer cases from one Local Court to another or to the District Court, before judgment.[87] Thus the Local Courts Ordinance maintained the power of administrative officers over the courts of Africans, and in many ways were not a substantial departure from the previous system.

Nonetheless, the ordinance was of great practical and symbolic importance to the High Court because it officially reintegrated a High Court judge into the appeals process for the first time in over 20 years. It replaced the Governor's Appeal Board with the Central Court of Appeal and put a High Court judge at its heart, who presided over the new court as President.[88] He was nominated by the Chief Justice, giving the judiciary a role shaping who would serve on the Court.[89] The judge was accompanied by a Member of Local Government (such as the Minister for Provincial Affairs) and the Local Courts Adviser (a role created by the ordinance), with a total of three members.[90] The appointment of a High Court judge to the Central Court of Appeal re-established a relationship between the High Court and the Local (formerly Native) Courts that had been completely severed by the Native Courts Ordinance in 1929.[91]

Yet the Central Court of Appeal was neither a full reinstatement of the High Court's lost jurisdiction from 1929 nor the integration of the two systems. It created a single connection between the two systems, but it did not result in any substantial or meaningful integration. Provincial commissioners still 'filtered' which cases made it to the Court of Appeal, and the judge had to reach agreement with the other two members of the Court on decisions. If agreement was not reached, members voted and the majority determined the outcome, regardless of whether the judge as President agreed with it.[92] Moreover, the Central Court of Appeal remained the final layer of appeal available to cases generating from the Local Courts, and therefore there was no relationship between the court system for Africans and the Eastern African Court of Appeal and Privy Council, as there was for cases in the British court system.[93] Nevertheless, the Central Court of Appeal was a departure from the rigid separation of the two court systems and through it judges and advocates found their way back into the appeals process at the highest level.[94]

The measured progress towards integration of the court systems continued at the Judicial Advisers' Conference in 1953. The conference brought together judicial advisers from 11 British territories in Africa to discuss the state of Native Courts and the direction of British colonial justice systems on the continent. The role of judicial adviser involved advising the administration and judiciary on the activities and development of the courts and customary law, and served as a connection between the Native/Local Courts and the British Courts.[95] A few colonial governments in Africa created the post of judicial adviser before World War II, but nearly all British African colonies added the position to their governments after World War II at the behest of the Secretary of State for the Colonies.[96] In Tanganyika the post involved advising officials, as well as revising and adjudicating cases. To fill this role, the Secretary of State for the Colonies decreed that an officer should ideally have legal qualifications *and* experience working with African courts, emphasising the value of both types of knowledge.[97] In Tanganyika the Local Courts Adviser, P.H.W. Haile, was a barrister.[98] This new role was, however, attached to the Secretariat rather than the judiciary, although it was supposed to function 'independent[ly] of the executive'.[99]

The meeting of the judicial advisers at Makerere College, Uganda, under the Legal Adviser, Sir Kenneth Roberts-Wray, was a noteworthy moment in the development of colonial philosophy about the courts in Africa.[100] The conference placed the issue of control over the Native Courts at the top of its agenda and emphasised the integration of 'parallel' court systems as the 'ultimate objective' for colonial legal systems.[101] Morris argues that not only did it set the course for the eventual integration of the court systems in Tanganyika, but it also highlighted how truly separate the two systems were in practice.[102] The report of the conference drew attention to Tanganyika as a territory with a low degree of integration of its two court systems as compared with other African territories such as the Gold Coast, and used the Central Court of Appeal as an example of how 'parallel' systems could be first linked in other territories.[103] Ultimately, the principles the conference affirmed in 1953 were not realised in Tanganyika during British rule. Yet the conference did elucidate the elements of the 'parallel' colonial court systems, including the unity of executive and judicial powers in chiefs, which would be challenged and then changed during transition to national independence less than a decade later.[104]

These early efforts towards integrating the two court systems were contemporaneous with the first advancements in desegregating the Bench. In 1951 Tanganyika's administration appointed two African men to the magistracy for the first time in the territory's history. Their appointments mark the earliest inclusion of Africans as judicial authorities in Tanganyika's British court system. Edward Halwenge and Mdoe Bakari were both African administrative assistants who had worked under administrative officers in Tanganyika in the years preceding their appointments. They took the territorial law exam in 1951 and, after passing it, the government granted both men Third Class magisterial powers with jurisdiction over the entire territory.[105] The identical letters sent to the new magistrates congratulated them on being appointed 'one of the first two Africans to hold magisterial powers in Tanganyika in the Territorial Courts' and reminded them that they were 'responsible directly to the High Court'.[106] They were also warned that the colonial government would be watching their work with 'very great care'.[107]

During Halwenge's and Bakari's first years of service the administration required them to send the records of their court work for inspection by the High Court, but in 1954 the Court determined it had a favourable opinion of their work and no longer required it to be reviewed beyond the standard procedures for Third Class magistrates.[108] The Court suggested granting the two men Second Class magisterial powers, and Halwenge's magisterial powers were expanded in September 1954.[109] That same year, the Provincial Commissioners' Conference declared the 'experiment of employing African Administrative Assistants ... a success', with seven African men working in the role at that point.[110] From then on African administrative assistants, who were later called assistant district officers, were allowed to sit a law exam without pre-approval from the Court, becoming magistrates of the Third Class upon meeting the government's conditions and standards.[111] After two years of service at that grade, they were eligible to become Second Class magistrates.[112]

The American Consulate, observing these developments at the time, interpreted the appointments of Africans to the magistracy and to other spheres of the colonial government, such as the Legislative Council, as 'a further step in the attempt of the Government of Tanganyika to extend full recognition of competent Africans and to develop seeds of self-government in Tanganyika in accordance with the terms of the Trusteeship of the United Nations'.[113] These appointments did not, however, signify the opening of a passageway to the professional magistracy or High Court Bench. These African magistrates were not barristers and did not have the necessary qualifications to be appointed by the Colonial Office, even if the territorial government would have considered it. Nor did these appointments open the door to more senior levels of the administration to

Africans.[114] Yet they represented the first concrete move towards racial integration of the lower Bench and were useful for the colonial government because they helped it deal with the overwhelming number of cases in the British court system and the limited number of legal staff.

The 1950s were a period of growth for the ideas of integration and desegregation of the courts—a key element of the decolonisation of the colonial judiciary. The conversion of the Native Courts into Local Courts had little impact on the Africans using them but, due to the advent of the Central Court of Appeal, had a more substantial impact on the position and jurisdiction of High Court judges, who regained a role in deciding appeals from African courts. The appointment of the first African magistrates was likely driven by necessity rather than ideology, but the rhetoric accompanying the appointments marked a change in colonial views about who could be a part of the administration of colonial justice and was the beginning of the inclusion of Africans in the magistracy.

Increasing the Prestige and Improving the Position of the Colonial Bench in East Africa

Though colonial judges remained secondary to the administration during the 1950s, their position in colonial rule in Tanganyika, and in East Africa more broadly, was further entrenched and legitimised during this period. The growth and incorporation of Tanganyika's Bar, the establishment of a permanent Court of Appeal for Eastern Africa, and the invitation of colonial judges of the Empire to sit on the Privy Council, helped to increase the prestige of the colonial Bench and emphasised its importance in colonial rule. In the post-war era the High Court of Tanganyika reached a higher stature and became a more established element of British colonial rule.

Advocates had been working in Tanganyika since the early stages of British rule, but after World War II the number of those applying to appear before the High Court increased from 44 in 1946 to 187 by 1960.[115] Most advocates were Asian and earned a living representing parties in civil disputes before the High Court and professional magistracy. The government incorporated the Tanganyika Law Society as the institution responsible for organising the Bar in 1954, and in 1955 the Tanganyika Law Society became the keeper of the roll of all advocates who were qualified to practice in the territory.[116] The Advocates Ordinance of 1954 laid out the requirements of those on the roll and consolidated the laws on advocates practising in the territory. This formalisation of the Bar was a boost for the legitimacy of the entire legal community in the territory. It was also an indication of its permanence and importance to the economy in facilitating and responding to the growing commercial enterprises in the territory.

The establishment of a permanent Court of Appeal for the region in 1951 further embedded the British courts in Tanganyika, as well as East Africa more broadly. Before then, the Eastern African Court of Appeal had been comprised of regional territorial Chief Justices and convened at intervals in the territories under its jurisdiction. As High Courts across East Africa were faced with increasing criminal and civil caseloads in the post-war era, the Colonial Office (in consultation with territorial governments) decided to transform the institution into a permanent court called the Court of Appeal for Eastern Africa, with its own Bench based in Nairobi.[117] It was modelled after the West African Court of Appeal established three years earlier in 1948.[118] The main purpose was to reduce delays in court decisions in the region. The Court of Appeal's judges would only handle appeals, thereby expediting the hearing of appeals and removing the Court of Appeal caseload from the territorial judges. The Court of Appeal had jurisdiction over seven territories in the region—Kenya, Uganda, Tanganyika, Zanzibar, Aden, Somaliland, and the Seychelles—and, like its predecessor, it held sessions in large cities and towns in East Africa. The creation of the permanent Court of Appeal eased the workload of the High Court of Tanganyika, which no longer had to loan its judges to the Court, and enhanced the size and strength of the judiciary in East Africa through a new and elite institution.

Further validation of the importance and legitimacy of the colonial Bench followed the decision to allow colonial judges to sit on the Privy Council to hear appeals generating from colonial benches.[119] As the number of appeals from the colonies increased, the Privy Council decided to involve colonial judges in the Committee, indicating an appreciation of their knowledge of the colonies.[120] The measure was also perhaps an attempt to unify the colonial benches across the Empire through the highest body of appeal. Though no judges from Tanganyika sat on the Privy Council during this period, the move helped raise the status of colonial judges among the legal communities in colonies as well as in Great Britain.

The Colonial Legal Service After World War II: The Dispute over the Independence of Colonial Judges and the Battershill Committee

British investment in the regional colonial courts and discussion of the inclusion of colonial judges on the Privy Council illustrates that the Colonial Office ascribed a greater value to the colonial Bench in the post-war era and was increasingly willing to regard colonial judges as British judges. The increasing role and importance of colonial judges in the maintenance of British colonial rule gave them greater leverage in their assertion of independence from the executive.

The policy that colonial judges served at the pleasure of the Crown had been a subject of debate in the interwar era, but became an even more contentious issue in the 1950s when a colonial judge brought a case against the Secretary of State for the Colonies after he was forced to retire.[121] The judge, A.K. a'Beckett Terrell, had not been dismissed for challenging the colonial administration for misconduct, but had lost his position while he was on leave.[122] He had served as a judge of appeal for the Colony of the Straits Settlements and was in Australia when the Japanese invaded the Malayan peninsula in 1941.[123] Subsequently, the Colonial Office determined that his office had been abolished due to World War II and that it would not offer him another appointment between the end of his leave and before his scheduled retirement at the age of 62, as he was already over 60 years of age. The Secretary of State for the Colonies requested that he retire, but he refused because of the negative effect it would have on his pension, so the Secretary retired him 'against his wishes'.[124] Though the core of the actual legal dispute centred on whether the Act of Settlement was applicable to the Colony of Straits Settlements, the implication of the case was that it reinvigorated the debate surrounding whether colonial judges were entitled to the same safeguards as judges in Great Britain and therefore as independent from executive interference.[125]

The legal community in England was apparently 'shocked to discover from the decision ... that a superior judge in a colony was removable at the pleasure of the Crown'.[126] Though the Colonial Office had insisted that all cases of dismissal would be referred to the Privy Council, the forced retirement of Terrell highlighted the tenuous position of colonial judges.[127] The case was discussed in depth among the English Bar, motivating the

Conservative and Unionist Society of the Inns of Court to publish a pamphlet to rally public support for a change in policy.[128] It argued that under the current laws and practices,

> a judge has no better security of tenure in law than a civil servant. He is dismissable at 'Her Majesty's pleasure', which means in effect at the will of the Secretary of State for the Colonies. Yet there is no reason to suppose that the British subject in the colonies is less in need of defence against official disregard of his rights, or the judge in the colonies less in need of protection from official interference, than his brother at home.[129]

The Society framed the debate as representing efforts to shield colonial subjects from executive abuse of their rights through the independence of the colonial judiciary and to extend British notions of justice throughout the Empire.

From an historical perspective, the concerns over dismissal of colonial judges were overblown. It seems that there were virtually no documented cases that would qualify as dismissal 'at pleasure'.[130] Yet the case helped to reframe the colonial judiciary as a direct extension of the British judiciary and one which supposedly protected colonial subjects from potential administrative abuse. Steven Pfeiffer asserts that the debate may have 'inspired only cynicism' among Africans aware of the dispute, however, as the claims of judicial independence probably seemed far-fetched to those who had no right of appeal to colonial judges (in cases generated in African courts), as well as in cases where the judiciary was reinforcing administrative order rather than challenging it.[131] The uproar over the rights of colonial judges during the 1950s was, however, increasingly relevant as it became important for colonial judges to know whether they were disposable or could resist the actions of the colonial state in the context of an increasing number of resistance movements and for administrative expediency.

The position of the post-World War II colonial judiciary was directly relevant both to those already on the Bench, and for the recruitment of new officers to the Colonial Legal Service. After World War II the Colonial Office made efforts to expand the Colonial Service, increasing the quality and volume of new officers to carry out reconstruction and development policies. The expansion of the Service involved new policies and programmes to kick-start recruitment, especially among young and newly demobilised men. This was particularly necessary for the Colonial Legal

Service, which needed more officers to fill the growing Benches in the colonies and wanted to shake off the negative reputation of British colonial judges once and for all. In the years immediately following World War II, the Colonial Office struggled to find qualified barristers to help replenish flagging colonial court systems and to maintain law and order in occupied territories. The Service recognised the need in the short term to fill open posts and decided to hire solicitors, with the hopes of turning them into barristers, and to relax requirements relating to practical experience at the Bar.[132]

In 1944 the Colonial Office appointed the Battershill Committee, named for its Chair William D. Battershill, to make recommendations on how to improve recruitment training and competition for colonial legal officers.[133] The Committee suggested the development of a Legal Scholarship Scheme (later known as the Legal Probationership Scheme), which would provide financial assistance to barristers or aspiring barristers to obtain their call to the Bar and read in chambers so that they would be eligible to join the Colonial Legal Service.[134] The Colonial Office initiated the Legal Probationership Scheme soon after, but not all the Committee's recommendations were seen through.[135] For example, it had recommended increased training for legal officers focused on the places where they would serve, and greater encouragement of legal officers to learn about local law and custom.[136] The Colonial Office, however, did not elect to establish this training programme nor did it attempt to take in batches of officers as in the Administrative Service.[137] Instead, the Colonial Office continued the approach of selecting qualified individuals from 'the List' and sending them to the colonies. It simply aimed to have a longer list to choose from, with more desirable candidates.

The members of the Battershill Committee also raised questions about who would be eligible to be a part of the post-war Colonial Legal Service, both in terms of racial categorisation and educational background (as well as Bar membership). In light of the British government's declared policy that 'Africans should progressively be appointed to senior posts as and when suitable candidates become available', officers in the Colonial Office debated whether the new Probationership Scheme would be open to 'coloured' men.[138] The Colonial Office also began to reassess the value of qualifications from local teaching institutions in the colonies and promoted the idea of setting up a law college in West Africa to train lawyers to serve in the four British territories in the region.[139] West Africa already had a substantial number of Africans with legal qualifications from Great

Britain and by 1945 had 27 Africans in senior posts in judicial and legal departments in Nigeria, the Gold Coast, and Sierra Leone. No such suggestion was made for East Africa; however, as there were virtually no Africans with legal qualifications they therefore remained excluded from the Bench, except at the lower levels of the administrative magistracy.[140] While Africans were increasingly a part of the legal systems in Great Britain's West African territories, the colonial benches and bars in East Africa remained dominated by expatriate men in the Service, and the Probationership scheme did not increase the number of colonial subjects from the region entering the Service.

The Battershill Committee hoped that the revitalisation of the Joint Committee for the Inns of Court would attract aspiring barristers to the new scheme and draw in younger barristers already practising and eligible to join the Service. The Joint Committee had 'ceased to function' after the outbreak of World War II and Battershill envisaged that it would begin its work again, but this time with the aid of a liaison officer.[141] The first liaison officer appointed to the Inns was none other than Sir Alison Russell, the former Chief Justice of Tanganyika and member of the Battershill Committee. Russell had worked tirelessly after his retirement, following the Native Courts Ordinance of 1929, to improve the position of colonial legal officers throughout the Empire. In this new role he tried to make the Colonial Legal Service more appealing to potential recruits.[142] To this end he designed a pamphlet with photographs of the desirable lifestyle of judges in the colonies. Much to his chagrin, however, the ill-fated pamphlet was never published, as the Information Department apparently decided on 'something better'.[143] Yet the Committee's suggested efforts—shaped by its belief in the longevity of the Empire—did improve recruitment numbers to a degree in the early 1950s. The Colonial Office never achieved the volume of applicants they hoped for, however, and it seems that Russell and Furse were unaware of how soon their latest schemes would be nullified in the rapid transition of colonial territories to independent nations.

In 1954 the Colonial Office replaced the Colonial Service with Her Majesty's Oversea[s] Civil Service.[144] The new service was part of the Colonial Office's efforts to revise the idea of what a career in the colonies meant. It wanted to move towards the idea of 'a series of overseas assignments from a UK base' rather than a lifelong career in the colonies, as it became increasingly clear that some of the larger colonies would achieve independence in the coming decades.[145] Under the new Oversea[s] Service colonial judges were members of Her Majesty's Overseas Judiciary. The young officers who started their careers in this service did so with a higher status in the places they served and in the Empire, but with more limited prospects than their predecessors and superiors had enjoyed. They were not promised a career in the Empire—its future was increasingly in question—nor were they necessarily looking for one. Some of the recruits to the judiciary saw themselves as choosing a career and life *overseas*, rather than in the colonies.

A New Crop of Colonial Legal Officers

The new colonial legal officers arriving in Tanganyika in the 1950s benefitted from post-war policies and the enhanced presence and position of the judiciary in the territory. They were also shaped by previous years of British rule in the region and the outbreak of World War II. Their position and point of view on colonial rule after the conclusion of World War II gave them a different relationship to and experiences in Tanganyika than those of their pre-war predecessors. Members of this cohort had a much greater familiarity with East Africa, as some had previously lived in the region as children of men in the Colonial Service or of British entrepreneurs. Others had spent time in East Africa during World War II as soldiers. Furthermore, many young officers met their wives among the daughters of British colonial farmers and businessmen or among the new female recruits in the Overseas Civil Service, and started their families in the territory.[146] These factors encouraged members of this cohort to regard Tanganyika and East Africa as their second home rather than as a stop in a long series of overseas appointments.

An example of a judge whose background contains many of the characteristics common to the post-war judiciary is Justice Eric J.E. Law. Law was the son of Charles E. Law, a colonial judge and a member of the Bushe Commission, and he had lived in East Africa as a child during his father's tenure on Benches in the region.[147] He joined the military in 1939 after his call to the Bar and volunteered to go to East Africa to serve with the King's African Rifles. During the war he led African troops north to fight the Italians and served as an assistant judicial adviser to the Ethiopian government in 1942. After he was demobilised in 1944 he joined the Colonial Legal Service and was sent first to Nyasaland, where he met his wife, Patricia, the daughter of a member of the Colonial Audit Service. He occupied a number of junior posts in the Service in East Africa, including in Tanganyika, before finally joining the High Court Bench of Tanganyika in 1958. His interactions with Africans before his time in the Service and his lifelong relationship to East Africa were unparalleled among the pre-war judiciary, but are reflective of the experiences of many new junior legal officers of the 1950s.

As a result of this previous experience in East Africa, and an increased emphasis on basic language training for magistrates, a greater proportion of the legal officers in the 1950s passed the lower oral Kiswahili exam than had done before World War II.[148] This was made possible in part by the long period that some of the younger professional magistrates spent in Tanganyika. Some members of the High Court Bench in the early 1960s had been solely in the magistracy in Tanganyika and others had spent a period of time there, with interludes elsewhere (often in other East African territories), before returning to the High Court Bench.[149] This gave them the opportunity to learn the language while serving as magistrates in the territory—an opportunity that some of their predecessors had not enjoyed.

Despite these links to the territory Morris argues that colonial judges were 'even more remote from, and ignorant of, the social life of the African population than had been their predecessors'.[150] This may have been in part because the colonial legal officers of this period enjoyed a substantially improved quality of life and social life than their forerunners.[151] The expatriate social scene in the colony became more active after World War II, with larger numbers of British men and women working in the territory. Private parties at the homes of senior colonial officials, like judges, were reported in the newspapers. For instance, one newspaper reported that Law and his wife 'gave a most enjoyable sundowner on the grounds of their lovely home in Mwanza. Drink and a delicious variety of toasties were served in the garden, which was illuminated with multi-coloured lights.'[152] In addition to private gatherings, colonial social life for the most elite revolved around the Dar es Salaam Club, which was located near the High Court. Many senior officers of the Service were members and High Court judges visited frequently.[153] Africans were not allowed to enter the Club, except to serve members, and the social activities of colonial judges remained separated from those of Africans. The development of the colonial community and enhanced lifestyle, however, made Tanganyika more desirable for legal officers of this era and helped interest them in staying in Tanganyika, even after it gained independence.

The judges and magistrates of the 1950s had compelling social and professional reasons to hold on to their posts in Tanganyika. The bond of both attachment and necessity that some of these magistrates and younger judges had to Tanganyika would later become crucial to the survival of the British legal system—and specifically the High Court—at the time of independence.

The Judiciary and the Struggle for National Independence: The Trial of Julius Nyerere

The size and position of the colonial judiciary in the territory reached new heights in the late 1950s. This peak coincided with the greatest challenge the colonial administration had faced in the history of British rule in the territory: the struggle for national independence. The government attempted to contain Africans' efforts without using substantial force—for fear of provoking greater resistance—or losing credibility at home and on the international stage. It instead turned to the judiciary to legitimise its efforts. Rather than attempt to dissolve the independence movement through force, the administration put its leader on trial, apparently hoping that the judiciary would have the credibility and authority to snuff out the movement.

The role of courts and judges in colonial government responses to disorder and independence movements varied across the British Empire, even within Eastern Africa.[154] In Kenya, during the Mau Mau rebellion, colonial judges became the literal 'cutting edge of colonialism', handing down the death penalty to 1090 individuals accused of Mau Mau crimes.[155] In Nyasaland (Malawi), on the other hand, a British judge was employed to investigate the way in which the colonial government, especially the police, had responded to disorder in the colony.[156] In Tanganyika, however, the colonial government employed its judiciary to shield it from criticism that it was trying to impede the activities of the political organisation working towards independence: the Tanganyika African National Union (TANU).[157]

From 1954 TANU accelerated its work, increasingly challenging the actions of the administration and insisting on more roles in government for Africans. The Governor, Edward F. Twining, responded to the growing nationalist activities by 'tighten[ing] administrative control':

> the instrument was the Societies Ordinance of 1954, which required associations to seek government registration and obtain police permission before collecting subscriptions or holding public meetings … this machinery was very effective, although it also stimulated TANU to improve its organisation.[158]

As TANU grew in the mid-1950s, so did the profile of its leader, Julius K. Nyerere. Like most independence movements, Nyerere and TANU challenged the validity of Twining's government and of British colonial rule in Tanganyika.[159] TANU was effective at highlighting the contradictions inherent in British rule and the ways in which the colonial administration failed to live up to the principles the British espoused. The colonial court system was powerful proof that the British did not always practise what they preached.

In 1957 the government banned Nyerere from public speaking because it regarded his speeches as too hostile towards colonial authorities. It lifted the ban later that same year to avoid accusations from the United Nations that it was oppressing politically active Africans and delaying political progress in the territory, but continued to attempt to limit the activities of TANU branches in districts throughout the country as they became active loci of resistance to the colonial government.[160] The government's punitive actions towards TANU infuriated Nyerere, who wrote an article in the organisation's newspaper, *Sauti ya TANU*, on 27 May 1958 criticising two district commissioners. He claimed they were shutting down TANU branches in Geita and Mahenge and conspiring to remove an African chief from his position without appropriate cause.[161] Nyerere wrote that 'These same officials would have people committing perjury in court if only to vilify TANU. These same people who intimidate and punish innocence, cajole and reward crookery, have the temerity to invoke law and order.'[162] Twining was ambivalent over how to respond to Nyerere's claims and his Executive Council debated whether to bring charges against him for libel.[163] Trying him carried the risk of fuelling the independence movement, but also offered the possible reward of the 'collapse' of TANU if Nyerere was put in prison.[164] Ultimately, the government brought charges against Nyerere. His trial illustrates how the colonial government attempted to use the professional judiciary as a lawful route to containing the activities of the independence movement.[165]

The government charged Nyerere with three counts of criminal libel. It asserted that he had libelled the two district commissioners by accusing them of arbitrarily closing two of TANU's branches, encouraged perjury in court, and published a statement in the newspaper claiming the two men were 'rewarding crookery'.[166] Nyerere's trial commenced on 9 July 1958 at the District Court of Dar es Salaam before a professional magistrate, L.A. Davies. Defended by a British barrister, D.N. Pritt, and two Asian advocates from Tanganyika, Kantilal L. Jhaveri and M.N. Rattansey, Nyerere plead not guilty to the three charges.[167] Huge crowds attended the 'tense' trial in which Nyerere reportedly 'took full responsibility for the article and said that he had written it to draw the attention of the government to certain complaints'.[168] The prosecution claimed that Nyerere had written the statements 'for publicity' and that they constituted 'very grave libel'.[169] The prosecution also made a crucial argument about the significance of Nyerere's actions for the administration of justice. The lead prosecutor, Solicitor General John Summerfield, argued that what Nyerere had written 'had great implications to the relationship between the DCs and the citizens particularly considering the fact that the DCs were also magistrates by virtue of their positions'.[170] Therefore, the prosecution transformed Nyerere's supposed libelling of two individuals into an assault on not only administrative authority and actions, but also on the credibility of the legal system. The concern that Nyerere was discrediting the magistracy as well as the actions of the provincial administration increased the stakes in his case, as the dual role of administrative officers, like these district commissioners, remained a target of criticism. The two supposedly libelled district commissioners never testified in Court and one of the counts was dropped during the trial.[171]

The trial concluded on 18 July 1958 and less than one month later, on 11 August, Nyerere was found guilty on two counts of libel.[172] He was fined a total of £150 and was given an alternative of six months in prison.[173] He elected to pay the fine using funds raised on his behalf.[174] In his memoir Jhaveri summed up the impact of the trial, asserting that, 'even though the fine was small, the political implications were great'.[175] Nyerere's conviction enhanced his credibility in Tanganyika to Africans and the colonial government, further solidifying his position as the leader of the independence movement and TANU as the vanguard of African resistance to British rule. It also reframed his relationship with the new colonial governor, Richard G. Turnbull, who had started his tenure during Nyerere's trial.[176] Turnbull would probably have been faced with public outrage and possibly violence if Nyerere had chosen 'martyrdom' by going to prison instead of paying the fine.[177] Though Nyrere's conviction of libel remained of concern to his attorney Pritt, the independence movement on the whole was buoyed by the trial and Pritt described this outcome as 'really a victory'.[178] After the trial, in speeches throughout the country, TANU members framed the trial as the government's attempt to 'kill' the movement and the outcome, despite his conviction, as a triumph.[179]

Nyerere's trial thrust the judiciary into a new role in the territory. Twining's administration had attempted to use the courts to contain TANU's activities, and the magistrate had convicted Nyerere accordingly. Yet, while the decision in the case against Nyerere supported the administration by reinforcing colonial law and administrative control, it also imposed a relatively lenient sentence on Nyerere as compared with the penalties faced by other independence movement leaders in other British territories.

The involvement of Tanganyika's judiciary in responding to the independence movement differs from the roles of judiciaries in other British colonial territories. In neighbouring Kenya, the judiciary became a brutal arm of the colonial state as it attempted to contain the Mau Mau rebellion.[180] Ghai and McAuslan assert that the judiciary in Kenya proved to be 'less humane and impartial than they thought. The courts, no less than the administration, were part of the new colonial order, and had to and were prepared to support that order when it was essential to do so'.[181] The prosecution of Nyerere in Tanganyika, however, shows that just as colonial governments responded to independence movements in a variety of ways, so did colonial judiciaries. There was not a standard role for the judiciary in this process across British Africa and judges' decisions often depended on the nature of colonial rule and colonial institutions in a particular territory. In Tanganyika the British courts ultimately became more of a buffer than a weapon against challenges to British authority and prosecution substituted for the use of raw force in this case.

Conclusion: The High Court as the Legacy of British Colonial Rule

The post-war era was one of growth for the colonial judiciary. As the colonial administration transitioned from its emphasis on indirect rule to a focus on colonial development, the status of the colonial judiciary slowly improved. The size and infrastructure of the judiciary expanded, allowing it to hear more cases and have a greater presence outside Dar es Salaam.

Its position in the territory relative to the administration also changed, as it regained a role in deciding cases from African courts. The enhanced standing of colonial judiciaries and judicial institutions in East Africa, as well as throughout the remaining parts of the Empire, allowed Tanganyika's judges to benefit from a greater prestige and influence than that afforded their forebears.

Colonial rhetoric about 'just' court systems transformed during this period and the government took the first small steps towards integrating the 'parallel' court systems and magistracy. Though there was little meaningful change at the time, these early steps laid the groundwork for a restructured system after national independence. As the political and social movement towards independence hastened in the 1950s, the administration turned to the post-war judiciary to help it maintain legitimacy and authority in the face of challenges to both. It described the judiciary not only as an independent body, but also as an arm of the colonial state.

With political progress towards national independence, the judiciary and the common law became central to the government's attempts to reimagine its legacy as one of 'justice'. The judiciary and the courts were invoked as *the* symbols of British activities in the territory and the physical embodiment of this rhetoric was the new High Court building, which opened in Dar es Salaam on 17 May 1958.[182] Since the 1920s members of the Bench had been requesting a purpose-built British courthouse to replace the old German building. In 1953, in the context of many colonial building projects and when 'independence was not regarded [by the British] then as a practical possibility for at least another generation', the government approved the plans for a new courthouse building.[183] The High Court building was a substantial financial venture, including many amenities like air conditioning and accommodation for visiting Court of Appeal judges.[184] The administrators and judges planning the courthouse in the early 1950s regarded it as an investment in the colonial state and new infrastructure.

By the time it opened, however, the courthouse (shown in 2008 in Fig. 4.1) became a sort of parting gift and memorial to British colonial justice, and one which the Colonial Office and government were keen to use to reframe the history of British rule. Though the new building opened amid much pomp and circumstance in 1958, and was celebrated as 'another major step forward in the continuing development of Tanganyika', it was also framed as a 'mark of what has already been achieved'.[185] In the Lord Chancellor of Britain's speech at the opening ceremony, he further

Fig. 4.1 The High Court of Tanzania in December 2008 (Photo by A.K. Dewar and E.R. Feingold, Dar es Salaam, December 2008. Photos taken and reprinted with the permission of the photographers and the Court of Appeal of Tanzania)

described the courts and the common law as Britain's most significant 'contribution to the world', framing the judiciary and its new courthouse as symbols of this honourable legacy.[186] At the opening ceremony one British official reportedly pointed to a flourishing mango tree in front of the new building and proclaimed, 'We English, everywhere we go we plant the seeds of justice.'[187] Colonial authorities somewhat ironically also expressed the hope that judicial institutions would be a 'safeguard against possible autocratic tendencies' in the future.[188] They espoused their belief that British actions had instilled values through the administration of justice that 'having once learnt, as you [Tanganyikans] have, that the impartial doing of justice between man and man is the foundation of a truly civilised society, it is a lesson which you will never forget'.[189] The judiciary's role as the 'civilisers' through the application of the law was certainly a part of interwar rhetoric, but the reframing of the administration of justice as the main purpose of colonial rule made the symbolic significance of the judiciary even more important to the British colonial project in Tanganyika, even near its end.

Fig. 4.2 The mural at the High Court of Tanzania (Photo by A.K. Dewar and E.R. Feingold, Dar es Salaam, December 2008. Photos taken and reprinted with the permission of the photographers and the Court of Appeal of Tanzania)

The opening of the new courthouse not only provided an opportunity for colonial authorities to reframe the legacy of the Bench and British courts, it also enshrined indirect rule and the racially divided and 'parallel' court systems in the courthouse itself. At the top of the staircase inside of the courthouse the government commissioned a mural with two panels (see Fig. 4.2), in which British colonial justice is reimagined.[190] The official documentation on the opening of the courthouse describes the individuals depicted in the pictures as 'the administrators of the law, past and present'.[191] The two panels were intended to show the 'progress from trial by tribal elders and witchdoctor to the administration of British justice through the district officer and the High Court judge'.[192] The period before colonial rule is depicted as lacking order and justice in the left panel (see Fig. 4.3) while the colonial period appears orderly and just in the right panel (see Fig. 4.4). The portrayal of the two different types of justice on two different panels also can be interpreted as showing the 'parallel' court systems, which were still in use at the time. The left panel depicts African and Arab authorities in the Local Courts, while the right panel features the British courts.[193] Though the mural does not accurately or completely capture and

Fig. 4.3 Left panel of the mural at the High Court of Tanzania (Photo by A.K. Dewar and E.R. Feingold, Dar es Salaam, December 2008. Photos taken and reprinted with the permission of the photographers and the Court of Appeal of Tanzania)

convey the past method of administration of justice, or the dual courts structure at the time of the mural's creation in 1958, it does portray some of the main divisions of the court systems in place under British rule—divisions that would become the primary target of structural reforms to the court system during the process of decolonisation.

Fig. 4.4 Right panel of the mural at the High Court of Tanzania (Photo by A.K. Dewar and E.R. Feingold, Dar es Salaam, December 2008. Photos taken and reprinted with the permission of the photographers and the Court of Appeal of Tanzania)

Notes

1. A.H.M. Kirk-Greene, *On Crown Service: A History of HM Colonial and Overseas Civil Service, 1837–1997* (London, 1999), p. 59.
2. J. Iliffe, *A Modern History of Tanganyika* (Cambridge, 1979), p. 376.

3. See Article 76 of the Trusteeship Agreement. It is reprinted in: B.T.G. Chidzero and the Royal Institute of International Affairs, *Tanganyika and International Trusteeship* (Oxford, 1961), pp. 263–268.
4. M.L. Bates, 'Tanganyika under British Administration, 1920–1955', D.Phil. thesis (University of Oxford, 1958), p. 546.
5. Iliffe, *A Modern History*, p. 436.
6. Ibid., p. 356.
7. J.D. Graham, 'Indirect Rule: The Establishment of Chiefs and Tribes in Cameron's Tanganyika', *Tanzania Notes and Records*, 77 (1976), p. 9.
8. On the status of tenure of colonial judges prior to the twentieth century, see: J. McLaren, *Dewigged, Bothered, and Bewildered: British Colonial Judges on Trial, 1800–1900* (Toronto, 2011), especially pp. 16–18; J. McLaren, 'Navigating the Scylla of imperial politico-legal aspirations and Charybdis of colonial micro-politics in the British Empire', in S. Dorsett and J. McLaren (eds.), *Legal Histories of the British Empire: Laws, Engagements, and Legacies* (New York, 2014), p. 16.
9. The metaphor of the judiciary as a plant was inspired by Morris' description of English law as a 'hardy plant in an alien soil'. H.F. Morris, 'English Law in East Africa: A Hardy Plant in an Alien Soil' in H.F. Morris and J.S. Read, *Indirect Rule and the Search for Justice: Essays in East African Legal History* (Oxford, 1972), p. 73.
10. A list of those who testified is available at the end of the Report, see: The Bushe Report, pp. 100–102. Few Africans, however, were given the opportunity to offer their views on the administration of justice. The Africans who were able to give testimony to the Commission were primarily chiefs and headmen, whose elite though subordinate position within the judicial system should be taken into account when assessing the opinions they offered.
11. The Bushe Report; Great Britain, *Commission of Inquiry into the Administration of Justice in Kenya, Uganda, and the Tanganyika Territory in Criminal Matters, Minutes of Evidence and Memoranda Submitted to the Commission* (London, 1934). A number of works examine the Bushe Commission in detail, see, for example: H.F. Morris, *Evidence in East Africa* (London, 1968); Y.P. Ghai and P. McAuslan, *Public Law and Political Change in Kenya: A Study of the Legal Framework of Government from Colonial Times to the Present* (Nairobi, 1970), pp. 139–147; H.F. Morris, *Some Perspectives of East African Legal History* (Uppsala, 1970), pp. 24–25; D. Anderson, 'Policing, Prosecution and the Law in Colonial Kenya, c. 1905–39' in D. Anderson and D. Killingray (eds.), *Policing the Empire: Government, Authority and Control, 1830–1940* (Manchester, 1991), pp. 188–191; D. Anderson, 'Kenya, 1895–1939: Registration and Rough Justice' in D. Hay and P. Craven (eds.), *Masters,*

Servants, and Magistrates in Britain and the Empire, 1562–1955 (London, 2004), pp. 498–528; E.R. Feingold, 'Power, Procedure, and Punishment: The Administration of Criminal Justice in East Africa c.1933', M.Sc. thesis (University of Oxford, 2007).

12. On the codes introduced to East Africa in 1930 see: H.F. Morris, 'A History of the Adoption of Codes of Criminal Law and Procedure in British Colonial Africa, 1876–1935', *Journal of African Law*, 18 (1974), pp. 13–17; C.C. Roberts, R.P. Nicholson, and G.S.J. Orde-Browne, *Tangled Justice: Some Reasons for a Change of Policy in Africa* (London, 1937), pp. 48–55.
13. H.F. Morris, 'The Reception and Rejection of Indian Law' in H.F. Morris and J.S. Read, *Indirect Rule and the Search for Justice: Essays in East African Legal History* (Oxford, 1972), p. 119.
14. The Bushe Report, p. 2. Respectively: A.D.A. MacGregor, W. MacLellan Wilson, P.E. Mitchell, J.B. Griffin, and C.E. Law.
15. There was one exception. Justice C.E. Law noted a reservation to the Report's findings on the admissibility of evidence and confessions to police. The Bushe Report, p. 99.
16. Griffin was appointed the Chief Justice of Uganda, Law the Chief Justice of Northern Rhodesia, and MacGregor the Chief Justice of Hong Kong.
17. The Bushe Report noted that all witnesses were in agreement that there were problems with the courts in Tanganyika. The Commission made the claim that conditions in Tanganyika were worse than in Kenya and Uganda. The Bushe Report, pp. 9, 14, 16.
18. A. Russell, 'The Administration of Justice in East Africa', *Journal of Comparative Legislation and International Law*, 17 (1935), p. 11.
19. The Bushe Report, pp. 8–9.
20. Ibid., p. 10.
21. Ibid., pp. 13–14.
22. For comparison, the Commission recommended increasing the size of the High Court Benches of Kenya and Uganda by one judge each. Ibid., p. 96 (Rec. v).
23. Ibid., p. 96 (Rec. vi). The Commission suggested that these trials should take place without reference to the High Court because it would increase delays. Ibid., p. 25.
24. Ibid., pp. 23, 96 (Recs. viii & xi).
25. Ibid., p. 96 (Recs. ii & vii).
26. Morris, 'English Law in East Africa', p. 100.
27. Ibid., p. 102.
28. Feingold, 'Power, Procedure, and Punishment', pp. 1–2.
29. Ghai and McAuslan, *Public Law*, p. 146.
30. The response of each of the three governors was published along with the Report. The Bushe Report, pp. 104–160.

31. Morris, 'English Law in East Africa', p. 100. For instance, the East African governments accepted the Bushe recommendation that there should be a public defender for poor defendants, but could not afford to hire the additional staff and therefore never introduced one during this period. Ibid., pp. 94–95.
32. Some, such as R. Hamilton, acknowledged the financial implications of the recommendations, but still expressed the hope that the territories would not allow finance to stand in the way of what he believed were necessary and principled changes. R. Hamilton, 'Criminal Justice in East Africa', *Journal of the Royal African Society*, 34 (1935), p. 17.
33. Unknown, 'Criminal Justice in East Africa', *The Times*, 6 December 1934, p. 4.
34. Morris, 'English Law in East Africa', p. 102.
35. RHL, MSS. Brit. Emp. s. 415, Ralph Furse Papers, Box 6/7, R. Furse, 'Legal', n.d., p. 2.
36. A.H.M. Kirk-Greene, *Britain's Imperial Administrators, 1858–1966* (Basingstoke, 2000), p. 188.
37. R. Collins, 'The Sudan Political Service: A Portrait of "Imperialists"', *African Affairs*, 71 (1972), p. 300.
38. Kirk-Greene, *Britain's Imperial Administrators*, p. 188.
39. RHL, MSS. Brit. Emp. s. 415, Ralph Furse Papers, Box 6/7, R. Furse, 'Legal', p. 2.
40. For example see: H.G. Bushe, 'Criminal Justice in East Africa', *Journal of the Royal African Society*, 34 (1935), pp. 117–128; Hamilton, 'Criminal Justice'; Russell, 'The Administration of Justice in East Africa'; Unknown, 'Criminal Justice in East Africa'; H.R. Hone, 'The Native of Uganda and the Criminal Law', *Journal of Comparative Legislation and International Law*, 21 (1939), pp. 179–197.
41. Ironically, by the time the Colonial Office and East African Governments began to make some of the changes advocated by Bushe after World War II, he was no longer Legal Adviser but had become an administrator himself: The Governor of Barbados.
42. TNA (UK), CO 691/191/10, [CO] Scott to unknown [CO], 24 April 1944.
43. TNA (UK), CO 691/191/10, W.E.F. Jackson to G.H. Gater, 23 August 1944, p. 1.
44. Ibid.; TNA (UK), CO 691/191/10, unknown [CO] to unknown [CO], 1 May 1944, p. 2.
45. Justice R.M. Cluer wrote a scathing letter on the state of the administration of justice in Tanganyika to the Colonial Office in 1943, complaining that many of the concerns raised by Bushe remained unresolved. The memo was also signed by two other judges of the High court, Justice

G.A.K. McRoberts and Justice M. Wilson, and can be regarded as expressing views held by a significant portion of the High Court at the time. TNA (UK), CO 691/191/10, 'Memorandum by Mr. Justice Cluer', 31 December 1943.

46. TNA (UK), CO 691/191/10, W.E.F. Jackson to G.H. Gater, 23 August 1944, p. 1.
47. Ibid. The Governor advised the Colonial Office to promote Mark Wilson to Chief Justice outside Tanganyika. He was eventually appointed Chief Justice of the Gold Coast in 1948.
48. For example, see: TNA (UK), CO 323/1925/3, C. Mathew to K. Roberts-Wray, 15 June [c. 1951]. Administrative officers from the late 1950s described a working relationship between the branches of the government that was typically cordial, but at times strained. One officer summed up the relationship between the administration and judiciary as one where each branch had 'fairly healthy contempt for the other'. Bryan McCleery, interview with author, Templecombe, 23 April 2009.
49. These modifications are discussed later in this chapter.
50. Morris, 'English Law in East Africa', p. 103.
51. Ibid.; J. Cooke, *One White Man in Black Africa: From Kilimanjaro to Kalahari 1951–1991* (Thornhill, 1991), p. 44.
52. TNA, 43474, 'High Court Circular No. 10 of 1953: The Expansion of the Judicial Department', 5 August 1953.
53. Morris, 'English Law in East Africa', p. 103.
54. Tanganyika had approximately seven professional magistrates in 1933, which increased to 32 by 1959. Data from: COL 1933, p. 459; TSL 1959, pp. 217–219.
55. Two of the four senior resident magistrates in the late 1950s were promoted to the High Court Bench of Tanganyika: D.J. Williams in 1960 and M.C.E.P. Biron in 1961. Magistrates of this rank were also called upon to serve as acting judges in the absence of a judge from the territory. For instance Biron was an acting judge for part of 1957. Tanganyika Territory, *Staff List July 1957* (Dar es Salaam, 1957), p. 5.
56. TNA, 43474, 'High Court Circular No. 10 of 1953: The Expansion of the Judicial Department', 5 August 1953.
57. TNA, 43474, L.M. Heaney to H.R.F. Butterfield, 4 September 1953.
58. TNA (UK), CO 691/191/10, 'Memorandum by Mr. Justice Cluer', 31 December 1943.
59. RHL, MSS. Afr. s. 592, Mark Wilson Papers, Box 5/1, M. Wilson, 'Memorandum: Proposals for Post-War Developments and Improvements in the Administration of Justice in the Tanganyika Territory', 25 May 1945, pp. 6–9.
60. Ibid., p. 9.

61. ARJ 1950, p. 6.
62. TNA, 38775, E.W. Pennefather to R. de Z. Hall, 23 December 1949, p. 1; TNA, 38775, R. de Z. Hall to E.R.E. Surridge, 9 January 1950.
63. TNA, 38775, E.W. Pennefather to R. de Z. Hall, 23 December 1949, p. 1; ARJ 1951, p. 3.
64. ARJ 1953, p. 2.
65. Salaries of the Court are also indications of the administration's increasing valuing of the judiciary. The actual salaries of the judiciary and their relative salary to the Governor and Chief Secretary, increased during the 1950s. Though Chief Justice Sheridan had increased the salaries of the Court in the 1930s, after World War II the Chief Justice's salary increased relative to the Governor's gross salary from 36% of the total value in 1940 to 43% by 1956. The Chief Justice's salary remained a small amount above that of the Chief Secretary's, a minor but perhaps symbolically important difference of approximately 100 GBP per year. The value of the Puisne judges' salary relative to the Chief Secretary increased from 70% of the gross salary to 85% of the gross salary over the same period. Salary data from: COL 1940, pp. 489–490; TSL 1956, pp. 1–2.
66. ARJ 1954, p. 1.
67. ARJ 1958, p. 1.
68. Bodleian Law Library, Cw Gen 510 A258.4a, R.E.S. Tanner, 'Reflections on the Legal System of Colonial Tanganyika: Failure, Misunderstanding, or Interlude' in *Africa in the Colonial Period Conference, Symposium Number Five: The Administration of Law in British Africa*, University College, Oxford, 1–2 July 1980, p. 15.
69. TNA, 205-78 Vol. II, 'High Court Circuits—1958', 23 November 1957.
70. TNA, 205-78 Vol. II, M.J.R. Coakley to J.S.R. Cole, 20 March 1958.
71. J.K. Williams, *Black, Amber, White: An Autobiography* (Worthing, 1990), p. 118.
72. Ibid., p. 108.
73. RHL, MSS. Afr. s. 592, Mark Wilson Papers, Box 5/1, M. Wilson, 'Memorandum: Proposals for Post-War Developments and Improvements in the Administration of Justice in the Tanganyika Territory', 25 May 1945, pp. 3–4.
74. Ibid., p. 20; Morris, 'Native Courts', p. 135.
75. RHL, MSS. Afr. s. 592, Mark Wilson Papers, Box 5/1, M. Wilson, 'Memorandum: Proposals for Post-War Developments and Improvements in the Administration of Justice in the Tanganyika Territory', 25 May 1945, p. 21.
76. NACP, Record Group (RG) 59, 4036, [file untitled], American Consulate Dar es Salaam to Department of State, 15 August 1950, p. 1.
77. J.S.R. Cole and W.N. Denison, *Tanganyika: The Development of Its Laws and Constitution* (London, 1964), p. 102.

78. Morris, 'Native Courts', p. 160.
79. The courts did not have jurisdiction in cases where an African was charged with an offence resulting in a death—or for an offence which could result in the death penalty—non-customary marriage disputes, proceedings affecting ownership of land, and proceedings involving claims of witchcraft. Local Courts Ordinance 1951, s 10–13. The ordinance roughly defined Africans as the people of tribes within the territory and surrounding territories, for the exact definition, see s(2).
80. Local Courts Ordinance 1951, s 10(1).
81. Ibid., s 15(a).
82. Secretary of State for the Colonies, 'Judicial Advisers' Conference 1953', *Journal of African Administration*, Special Supplement (1953), p. 21. Hereafter cited: Judicial Advisers' Conference 1953.
83. Morris, 'Native Courts', pp. 160–161.
84. Additional authorities were also given various supervisory and revisionary powers including the local courts adviser (a post created through the ordinance under section 3), district commissioners, and provincial local courts officers (also created under the ordinance, section 3, although none had been appointed as of 1961). Cole and Denison, *Tanganyika*, p. 105. For details of the powers of administrative officers over the Local Courts see: Local Courts Ordinance 1951, s 4–6 & 34.
85. Cole and Denison, *Tanganyika*, p. 103.
86. Local Courts Ordinance 1951, s 38(1).
87. Transfers could not, however, go the other direction. On the directions of transfers, see: *Regina v. Lamba s/o Mkenga* and *Regina v. Alute s/o Makiya* (1953) 2 T.L.R. (R), 63; Local Courts Ordinance 1951, s 35.
88. Local Courts Ordinance 1951, s 39(1–2). Judges could be invited to serve on the Governor's Appeal Board prior to the ordinance, but it was not until 1951 that a judge was officially given a position on and the presidency of the appeals body. On appeals up to 1953, see: Tanganyika, *Digest of Appeals from Local Courts* (Dar es Salaam, 1953). From 1953 the colonial government published a yearly Digest of Appeals from Local Courts until 1964.
89. Local Courts Ordinance 1951, s 39(2).
90. A local courts adviser had the power to revise decisions in Local Courts and the ability to transfer cases. The role replaced the pre-existing Native Courts adviser, which was established in 1948 to assist with the supervision of Native Courts and to serve on the Governor's Appeal Board. African Studies Branch, 'A Digest', p. 22.
91. A.N. Allott, 'The Development of the East African Legal Systems During the Colonial Period' in D.A. Low and A. Smith (eds.), *History of East Africa* (3 vols., Oxford, 1976), iii, p. 376.

92. Local Courts Ordinance 1951, s 39(3).
93. Ibid., s 39(4); J.H. Jearey, 'The Structure, Composition and Jurisdiction of Courts and Authorities Enforcing the Criminal Law in British African Territories', *The International and Comparative Law Quarterly*, 9 (1960), p. 413.
94. Though advocates remained barred from the Local Courts, they were permitted for the first time in appeals to the Central Court of Appeal under the ordinance. Cole and Denison, *Tanganyika*, p. 103. While judges were regaining some lost ground in Tanganyika, in Kenya the position of the Supreme Court relative to 'native' tribunals was transforming in the other direction. In 1951 Africans' tribunals were completely separated from the court system under the judiciary. Shadle, 'African Court Elders', p. 181.
95. Judicial adviser was a generic title for individuals appointed to the specific role of supervising and 'guiding the progress of African courts'. These individuals had a variety of titles and a range of duties depending on the position of the Native or African courts relative to the British courts in their territory. Judicial Advisers' Conference 1953, pp. 2, 39; W. Twining, *The Place of Customary Law in the National Legal Systems of East Africa: Lectures Delivered at the University of Chicago Law School in April-May 1963* (Chicago, 1964), p. 28.
96. The despatch from the Secretary of State urging African territories to create a judicial adviser post after World War II is reprinted in Appendix B of the report of the conference, and see p. 11.
97. Ibid., p. 40. The positions were initially supposed to be open to members of the legal and administrative services. Ibid., p. 12.
98. Tanganyika Territory, *Staff List February 1953* (Dar es Salaam, 1953), p. 3.
99. Judicial Advisers' Conference 1953, p. 14.
100. Though it should be noted that there are examples of judicial advisers advocating for the integration of the court systems in British colonies in Africa the years preceding the first Judicial Advisers' Conference see: A.J. Loveridge, 'The Future of Native Courts', *Journal of African Administration*, 1 (1949), pp. 7–18.
101. Ibid., p. 5.
102. Morris, 'Native Courts', p. 161. Morris notes, however, that the advisers and their governments did not expect integration to be carried out quickly.
103. Judicial Advisers' Conference 1953, p. 7. The only system with a greater degree of separation was Kenya, which had completely parallel court systems. Secretary of State for the Colonies, 'Judicial Advisers' Conference 1956', *Journal of African Administration,* Special Supplement (1957), p. 4. Hereafter cited: Judicial Advisers' Conference 1956.

104. Judicial Advisers' Conference 1953, p. 15; S.B. Pfeiffer, 'The Role of the Judiciary in the Constitutional Systems of East Africa', *The Journal of Modern African Studies*, 16 (1978), p. 41.
105. Halwenge had been in the government since 1940 and was made an African administrative assistant in 1950, one year before he took his law exam. Bakari began working for the government in 1948 after attending Makerere College in Uganda. NACP, RG 59, 4035, [file untitled], American Consulate Dar es Salaam to Department of State, 30 June 1951. Their appointments were announced early in the summer of 1951. C. Mathew, 'General Notice 1073—Appointment of Magistrates', *Tanganyika Gazette*, 6 July 1951.
106. TNA, 41755, R. de Z. Hall [also stamped with signature of T.J. Tawney] to E. Halwenge, 6 July 1951; TNA, 41755, R. de Z. Hall [also stamped with signature of T.J. Tawney] to M. Bakari, 6 July 1951.
107. Ibid.
108. TNA, 41755, 'Extract from the Honourable Mr. Justice Crawshaw—date 5.28.1953', 4 June 1953.
109. A.J. Grattan-Bellew 'General Notice 1771—Appointment of Magistrate', *Tanganyika Gazette*, 14 September 1954.
110. TNA, 41755, 'Extract from Minutes of the Meeting of the Provincial Commissioners' Conference—January 1954', n.d., p. 1.
111. To become an assistant district officer these men had to meet a number of requirements, many of which were similar to those for district officers. For the requirements see: TNA, 41755, 'Extract from Minutes of the Meeting of the Provincial Commissioners' Conference—January 1954', n.d., p. 1.
112. Ibid.
113. NACP, RG 59, 4035, [file untitled], American Consulate Dar es Salaam to Department of State, 30 June 1951.
114. On the entrance and position of African employees in the lower levels of colonial government after World War II, see: A. Eckert, 'Cultural Commuters: African Employees in Late Colonial Tanzania' in B.N. Lawrance, E.L. Osborn, and R.L. Roberts (eds.), *Intermediaries, Interpreters, and Clerks: African Employees in the Making of Colonial Africa* (Madison, 2006), pp. 250–253.
115. ARJ 1946; ARJ 1960. Advocates in Tanganyika had a fused role as barrister and solicitor, since the colonies had 'too few lawyers … to allow such a split'. F. Twaib, *The Legal Profession in Tanzania* (Bayreuth, 1997), p. 15.
116. Tanganyika Law Society Ordinance 1954, s 3; Advocates Ordinance 1954, s 7.
117. TNA (UK), CO 822/124/1, 'Memorandum by Sir Barclay Nihill, Chief Justice of Kenya', 8 July 1948, p. 2. There was substantial debate over its placement in Kenya because the Government of Uganda regarded the

move as disadvantageous to it and to Tanganyika, which had more appeals to the Court of Appeal than Kenya. TNA (UK), CO 822/124/1, 'Memorandum by the Government of Uganda—Annexure 2', 2 September, 1948, p. 1.

118. TNA (UK), CO 822/124/1, 'Memorandum by Sir Barclay Nihill, Chief Justice of Kenya', 8 July 1948, p. 2.
119. This move had been considered at numerous points, but was not enacted until after World War II.
120. The extensive debate surrounding the inclusion of colonial judges in the Privy Council is documented in: TNA (UK), Lord Chancellor's Office (LCO) 2/5788; CO 1026/114. See also: B. Ibhawoh, 'Asserting judicial sovereignty: The debate over the abolition of Privy Council jurisdiction in British Africa' in S. Dorsett and J. McLaren (eds.), *Legal Histories of the British Empire* (Oxford, 2014), pp. 31–35.
121. *Terrell v. Secretary of State for the Colonies* (1953) 2 Q.B. [Queen's Bench] 482.
122. Inns of Court Conservative and Unionist Society, *British Colonial Judges: Their Appointment and Tenure of Office* (London, 1956), p. 10.
123. S.A. de Smith, 'Tenure of Office by Colonial Judges', *The Modern Law Review*, 16 (1953), p. 502.
124. Ibid.
125. Ibid., p. 503.
126. Ibid., p. 502. Roberts-Wray, Legal Adviser to the Colonial Office, asserts that while there was a 'stir' among the legal community in England over the case, that it provoked 'very little reaction among the overseas judges themselves'. K. Roberts-Wray, *Commonwealth and Colonial Law* (London, 1966), p. 496.
127. Smith, 'Tenure of Office', pp. 505–506.
128. Roberts-Wray challenges the validity of the pamphlet in: Roberts-Wray, *Commonwealth*, pp. 497–498.
129. Inns of Court Conservative and Unionist Society, *British Colonial Judges*, pp. 17–18.
130. One British judge asserted that the practice of referring cases of dismissal to the Privy Council had been 'undeviating' since the 1929 circular outlining the policy and referred to the practice as an 'impregnable … safeguard for their [colonial judges'] independence of the Executive as that enjoyed by their English brethren'. TNA (UK), CO 1026/34, N. Birkett, 'Independence of the English Judges', n.d., pp. 19–20.
131. Pfeiffer, 'The Role', p. 44.
132. TNA (UK), CO 877/23/2, unknown to unknown, [first words: 'In the absence of barrister candidates'], 5 September 1945; K.O. Roberts-Wray, to J.B. Gardener, 21 November 1945.

133. Battershill briefly served as Governor of Tanganyika, his short tenure resulted from an extended illness, which ultimately led the Secretary of State for the Colonies to encourage him to resign. J.M.M.H. Listowel, *The Making of Tanganyika* (London, 1965), p. 156; TNA (UK), CO 850/209/10, 'Report of a Committee appointed by the Secretary of State for the Colonies: Colonial Legal Service', 16 February 1945, p. 1. Hereafter cited: Battershill Committee.
134. Ibid., p. 4.
135. The details of the scheme, including the types of probationerships and relevant financial assistance for new recruits, are outlined in: Great Britain Colonial Office, *Appointments in Her Majesty's Overseas Civil Service, and Other Appointments in Colonial and Overseas Territories* (London, 1957), pp. 74–76.
136. Battershill Committee, p. 5.
137. In the post-war era, the training courses for administrative officers were revamped, and the inaugural First Devonshire Course opened in 1946. Devonshire courses included more legal training for administrative officers, perhaps an indication that they would continue to administer justice and that they would need more training in order to stand up to increasing scrutiny of their role as magistrates.
138. Battershill Committee, p. 8; TNA (UK), CO 877/31/3, R. Furse to C. Jefferies, 13 March 1947, p. 1.
139. Battershill Committee, Appendix V, pp. 19 and 9.
140. Ibid., p. 8.
141. Ibid., p. 12.
142. The role of liaison officer and the procedure for applying to the Colonial Legal Service via the Joint Committee is outlined in: TNA (UK), CO 877/24/8, 'Method of Dealing with Applications for Appointment to the Colonial Legal Service from Members of the Four Inns', n.d.
143. TNA (UK), CO 877/31/1, A. Russell to R. Furse, 4 March 1948, p. 2.
144. The transition from Her Majesty's Civil Service was a long process, but the Oversea Service was officially born on 1 October 1954. The Colonial Office added the 's' in Overseas at a later date. Kirk-Greene, *On Crown Service*, pp. 62 and 68.
145. Ibid., pp. 65 and 93.
146. For example: Patrick Ellis, interview with author, Bishops Stortford, 25 March 2009.
147. The details in this section on Justice Law's life and career generate from an interview with his widow, except where cited otherwise. Patricia Law, interview with author, Canterbury, 14 May 2009.
148. Data from: TSL 1942, p. 24; TSL 1950–1959 (under the section entitled 'Judicial').

149. For instance, Justice Biron was first appointed to the magistracy in Tanganyika in 1950 and remained there for the following 11 years of British rule.
150. Morris, 'English Law in East Africa', p. 104.
151. For Justice Williams' description of this comfortable lifestyle see: Williams, *Black*, p. 85.
152. Charles Law Personal Papers, Canterbury, 'Garden Sundowner', excerpt from newspaper in Tanganyika (title and exact date unknown).
153. Patricia Law, interview with author, Canterbury, 14 May 2009.
154. For a comparative study of the responses of colonial governments to disorder in colonies in the mid-twentieth century, see: R.F. Holland, *Emergencies and Disorder in the European Empires after 1945* (London, 1994).
155. The phrase 'cutting edge of colonialism' is used by Chanock to describe the law, but is extended here to refer to judges handing down the death penalty. Chanock, *Law, Custom, and Social Order*, p. 4; D. Anderson, *Histories of the Hanged: Britain's Dirty War in Kenya and the End of Empire* (London, 2005), pp. 6–7.
156. A.W.B. Simpson, 'The Devlin Commission (1959): Colonialism, Emergencies, and the Rule of Law', *Oxford Journal of Legal Studies*, 22 (2002), p. 17.
157. The foundational works on TANU include: Iliffe, *A Modern History*, pp. 507–520; C. Pratt, *The Critical Phase in Tanzania, 1945–1968: Nyerere and the Emergence of a Socialist Strategy* (Cambridge, 1976), pp. 23–59; Listowel, *The Making*, pp. 218–238. On the role of women in TANU, see: S. Geiger, *TANU Women: Gender and Culture in the Making of Tanganyikan Nationalism, 1955–1965* (Oxford, 1997). See also: P. Bjerk, *Building a Peaceful Nation: Julius Nyerere and the Establishment of Sovereignty in Tanzania, 1960–1964* (Rochester, 2015).
158. Iliffe, *A Modern History*, pp. 553–554.
159. For an account of Twining's tenure in Tanganyika see: D. Bates, *A Gust of Plumes: A Biography of Lord Twining of Godalming and Tanganyika* (London, 1972), pp. 202–281.
160. Iliffe, *A Modern History*, p. 554. Mwakikagile claims that as many as twelve branches were closed down during 1958–1959. G. Mwakikagile, *Life in Tanganyika in the Fifties* (Pretoria, 2009), p. 140.
161. Listowel, *The Making*, p. 326. The two men were F.B. Weeks, District Commissioner of Musoma, and G.T.L. Scott, District Commissioner of Songea.
162. As quoted in: Listowel, *The Making*, p. 326.
163. Ibid., pp. 166 and 327.

164. Ibid., p. 327.
165. The case file of the trial is not accessible in Tanganyika or the UK. One work alleges that, 'the colonialists might have taken it when they left [Tanganyika] as they did with several other documents'. Court of Appeal of Tanzania, *The History of the Administration of Justice in Tanzania* (Dar es Salaam, 2004), p. 95. Extensive searching for material on the case resulted in secondary sources, cited in this section, and two firsthand accounts: S. Ngh'waya, *Kesi ya Julius Kambarage Nyerere, rais wa Tanganyika African National Union, kwa 'kashfa' dhidi ya maDC wa kikoloni wawili 1958* (Dar es Salaam, 1990); K.L. Jhaveri, *Marching with Nyerere: Africanisation of Asians* (Delhi, 1999). The only primary sources, other than newspapers, that were located were the papers of one of Nyerere's attorney's, D.N. Pritt, at the London School of Economics and Political Science Archive (LSE), and an interview with another attorney on the case, Jhaveri, respectively: LSE, Pritt_1.35; Kantilal Jhaveri, interview with author, Dar es Salaam, 16 December 2008.
166. J.C. Taylor, *The Political*, p. 167.
167. Pritt defended numerous other high-profile Africans working for independence in other colonies; Listowel, *The Making*, p. 327.
168. This material comes from an article in the November 1958 edition of *Drum* magazine and is reproduced in: Mwakikagile, *Life*, pp. 141–142.
169. Kantilal Jhaveri, interview with author, Dar es Salaam, 16 December 2008.
170. Court of Appeal of Tanzania, *The History*, p. 99.
171. Ibid.
172. During the trial the first count was withdrawn and the third was modified. For a discussion of the events that led to these alterations, see: Listowel, *The Making*, pp. 328–331.
173. Ibid., p. 332.
174. Ibid.
175. Jhaveri, *Marching with Nyerere*, p. 56.
176. Turnbull was sworn in on 15 July 1958.
177. Listowel, *The Making*, pp. 332–333; Iliffe, *A Modern History*, p. 564.
178. LSE, Pritt_1.35, D.N. Pritt, draft letter to J.K. Nyerere, n.d.
179. TNA (UK), CO 822/1325, 'African Political Affairs', n.d., pp. 6 and 11.
180. Anderson, *Histories*, pp. 6–7.
181. Ghai and McAuslan, *Public Law*, p. 173.
182. ARJ 1958, p. 1.
183. Bates, *A Gust of Plumes*, p. 225.
184. Tanganyika Public Relations Department, *Official Opening of New High Court at Dar Es Salaam, on 17th May 1958* (Dar es Salaam, 1958), pp. 3 and 6.

185. Unknown, 'The Highest Court in the Land', *Sunday News*, High Court Supplement, 18 May 1958, [accessed in NACP, RG 59, 3698, 778.13/11-459]; TNA (UK), LCO 2/5831, Draft for the Lord Chancellor's Speech at Opening of the High Court in Tanganyika, p. 3.
186. TNA (UK), LCO 2/5831, Draft for the Lord Chancellor's Speech, p. 3.
187. Leopold Kalunga, interview with author, Dar es Salaam, 31 October 2008.
188. Morris, 'English Law in East Africa', p. 104.
189. TNA (UK), LCO 2/5831, Draft for the Lord Chancellor's Speech at Opening of the High Court in Tanganyika, p. 4.
190. The mural is the work of artist Mrs. J.W. McKeon, who lived in Dar es Salaam in the late 1950s. The painted panels were originally 'linked by a cast plaster frieze picked out in gold', but the gold decoration was no longer apparent as of 2008. Tanganyika Public Relations Department, Official Opening, p. 6. A British expatriate who lived near the artist in Dar es Salaam, recalled seeing the people who served as models for the mural. She recollected that hearing some noise near her home in Dar es Salaam, she 'caught sight of it [the cause of the noise], it was led by a female witch-doctor, and she and her retinue were all dressed in colourful costumes, their full regalia, preceded by all manner of instruments being banged. I was much relieved when they passed by my bungalow and headed for one several doors away. I found out they were there to be photographed and drawn by an artist living there who had been commissioned to paint murals on the new Law Courts'. Mary Johnson, correspondence with author, 14 July 2008, p. 1. In the early 2000s the mural was repainted to refresh its colours and some may have been altered in the process, but the scenes in the mural have not been changed in any other way since its creation. Barnabas Samatta, interview with author, Dar es Salaam, 3 December 2008.
191. Tanganyika Public Relations Department, 'Official Opening', p. 6.
192. G. Rockey, 'The First of "Little Whitehall"', *Sunday News*, High Court Supplement, 18 May 1958, [accessed in NACP, RG 59, 3698, 778.13/11-459].
193. The Islamic courts are an interesting exception, however, as they are depicted on both sides of the mural.

PART II

Decolonising the High Court of Tanganyika, 1959–1971

CHAPTER 5

Restructuring Colonial Justice, Empowering the High Court, 1959–1964

Political progress towards independence in Tanganyika rapidly accelerated in the late 1950s, with a chain of general elections during 1958–1960 and the subsequent establishment of full internal self-government in May 1961.[1] Violent clashes in neighbouring Kenya and Nyasaland in 1959—and a strong desire in London to avoid similar events in Tanganyika—helped expedite Tanganyika's final independence negotiations.[2] On 9 December 1961 Tanganyika became the first territory in East Africa to become independent from Great Britain. Though the 'wind of change' was blowing powerfully in the political spheres of Tanganyika, it stopped at the doors of the new High Court in Dar es Salaam.[3] Initially, it seemed the High Court was in the eye of a storm, remaining unaltered while political and social change swirled around it. One officer working at the High Court at the time recalled that he felt 'protected from changes so far behind the portals of the High Court' although there were 'rapid changes going on' outside.[4] Inside the courtroom trials carried on as they had before independence and there were few indications of the momentous transformations taking place in the Tanganyikan government.

After national independence in 1961 Tanganyika's political leadership had to decide whether and how to integrate the colonial courts into the new government. The changes the government chose to make to the colonial court systems were reactions to the ways in which the jurisdictions and authorities of the courts, as well as their position relative to the

E.R. Feingold, *Colonial Justice and Decolonization in the High Court of Tanzania, 1920–1971*, Cambridge Imperial and Post-Colonial Studies Series, https://doi.org/10.1007/978-3-319-69691-1_5

administration, had reinforced British administrative hegemony. Africans had been prevented from accessing the High Court, their cases placed under the supervision of administrators, and they had been barred from participating in the administration of justice outside the sphere of the Local Courts. The government addressed these forms of exclusion through a series of changes to the court system that can be divided into two categories: structure and personnel. The government's first priority in relation to the courts was to remove the legacy of racial inequality before the courts that had limited Africans' access to the High Court. Therefore, the government sought to alter the 'parallel' structure of the court systems that had reflected and reinforced colonial racial divisions, replacing the colonial court systems with a single system equally accessible to everyone. It then began to increase the participation of Africans in the administration of justice at the highest levels through making efforts to replace colonial judges with African judges. This chapter examines how the government approached decolonising the structure of the colonial court systems and the judiciary's relationship to the executive. The following two chapters examine the decolonisation of the High Court Bench and the individual judges who were a part of this process. Taken together these three chapters offer an approach to assessing how colonial High Courts transitioned to local institutions.

The government's decisions in relation to decolonisation of the structure of the colonial court systems were connected to Nyerere and TANU's political agenda. In the early 1960s the country's political leadership regarded economic development and the growth of national unity as essential components in the creation of a state. The political leadership in power at the time viewed the common law system as a precondition of economic stability and as a means for building the united political community it sought.[5] They may have also wanted to use the common law to help diminish local reliance on customary traditions that the government thought entrenched the divisions between ethnic groups in the country.[6] Therefore, as an institution, the High Court survived after national independence because the government determined that the maintenance of the common law system was essential for national political progress.

Though the preservation of the High Court in its colonial form made it appear unchanged as an institution, this was a period of great structural transformation in the court system. Between 1959 and 1964 the High Court's relationship to the other branches of government, the country's African population, and the courts and judicial officials beneath and above it fundamentally changed. The structural transformation of the High Court's relationships to the executive and colonial court systems occurred in three stages between 1961 and 1964. First, in 1961 the High Court gained a greater degree of independence from executive authority through provisions protecting judges' security of tenure, which they had lacked during British rule. Tanganyika's independence Constitution established three separate branches of government and outlined the relationships between them, as well as the High Court's relationship to the monarchy of Great Britain via the Privy Council. It made the judiciary a separate branch of government and established provisions to protect it from interference by the executive and legislative branches. Though the government replaced the independence Constitution with the republican Constitution in 1962, the judiciary continued to enjoy most of the protections established in the first Constitution. The new Constitution did, however, sever the state's constitutional links with Great Britain, and therefore the judiciary's relationship to the Privy Council. This increased the Tanganyikan state's authority over the appointments and employment of judges, making it more of a national, rather than colonial, body.

The second stage of structural transformation affected the High Court's relationship to Africans and the Local Courts. In 1961 the government began to chip away at the 'parallel' colonial court systems by creating connections between the Local Courts and the British court system. The aim was to remove the elements of the court systems that symbolically represented and practically facilitated indirect rule, namely the barriers preventing Africans from accessing the High Court through appeals and the granting of magisterial powers to administrators. By creating a link between the High Court as institution and the Local Courts system, as well as removing judicial powers from administrators, the government was able to make progress towards its goal of racial equality before the courts and the separation of powers between judicial and executive officers. The result of these measures for the High Court was that it regained the appellate jurisdiction it had lost in 1929 with the enactment of Governor Cameron's Native Courts Ordinance, giving it greater jurisdiction and authority in the sphere of the administration of justice.

In the third and final stage, the High Court and its judges became the apex of Tanganyika's new unified court system and professionalised judiciary. The Magistrates' Courts Act, which came into force in 1964, replaced all the courts that were operating in the country—other than the High Court—with a unified three-tier court system that was, by law, equally accessible to everyone in the country. All the courts in the system were staffed by judicial officers, whose duties were solely judicial, and who were under the auspices of the High Court, which comprised the top tier of the system. The High Court's position in the new court system further increased its authority. The role of High Court judges as leaders of the new cadre of magistrates made them the head of an expanded judiciary, giving them supervision and control over judicial offices at all levels—a prominent role they had not had under British rule.

Through these three stages of transformation the Tanganyikan government revised the structure of the colonial court systems and institutional relationships designed by colonial authorities during British rule. The way in which the government approached changing the court systems indicates that, from the perspective of the political leadership in the early 1960s, decolonising the courts in Tanganyika did not mean removing all traces of the British legal system, just the structures that made the judiciary subordinate to the executive and entrenched racial and ethnic divisions underpinning indirect rule in Tanganyika. These efforts helped bring the courts into line with the dominant political ideology and constitutional structure in place at the time, further integrating them into the machinery of the state. This chapter demonstrates how these changes elevated the High Court to the pinnacle of its power since its establishment in 1921.

The Common Law System and TANU's Political Agenda

During the transition to independence the government of Tanganyika maintained the common law system and British courts that had been introduced by British colonial authorities. In the process of decolonisation in the twentieth century it was the norm for newly independent countries to maintain the legal traditions they inherited from their European predecessors. Therefore, that the common law system would survive was an assumption underlying political rhetoric at the time and was, according to Shirley Castelnuovo, 'never seriously questioned'.[7] There certainly were no substantial movements in mainland East Africa in the 1960s calling for the new governments to scrap their British legal systems entirely.[8] Yet, upholding the system in Tanganyika was more than a default decision; rather, it was crucial to the government's political efforts to develop a modern and unified post-colonial state.

Widner offers three main explanations for why many African postcolonies preserved their colonial common law systems.[9] First, former colonial subjects wanted 'equal treatment under the law' and that meant having the same law in the independent state that applied to citizens of the colonial state. Second, it would have been costly and difficult to review and replace the statutes in place at the time of independence. Third, while it would have been possible for governments to seek out other traditions to follow, 'no one bothered to think in such grand terms' about the legal system with so many other urgent challenges facing the nation. While these 'emotive' and 'practical' explanations provide a starting point for understanding this phenomenon, they overlook the role the common law system played in the government's efforts to develop a national economy and unify its citizens into a political community.

The British legal system helped to facilitate the early development of a market economy in the territory by providing a mechanism to enforce contracts, protect personal property, and resolve disputes over commercial transactions. Over the 40 years of colonial rule the courts had been integral to the operation of the economy and had played a role in creating conditions that allowed businesses to function according to the same principles as they had in Britain and in most colonies throughout the Empire. During the transition to independence economic development was one of TANU's main concerns, and removing the system in place would have called into question the principles on which the formal economy in the territory had developed and was developing, and through which businesses and individuals engaged in transactions.[10] The political leadership regarded the common law system as part of the foundation of the economy and therefore, at the time, did not frame it politically as a symbol and tool of colonial domination, but, rather, as a necessary component of a market economy.

Maintaining the foundations of the economy was of paramount political and practical importance to the country's leadership, but creating unity among a large and diverse constituency was also a top priority for the government. As shown in the previous chapters, during British rule the 'parallel' court systems had not only created a separate set of courts and procedures for Africans and non-Africans, but had also required Africans to live under the enforcement of perceived local notions of customary law. The colonial administration had used custom as a means of differentiating communities from one another and thereby facilitated the creation of separate identities along ethnic lines. After independence the government began its political efforts to create a single national community by inculcating a shared identity among the more than 120 ethnic groups in the country. Its approach was to emphasise the similarities and unity among Tanganyikans, rather than differences and local attachments, which had been the organising principle of indirect rule.

The unified court system was central to the national political project. Legal development can be a powerful instrument for shaping society and was a means through which African governments attempted to establish unified national identities in new countries in the mid-twentieth century.[11] Castelnuovo argues that the Tanganyikan government decided to create a single legal and judicial system as a part of its 'broad scheme (political, social, and economic) to reinforce national unity'.[12] The legal pluralism sanctioned under indirect rule was also a threat to the new central authority and by limiting it the government aimed to create a more centralised state.[13]

Therefore, during the transition to independence, the key question for Tanganyika and post-independence governments across Africa was how customary and Islamic law would be integrated into a system based on common law.[14] The options for integrating customary law were debated in both practical and theoretical terms among judges, political leaders, and academics at the time.[15] A series of conferences in the early 1960s on African law and its relationship to post-colonial national legal systems provided a platform for, and helped shape discussions about, the main issues at stake and the range of approaches governments could take in integrating customary law into national systems across Africa.[16]

In 1961 Nyerere announced that the government would begin the process of codifying customary law and integrating it with the law in force in the country. He initiated the Customary Law Codification and Unification Project and its first task was to record the customary law and unify it. Unification involved writing down the principles of custom, emphasising the similarities while minimising and modifying differences between communities' asserted customs.[17] The ultimate goal was a single written work covering the main elements of customary law (excluding land law) among those people classified as members of 'Bantu patrilineal tribes'.[18] The intention was that this work would then become recognised as statute law and would be applied to the relevant tribes, who made up approximately 75% of the population at the time.[19] The product of these efforts was the local Customary Law (Declaration) Orders in 1963, which facilitated the application of the codified customary law to specified districts and types of cases.[20] The declarations of customary law can also be understood, however, as a part of a larger effort to preserve and develop the British legal traditions in place at the end of British rule. They allowed the government to maintain elements of custom while continuing to use a common law system. However, the customary law codes were, according to Castelnuovo, 'not known and accepted by customary law communities', and can be seen as an attempt to 'invent' or manipulate custom for political and administrative aims, as colonial authorities had arguably done during British rule.[21] Nevertheless, the creation of the codes was a crucial part of facilitating the unification of the court systems, because it defined the customary law the courts could apply.[22]

The preservation of the common law system and codification of customary law was a part of the government's larger efforts to shape the new nation in the early 1960s. This was both a shrewd political move and a response to practical needs at the time. The importance of the courts to the economy and their role in reinforcing national unity illustrate how the justice system was a political device in Tanganyika. With these underlying motivations, the survival of the High Court was secure. Exactly what role it would play in the new state and its relationship to other government bodies, however, were under consideration and negotiation in the early 1960s.

The High Court and the Constitutions

Tanganyika's transition to independence hinged on negotiated agreement between Tanganyika and Great Britain on the nation's first Constitution. In this process Great Britain sought a careful transition in the context of political and social upheaval in many of its other colonies. Seeking proof of its ability to transfer power to democratic governments without violence, Britain wanted Tanganyika's transition to independence to progress smoothly but also slowly, so as to facilitate an economic and political relationship between the two countries that would continue to tie them to one another and allow for the persistence of British policies and institutions on the ground.[23] TANU wanted independence as quickly as possible, aiming to achieve it in 1961. Its leaders were unwilling to put off independence as the British had hoped and refused to accept a government on any other basis than that of majority rule, which was the primary political aspiration of the party and the main justification for its opposition to British rule.[24] Yet TANU needed economic support for development and to help alleviate widespread poverty in the country, and therefore could not disregard Britain's interests in the process. Furthermore, Nyerere believed that achieving independence without violence would help accomplish these goals as well as demonstrate to other colonies that they could achieve independence as multi-racial and democratic African countries, rather than seeing power consolidated in white administrations as in South Africa and Southern Rhodesia.[25]

These combined motivations and the agreement between Britain and Tanganyika that the new country would become a democracy allowed Britain to press TANU to accept most of the provisions and structures in its 'standard form' independence Constitution.[26] The standard form was a model produced by the Colonial Office for colonies to adopt as they became independent. It called for a government based on the separation of power between the executive, legislative, and judicial branches. That model was then modified at constitutional conferences, which were held for each colony. At a nation's constitutional conference, representatives of the British government and the African political leadership negotiated the details of the Constitution that would make the nation legally and officially independent from colonial rule. Tanganyika held its conference in Dar es Salaam in 1961 and it resulted in an agreement on the provisions making up the country's independence Constitution.[27] Roland Brown, an adviser to TANU in its negotiations and the nation's first Attorney General, recalled in his unpublished memoir that 'not everything put on the table by the British was to their [TANU's] liking, but there was nothing in dispute which was worth a real showdown that might prevent or delay agreement on an early date for independence'.[28]

Tanganyika's Constitutional Conference yielded the country's first Constitution, which came into force on 9 December 1961. Under the Constitution Tanganyika became a parliamentary democracy with a connection to the monarchy of Great Britain. The main components of the state were the Parliament (the National Assembly and the Crown), the Governor-General (who exercised the Executive Authority of the Crown), and the Prime Minister (who was appointed by the Governor-General).[29] The Constitutional Conference in 1961 and the related process of drafting Tanganyika's independence Constitution provided an opportunity for the redefinition of the position and role of the judiciary in the state.[30] Nyerere framed the position of the judiciary as a part of the realisation of independence from colonial rule. He declared that 'real freedom' meant that every citizen would be 'confident that his case would be impartially judged' and that an independent judiciary was a part of ensuring that freedom and therefore realising independence from colonial rule.[31] To this end the Constitution made the judiciary a separate branch of government, re-establishing the High Court of Tanganyika as the most superior court in the country.[32] Parliament passed a related act outlining the Court's jurisdiction and the law it would administer, granting it 'full jurisdiction, civil and criminal' in Tanganyika.[33]

The Constitution laid out the position of the judiciary relative to the other branches of government.[34] The provisions relating to appointment, tenure, and dismissal established the judiciary as a separate branch of government with a substantial degree of independence, although there was not a complete separation of powers.[35] This was a significant departure from the policies of the Colonial Office and territorial administration, which had exercised more control over the activities of the High Court during the colonial period than the new Constitution allowed.

Under the 1961 Constitution the Governor-General was responsible for the appointment of the Chief Justice (in consultation with the Prime Minister) and the puisne judges (on advice of the Judicial Service Commission).[36] This was a significant change from the colonial period—while appointments were still in the hands of an executive, it was the head of the independent state rather than the Colonial Office (and colonial administration) who made the decision about whom to appoint.

Once in office, High Court judges enjoyed greater security of tenure under the Constitution than they had experienced under colonial rule. Similar to the colonial period, the retirement age for High Court judges was 62, with the ability to extend until 65, but, unlike the colonial period, judges of the High Court were protected from transfers to any other place or role.[37] They could only be removed from their posts in the case of misbehaviour or the inability to perform the required functions.[38] The Constitution stipulated that any cases of removal would ultimately be decided by the Privy Council, and would only reach the Privy Council by the permission of the Governor-General after being investigated first by a tribunal of at least three judges.[39] The Colonial Office claimed to provide reviews by the Privy Council of removals of colonial judges, but they technically served 'at pleasure', regardless of the procedures the Colonial Office asserted were in use during colonial rule. Therefore, the enactment of the Constitution marked the first time in Tanganyika's history that High Court judges had the legal right to have their fates decided by the Privy Council in case the administration sought their dismissal.

Other than removals sanctioned by the Privy Council, the Constitution protected judges from all other forms of punishment or harassment, such as having their offices abolished during their tenure and their salary altered to their disadvantage, which Governor Cameron had arguably done to Chief Justice Russell in the late 1920s.[40] These provisions increased the independence of the High Court Bench from executive intervention and formalised High Court judges' relationships with Great Britain.

The Constitution and subsequent legislation also enhanced the security of tenure for lower judicial officers through the establishment of a body called the Judicial Service Commission.[41] This Commission dealt primarily with overseeing judicial officers below the level of the High Court and made decisions on their appointments, disciplinary measures, and dismissals.[42] The establishment of this independent body was a marked departure from the colonial system, when the fate of these more junior officers was determined by the territorial administration and Colonial Office.[43] The Constitution specified that the Chairman of the Judicial Service Commission was the Chief Justice and that other judges (chosen by the Governor-General in accordance with the advice of the Prime Minister) would be members, as would the Chairman of the Public Service Commission.[44] Therefore, while the executive maintained a role in shaping the Judicial Service Commission, the Constitution limited that role and gave judges controlling positions in matters relating to the employment of members of the Judicial Service.

The requirements in the Constitution relating to who could become members of the Bench ensured that it would be an experienced community of barristers with British legal qualifications. The provisions essentially relied on the requirements laid out in the Advocates Ordinance (with subsequent amendments to the original 1954 ordinance), and specified that an individual's legal qualifications must be held for at least five years before appointment, or that an appointee had experience on a superior Bench in the Commonwealth, or outside of it as prescribed by Parliament.[45] One impact of upholding British colonial standards for appointments to the Bench made it impossible for almost any Africans living in Tanganyika to become judges because virtually none were able to meet these requirements.

The Constitution also specified the minimum size of the Bench, requiring at least six puisne judges as well as a Chief Justice.[46] The size of the Bench had been a source of fierce debate during the colonial period, especially the interwar years when it was approximately half the size the 1961 Constitution required. The Constitution required that the size of the colonial Bench in 1961 remain unaltered, thereby preventing any other branches of government from pushing for a reversion to a smaller Bench.

Cases in the High Court could be appealed to another court in the region, namely the regional Court of Appeal (referred to as the Eastern Africa Court of Appeal after 1961), on prescription from the national Parliament.[47] The highest level of appeal remained the Privy Council, as it had been during British rule.[48] The only exception to this was that matters relating to the interpretation of the Constitution could not go to the Eastern Africa Court of Appeal before appeal to the Privy Council, but had to be appealed directly from the High Court to the Privy Council, whose decision was final.[49] Thus the High Court remained under the umbrella of Britain's courts and in line with the state as a whole, which was constitutionally connected to Great Britain.

Tanganyika's first Constitution was the political mechanism through which it became a nation. Yet TANU members reportedly felt 'dissatisfaction' with some of the provisions of the Constitution and sought a fast transition to a Republic.[50] TANU wanted a stronger executive President as the head of state with the power to effect the changes the party wanted.[51] It also aimed to eliminate the constitutional links between Tanganyika and the monarchy. According to TANU the monarchy was an 'alien institution' and therefore the relationship to it in the first Constitution was inappropriate for a truly independent African state.[52] The replacement of the independence Constitution with the republican Constitution in 1962 'cut the last colonial links', including those in the judiciary.[53] As the country as a whole severed political ties with Great Britain, the judiciary's evolving relationship to the Crown reflected this transition.

Preserving the rule of law remained a part TANU's stated vision for governing and was therefore one of the main principles upon which the government developed the republican Constitution.[54] To uphold the rule of law the government wanted the Constitution to ensure the 'equal and impartial administration of the law'.[55] The High Court was the main and most superior institution in which it continued to entrust that responsibility. Therefore, the new Constitution maintained the separation of powers and most of the provisions relating to safeguarding the independence of the judiciary through security of tenure for its judges. The conditions and protections relating to grounds for removal, retirement age, membership and powers of the Judicial Service Commission, qualifications for appointment, security of salary, protection of office, and minimum court size (it added one more High Court judge for a minimum of seven) remained intact.[56]

The processes for appointment and dismissal, however, changed relative to the establishment of a new executive and the removal of a constitutional relationship to the monarchy. The office of President created under the new Constitution, occupied by Nyerere, gained the power to appoint the Chief Justice, and the puisne judges in consultation with the Chief Justice.[57] Through this provision the powers of the President over the Court were enhanced, but the Chief Justice also gained a guaranteed legal right to help decide on appointments of puisne judges for the first time in Tanganyika's history.

In cases where the President wanted to remove a judge from office, he had the authority to appoint a tribunal of at least three members who had been or were presently judges to determine the outcome.[58] That tribunal's decision, however, was final, and therefore the link to the Privy Council was severed only one year after it had become law. The relationship to the Privy Council was also removed in the appeals process, which continued to allow Parliament to stipulate appeals to the Eastern Africa Court of Appeal, except on matters relating to the interpretation of the constitution, but no longer made any prescription for appeals to the Privy Council. In 1962 Parliament acted to officially end appeals to the Privy Council.[59] Under the republican Constitution, the High Court had original and final jurisdiction over cases relating to the interpretation of the Constitution, and therefore cases of this nature could not be appealed at all from the High Court as the 1961 Constitution had permitted.[60]

Overall, the 1962 Constitution did not drastically alter the position of the Court or the provisions aimed at maintaining the independence of the judiciary from encroachment by other branches of government. It did, however, break all judicial links with the Privy Council and increased the power of the new executive President over the High Court. Confining most judicial matters within the country was a part of TANU's efforts to move away from political dependence on the former colonial ruler. The effect of this change on the High Court was that it helped make it more an internal institution of the state.

Through Tanganyika's first two constitutions the judiciary gained greater security of tenure and increased protection of its independence than it had had during British rule. These provisions defined the parameters of the new relationship between the Court and the other branches of government. They did little, however, to clarify the Court's new relationship to the people of Tanganyika, only enabling Parliament to enact laws defining how the High Court would carry out its work and the nature and activities of the courts beneath it. These relationships were still fluctuating and had not yet been tested, as they would be in the late 1960s when the government began to encroach on the independence of the judiciary. With this constitutional framework in place, the government began to enact legislation to implement the constitutional provisions for the judiciary and revise the court systems of indirect rule.

The High Court and the Dismantling of the 'Parallel' Colonial Court Systems

The reforms in the early 1960s focused on two key elements of the colonial court system: the role of race in dividing the 'parallel' court systems; and the dual role of administrators as magistrates. As shown above, these attributes had been central to indirect rule in Tanganyika and symbolised, for TANU, the racial policies and undemocratic nature of British rule.[61] They were also out of step with the government's broader political rhetoric and vision for the state. Therefore, Nyerere swiftly targeted these elements of the courts for reform, advocating a single national court system with a judicial service separate from the administration.

The direction of government reform of the courts following independence had already been articulated by colonial courts officers at the Judicial Advisers' Conferences in the 1950s. They had declared the eventual need to transfer judicial power from administrators to judicial officers and create more integrated court systems in African colonies.[62] Yet neither of these goals had ever come close to being accomplished in Tanganyika during British rule. After independence the new government followed the trajectory outlined by these conferences and began to chip away at the structure of the colonial court systems. During Tanganyika's first year as an independent state it made substantial 'progress towards achieving the unification of the court systems'.[63]

The initial phase of integration of the Local Courts into the British court system occurred in the year following independence. The Local Courts (Amendment) Ordinance replaced the Central Court of Appeal, which had been the final court of appeal for the Local Courts since 1951, with the High Court. This gave the High Court the ability to hear appeals from cases that had been tried first in the Local Courts.[64] Though individual High Court judges had served on the Central Court of Appeal, this move increased the High Court's appellate jurisdiction and allowed the

High Court as an institution to hear appeals from the courts of Africans—ending Cameron's legacy of the severed relationship between the Native (later Local) courts and the High Court.

Under the previous system, appeals from Local Courts went first to Local Courts of Appeal and then to the district commissioner (still in his capacity as an administrator, not as a magistrate) or a provincial Local Courts officer before being appealed to the High Court, with permission of the administrative 'filter'.[65] The 1962 ordinance removed provincial commissioners—the filters—from the process and replaced them with a single new officer called the Local Courts appeals officer. This move ended the role of provincial commissioners in the administration of justice.

The appointment of the Local Courts appeals officer was the responsibility of the Minister for Legal Affairs who was required to consult the Chief Justice about his choice.[66] The officer was attached to, as well as supervised by, the High Court.[67] The role encompassed both elements of the work of the Local Courts adviser, who had previously acted as a nexus between administration and judiciary in the administration of justice, and of the colonial provincial commissioners, who had been responsible for making decisions about whether to allow appeals to reach the Central Court of Appeal.[68] His main responsibility was to make decisions on whether to allow appeals from Local Courts to be heard by the High Court.[69] John Lewis-Barned, who served in this role, asserts that the purpose of creating a new filter between Local Courts and the High Court, rather than removing all barriers at once, was to prevent the High Court from being inundated with appeals and to provide a mechanism for the processing and translation of records, which were in Kiswahili and other local languages.[70] The position was 'the first office of its kind to be established within the High Court of Tanganyika'.[71] While he was, in essence, a barrier between the Local Courts and the High Court, the officer's singular judicial duties and replacement of provincial commissioners in the appeals process was a break with local mechanisms for appeals, facilitating the integration of the court systems and the removal of high-level administrators from the judicial process. Appeals that were allowed by the Local Courts appeals officer were heard by at least one High Court judge sitting with two assessors, and that judge's decision was final.[72] The creation of this office was an early step in the process of connecting the two systems and preparing them for eventual integration.

The second phase of change to the colonial court systems after independence involved separating judicial and administrative power fused at the level of district commissioner. The government aimed 'to bring those whose sole function it is to judge within the judicial service'.[73] Its first step towards this goal was in 1962 with the Local Courts (Minister for Justice and Regional Local Courts Officers) Act, which gave the Minister for Justice the responsibility for Local Courts.[74] It ended the judicial functions of district commissioners including their supervisory and appellate powers over Local Courts.[75] Many of these powers were transferred to 42 officers, called regional Local Courts officers.[76] These officers acted as full-time magistrates and took over the responsibility for hearing appeals from the Local Courts from district commissioners, eventually also replacing the Local Courts of Appeal.[77] Former Regional Local Courts Officer Patrick Ellis recalled that he was expected to 'search out and train magistrates or justices of the peace' for the lower courts, as well as supervise the current work of the Local Courts and keep records relating to them.[78] The individuals working as regional Local Courts officers were a combination of former colonial officers, some of whom had a legal background, and Africans who had previously worked in the administration.[79] For instance, Ellis was a former administrative officer in the Colonial Service who was studying for the Bar during his service and became a regional Local Courts officer in 1963 as well as an acting resident magistrate for Iringa and Njombe. The government also sent many without legal backgrounds, such as African officials drawn from the regional administration, to attend 'cram courses' to prepare them for their new duties in this role.[80]

The significance of the transfer of magisterial and supervisory powers from administrative officers to the regional Local Courts officers, however, was that it not only removed the contentious legacy of district commissioners having judicial powers over the courts of Africans, but it also placed those with judicial powers under the auspices of the High Court and brought more Africans into judicial roles. It also helped to facilitate the establishment of a separate judicial service at the lower levels of the courts, thereby bringing the lower courts more into line with the separation of powers outlined in the Constitution for the High Court.

The fusion of judicial and executive power under British rule not only occurred with administrative officers, but also with African chiefs, who had often acted as the judges in the Local Courts. The process of endowing different individuals in each ethnic group with judicial and executive powers, rather than a single individual, began in the early 1950s.[81] But it was not until 1962, when the government abolished the entire system of chieftaincy, that the office of chief became devoid of all its former political and judicial powers.[82]

Frederic DuBow asserts that during British rule the office of chief had been 'so closely linked with the colonial regime that it could not survive long in the reorganisation of the administration after independence'.[83] The rule of chiefs was also in conflict with the political direction of the country and the government hoped its abolition would remove 'ethnic loyalties from the political arena' and thereby any challenges to the centralised authority of the new government.[84] A possible contributing factor to the full removal of the office of the chief from both its executive and judicial duties is that the Native Courts Ordinance in 1929 had fashioned chiefs into more effective tools of the colonial administration by granting them both types of power. This opened the chiefs up to the same criticisms regarding the lack of a separation of power as those levied against administrative officers, making it more difficult for chiefs to remain in their offices with either administrative or judicial powers after independence. The abolition of the office of chief thus created open positions in the Local Courts for the government to appoint individuals to these posts with the sole purpose of adjudicating low-level cases.

The initial measures carried out by the government between 1961 and 1963 linked the Local Courts system to the British court system and began the messy process of separating judicial and executive duties at the lower levels of the magistracy. These changes had a significant impact on the High Court because it gained the jurisdiction to hear appeals from the Local Courts, which it had been denied since 1929. High Court judges also acquired greater exclusivity in the administration of justice, removing those powers from officers whose office was administrative and not judicial. These early changes remedied the main concerns of Chief Justice Russell and the Bushe Report, which indicates that their objections to administrators having judicial powers in the 1930s may have been not only about the need for a separation of powers, but also over a concern for the way in which the courts strengthened colonial administrative authority.

These first two phases of change to the court systems were incremental, and did not realise the goal of a unified court system. They were, however, advancements that the government highlighted to illustrate that it was moving away from the racial divisions and inequality of colonial rule and that the judicial and legal systems would match the ideology and political priorities of TANU. The initial phases also helped to prepare practically for the final 'big task' of transitioning the dual court systems into the unified court system in 1964, which dissolved the remaining attributes of the courts that the government perceived as remnants of British rule.[85]

At the Peak of Its Power: The High Court and the Magistrates' Courts Act

In 1964 the High Court became the top tier of a single unified court system that replaced all the lower courts and the interim offices in use between 1961 and 1963. The mechanism for this, the Magistrates' Courts Act, affected a fundamental shift in the administration of justice and the history of the High Court in Tanganyika. The structure of the courts created by the Act was the product of proposals by the government and the efforts of the Working Party on the Integration of the Court Systems, comprised of a High Court judge, a parliamentary draftsman, and a specially appointed courts integration officer.[86] They first produced a preliminary report.[87] After negotiations among the relevant government offices, a bill was placed before the National Assembly in 1963 where it apparently 'passed almost without debate', according to British observers.[88] From 1 July 1964 Tanganyika had a single three-tier court system with jurisdiction over everyone in the country, regardless of race. The Primary Courts were the first tier, District Courts and Resident Magistrates' Courts the second tier, and the High Court the third and top tier.

The first tier Primary Courts were established in each district with specified civil and criminal jurisdiction.[89] They had the ability to administer customary and Islamic civil law as well as statutory law. Cases usually under the purview of custom (such as marriage, guardianship, inheritance under custom, and immovable property other than land) could not be commenced other than in the Primary Courts, except with specific permission.[90] The courts could not apply customary criminal law, which was no longer permitted.[91] Each Primary Court was normally convened by a single Primary Court magistrate, who was not professionally trained in the law, but was a member of the judiciary.[92] It was not practically possible at the time—or necessarily seen as desirable—for the Primary Court magistrates to be qualified professional lawyers, as their main purpose was to adjudicate cases involving custom as well as more minor crimes and disputes.[93] Instead, some of these magistrates took training courses at the Local Government Training Centre in Mzumbe.[94] Since the magistrates were not trained lawyers and because the courts were supposed to serve as 'a forum for efficient and inexpensive dispute resolution', advocates were not allowed in the Primary Courts.[95] The government wanted these courts to provide substantial justice without regard for legal 'technicalities'.[96]

Kiswahili was the official language of the Primary Courts and court officials kept the records in that language, but in an effort to make these courts accessible to the majority of the population the proceedings could take place in the local vernacular.[97] The magistrates were at first allowed and later required by law to sit with assessors in cases where Islamic or customary law was relevant.[98] Cases under the original jurisdiction of the Primary Courts could be appealed, subject to certain conditions, to the next tier in the court system, the District Courts, and the Act gave provision for transfer of cases between tiers.[99]

District Courts and Resident Magistrates' Courts comprised the tier above the Primary Courts. The District Courts had defined original civil and criminal jurisdiction as well as appellate and revisionary jurisdiction (and supervisory powers) for civil and criminal cases generating from the Primary Courts.[100] Each District Court had jurisdiction over the district in which it was established and was presided over by a District Court magistrate.[101] Assessors only sat with the district magistrate in cases appealed from the Primary Courts dealing with customary or Islamic law.[102] The District Court magistrates were not professional lawyers, but were given more extensive training than Primary Court magistrates for the duties of this new role by the government.[103] These courts could operate in either Kiswahili or English.[104]

Resident Magistrates' Courts, which were established by order of the Chief Justice and convened by a single magistrate, shared the second tier of the new system with the District Courts.[105] The order establishing the Resident Magistrates' Court defined its original jurisdiction, usually over an administrative region under the government's new regional organisation of the country.[106] This facilitated the continued functioning of resident magistrates already at work in the territory.[107] Resident Magistrates' Courts were staffed by magistrates with professional training in the law and usually functioned in English. Cases heard under original, appellate, or revisionary jurisdiction at either of the types of courts in the second tier could be appealed, subject to certain conditions, to the High Court.

As the top tier the High Court gained appellate and revisionary jurisdiction over cases originating in District Courts and Resident Magistrates' Courts, as well as in cases that had originated in the Primary Courts and were appealed first to the District Courts. This new jurisdiction was in addition to the original civil and criminal jurisdiction it already enjoyed.[108] The High Court also gained supervisory powers over all courts and the Chief Justice received the power to appoint supervisory magistrates to supervise the lower courts on the High Court's behalf.[109] In criminal appeals to the High Court that originated in the Primary Courts, a single judge heard the appeal, but civil appeals from Primary Courts went to a division for the High Court where they were heard by at least one judge with an associate judge.[110] The office of associate judge was a new post for legally qualified Africans who would arguably be in a better position than British judges (still on the Bench) to hear cases involving custom and in Kiswahili. The Court was also able to refer questions relating to customary law to a panel of experts.[111]

The significance of the creation of the new court system for the High Court was twofold. First, the High Court became the highest court in this unified system, gaining power over the cases in all the courts beneath it. Its powers of supervision and revision as well as its appellate jurisdiction elevated the High Court to the pinnacle of its power. The implication of these changes for Africans was that they gained access to the High Court without special filters making independent decisions on their cases.

Second, High Court judges became the leaders of a drastically expanded judiciary, as magistrates at every level of the court system, including those without professional qualifications, became members of the Judicial Service. High Court judges were not only the most senior members of the judiciary, but also had a key role in the bodies responsible for controlling the employment of magistrates. Depending on the court tier, decisions about discipline and dismissal were either directly in the hands of the Judicial Service Commission, as with higher level magistrates, or were made by regional bodies created specifically for supervision of the large lower magistracy, which were overseen by more senior members of the judiciary.[112] The professionalisation of the judiciary through the Magistrates' Courts Act made High Court judges the main authority of the Judicial Service, which now had exclusivity in applying the law.

The Structural Decolonisation of the Court Systems in Practice

The creation of the three-tier system was integral to the government's political efforts to incorporate the courts into its centralised and democratic state and reflected the principles of racial equality and the separation of powers. Though the ideals of access and equality framed the Constitution and ordinances in the early 1960s, the new courts were not necessarily more connected to ordinary Africans. The way in which the government approached creating the new court system, combined with its limited resources, meant that the courts were not always accessible to Africans, even if their rights of appeal and access under the law increased during this period. Government officials referred to the early difficulties facing the justice system as 'teething troubles', but, in reality, the unification of the courts was a very difficult process.[113] In fact, in the years following the creation of Tanganyika's first unified court system litigants would face some of the same challenges to accessing the courts and understanding them as they had during colonial rule, as well as new ones created by the unification process.

During the process of integration, the transfer of judicial powers from district commissioners to regional Local Courts officers caused a 'lack of continuity and of court coverage in a number of districts'.[114] Under the new unified system, initially there were only about 400 Primary Court magistrates, which was approximately half of the total number of Primary Courts that were established in the country and less than half of the total number of Local Courts—thought to be around 900—that had been in operation around the time of independence.[115] Thus new Primary Court magistrates were 'largely peripatetic' and 'only the busiest courts, mostly in urban areas' had full-time magistrates.[116] Many Primary Court magistrates covered two or more districts and 'travelling alone absorbed a considerable amount of their energy and time'.[117] The peripatetic model and related decrease in the number of people covering Local Courts caused greater delays than most Africans would have experienced when bringing cases to the Local Courts prior to 1964.[118] Moreover, although Africans could appeal to the High Court after 1962, it was still primarily based in Dar es Salaam. Though it was beginning to develop satellite stations and registries in various parts of the country, with the opening of a High Court in Mwanza before independence and another in Arusha in July 1962, most people would have only interacted with the High Court through judges on circuit, if at all.[119] As an institution, the High Court remained remote from the lives of most Africans.

There were also difficulties with weaning the system off its reliance on administrative officers and chiefs. Though chiefs and headmen were stripped of their powers in 1962, some did find employment as Primary Courts magistrates. It appears, however, that some of these officials failed to follow the procedures required by the Criminal Procedure Code and were unable or unwilling to improve even after being given training. Patrick Ellis theorised that this may have been 'due to lack of necessary educational background and the ability to absorb the new system'.[120] Yet for individuals going to the Primary Courts where a chief had formerly been the judge and remained so, the supposed changes to the courts may have seemed superficial. In many cases, however, chiefs and headmen were replaced by 'ordinary citizens' of 'varying different quality, some had standard 10 education some only had village education'.[121] While these officials did receive some training, one regional Local Courts officer observed that, for the most part, the Local Courts were being run by, 'African magistrates of low ability, poor training, little enthusiasm and small popular prestige'.[122] With these challenges the new courts had difficulty gaining legitimacy, as some Africans may not have recognised the people dispensing justice as having the authority to do so, or believed that they were sufficiently familiar with local custom and circumstance to administer justice.

Another factor creating challenges in the adoption of the new court system was the cost associated with these changes. Adopting the new system necessitated a substantial monetary investment to train and pay the new magistracy and to provide them with the resources they required to carry out their work. The difficult financial situation for the government forced the magistrates of the new system to continue to rely on the infrastructure of the old system in many parts of the country. The space in administrative buildings, which had been used for both executive and judicial duties during colonial rule, continued to be used for both purposes at Primary Court level.[123] Many of these offices were in a state of disrepair.[124] The appearance of the judicial and executive officers working side by side in the same location as before independence may have sent a message of continuity with the old system, rather than one of change.

Though by 1964 the justice system had, in principle, moved a long way from its colonial origins, in practice it faced troubles with delays, legitimacy, and resources, similar to those that had plagued colonial courts for the duration of British rule. One former regional Local Courts officer recalled that, from his perspective, 'for the ordinary African things carried on much as they were' before independence.[125] The process of decolonising the court systems in Tanganyika illustrates that while the government had a clear vision for its court system, the process of breaking away from colonial structures required greater financial resources and personnel than it had available in order to make the process happen effectively. This provides another example of the practical limits of national efforts for reform in the process of decolonisation.

Conclusion

In the early 1960s decolonising the court systems in Tanganyika meant altering the elements of the court systems that represented and strengthened British colonial rule. This national political process can be understood as a reaction to and rejection of mechanisms of indirect rule, but also as one that was, in practice, shaped by the needs and resources of the new state and its leadership. The enactment of the Magistrates' Courts Act in 1964 was a watershed moment in the history of Tanganyika's justice system. While the internal attributes and activities of the High Court were relatively unaltered, the Court's relationship to the executive, the courts beneath it, and Africans attempting to gain access to it changed substantially. As a result, the High Court became a more independent, legally accessible, and powerful institution than it had been.

The combination of changes in the High Court's relationship to the courts beneath it and the continuity of its activities and appearance as an institution made it an anomaly in the post-colonial state. By 1964, perhaps the most visible element of the continuity of the High Court with its colonial roots was the personnel on its Bench. Throughout the structural decolonisation of the colonial courts, the High Court Bench remained populated by former colonial judges and magistrates, who had stayed in Tanganyika after independence. This was because there were no Tanganyikan Africans who met the requirements set out in the Constitution for joining the Bench and replacing the colonial judges. The government's need for colonial judges to remain on the Bench during the period of reforming the court systems illustrates that structural decolonisation of the court systems in Tanganyika relied on participation from colonial judges. Paradoxically, the individual colonial judges who remained on the Bench enjoyed greater independence, security of tenure, jurisdiction over Africans, and supervision of the judicial officers beneath them than they had in the same position only a few years earlier when they were working for the colonial government.

Notes

1. On the constitutional developments in Tanganyika between 1958 and 1961, see: C. Pratt, *The Critical Phase in Tanzania, 1945–1968: Nyerere and the Emergence of a Socialist Strategy* (Cambridge, 1976), pp. 43–59.
2. On the international and national impetuses helping to accelerate decolonisation in Tanganyika, see: S. Stockwell and L.J. Butler, 'Introduction', in L.J. Butler and S. Stockwell, (eds.), *The Wind of Change: Harold*

Macmillan and British Decolonization (London, 2013), pp. 6–8. See also: J. Iliffe, 'Breaking the Chain at Its Weakest Link: TANU and the Colonial Office' in G. Maddox and J.L. Giblin (eds.), *In Search of a Nation: Histories of Authority & Dissidence in Tanzania* (Oxford, 2005), p. 169.

3. The 'wind of change' refers to a phrase in a speech given by the British Prime Minister, Harold Macmillan, on 3 February 1960 to the Cape Town Parliament. He famously proclaimed: 'The wind of change is blowing through this continent [Africa] and whether we like it or not, this growth of national consciousness is a political fact.' H. Macmillan, 'Wind of Change', speech in the Cape Town Parliament [South Africa], 3 February 1960. On the many significances of this speech, see: L.J. Butler and S. Stockwell (eds.), *The Wind of Change: Harold Macmillan and British Decolonization* (London, 2013).
4. J. Lewis-Barned, *A Fanfare of Trumpets* (Witney, 1993), p. 99. Another officer, working as Crown Counsel in Tanganyika at the time of independence, recalled that in the legal system it was 'business as usual'. Norman Macleod, interview with author, Loch Winnoch, 25 May 2009.
5. On the role of the legal system in Tanganyika as a mechanism for building national unity, see: S. Castelnuovo, 'Legal and Judicial Integration in Tanzania: A Study of Law and Political and Social Change', Ph.D. thesis (University of California, Los Angeles, 1969), pp. vi, 5.
6. Mkenda makes a similar point about using the law to minimise differences between communities in relation to marriage law in Tanzania in: F. Mkenda, 'Tensions, Threats, and a Nation's Weakest Link: Muslim–Christian Relations and the Future of Peace in Tanzania', unpublished paper (Campion Hall, Oxford, 2011), p. 10.
7. Castelnuovo, 'Legal and Judicial', p. 66.
8. H.F. Morris, 'English Law in East Africa: A Hardy Plant in an Alien Soil' in H.F. Morris and J. S. Read, *Indirect Rule and the Search for Justice: Essays in East African Legal History* (Oxford, 1972), p. 104.
9. J.A. Widner, *Building the Rule of Law: Francis Nyalali and the Road to Judicial Independence in Africa*, 1st edn (New York, 2001), pp. 78–79.
10. J. Iliffe, *A Modern History of Tanganyika* (Cambridge, 1979), p. 574. On the key sectors in the economy of Tanganyika in the early 1960s, see: A. Coulson, *Tanzania: A Political Economy* (Oxford, 1982), pp. 145–175.
11. Castelnuovo, 'Legal and Judicial', pp. vi and 1.
12. Ibid., p. vi. See also, W. Twining, 'The Restatement of African Customary Law: A Comment', *Journal of Modern African Studies*, 1 (1963), p. 226.
13. Castelnuovo, 'Legal and Judicial', p. 78. On the ongoing tension between the centralised court system and local anti-centralised system as a legacy of colonial rule, see: S. Falk Moore, 'Treating Law as Knowledge: Telling Colonial Officers What to Say to Africans About Running "Their Own" Native Courts', *Law & Society Review*, 26 (1992), p. 12.

14. Islamic law was not a part of the government's codification efforts discussed here, but Tanganyika did undertake a project to formally restate schools of Islamic Law in the 1960s. On the process for restating Islamic law, see: E. Cotran, 'Integration of Courts and Application of Customary Law in Tanganyika', *East African Law Journal*, 1 (1965), pp. 120–121.
15. Some of the key works from the period include: A.N. Allott, 'The Judicial Ascertainment of Customary Law in British Africa', *The Modern Law Review*, 20 (1957), pp. 244–263; E. Cotran, 'The Unification of Laws in East Africa', *Journal of Modern African Studies*, 1 (1963), pp. 209–220; Twining, 'Restatement'; J.S. Read, 'Crime and Punishment in East Africa: The Twilight of Customary Law', *Howard Law Journal*, 10 (1964), pp. 164–186; W. Twining, *The Place of Customary Law in the National Legal Systems of East Africa: Lectures Delivered at the University of Chicago Law School in April–May 1963* (Chicago, 1964); A.N. Allott, 'Towards the Unification of Laws in Africa', *International and Comparative Law Quarterly*, 14 (1965), pp. 866–889; A.N. Allott, 'Customary Law in East Africa', *Africa Spectrum*, 4 [Law in East Africa edition] (1969), pp. 16–22; A.N. Allott, *New Essays in African Law* (London, 1970), pp. 255–297.
16. The 1959–1960 conference is of particular note: *The Future of Law in Africa: Record of Proceedings of the London Conference, 28 December 1959—8 January 1960* (London, 1960).
17. Hans Cory was the anthropologist the government hired to carry out the codification project. He had been working in the territory since 1913 recording the customs of more than 20 different ethnic communities. He died shortly after the beginning of the project and his efforts were continued by an administrative officer appointed to complete the process of turning the recordings of custom into a definitive and unified text. For a summary of Cory's work on the customary laws of Tanganyika, see: Twining, 'Restatement', pp. 224–225; J. Beattie, 'Obituary: Hans Cory, O.B.E.', *Tanganyika Notes and Records*, 60 (1963), p. 1. For examples of Cory's published recordings of customary law in Tanganyika, see: H. Cory, *Sukuma Law and Custom* (London, 1953); H. Cory and M.M. Hartnoll, *Customary Law of the Haya Tribe, Tanganyika Territory* (London, 1971).
18. Twining, 'Restatement', p. 225.
19. On the process for recording the customary law and turning it into statute in Tanganyika, see: E. Cotran, 'Some Recent Developments in the Tanganyika Judicial System', *Journal of African Law*, Spring (1962), pp. 26–28; Twining, 'Restatement', pp. 224–225; R.E.S. Tanner, 'The Codification of Customary Law in Tanzania', *East African Law Journal*, 2 (1966), pp. 107–109.

20. On the process of districts adopting and applying customary law under these orders see: Twining, *The Place*, p. 66; Cotran, 'Integration' p. 120.
21. Castelnuovo, 'Legal and Judicial', p. 18. See the discussion in Chap. 3 on customary law and courts under colonial rule.
22. Tanner, 'Codification', p. 105; Castelnuovo, 'Legal and Judicial', p. 182.
23. Pratt, *The Critical Phase*, pp. 57, 58.
24. Iliffe, 'Breaking', p. 193.
25. Pratt, *The Critical Phase*, p. 88.
26. J.P.W.B. McAuslan, 'The Republican Constitution of Tanganyika', *The International and Comparative Law Quarterly*, 13 (1964), p. 502.
27. For a description of the Constitutional Conference for Tanganyika see: J.M.M.H. Listowel, *The Making of Tanganyika* (London, 1965), pp. 380–390.
28. Roland Brown Personal Papers, Copenhagen, R. Brown, untitled and unpublished memoir, [emailed to author, accessed on 4 July 2010], Chap. 5: 'Making of the First Constitutional Conference: Part 2', p. 1. Roland Brown was working in London at the Bar with a small practice in 1960 when Nyerere asked him to come to Tanganyika to provide legal advice in the transition to independence and then serve as the first Attorney General. Brown, by his own description, was not widely known and was therefore 'astonished' when asked to take on the position. Chapter 4, 'Making of the First Constitutional Conference: Part 1', p. 5. He recalled Nyerere telling him 'were not looking for a distinguished lawyer, we want a friend'. He agreed to work for the Tanganyikan government until the office could be filled by an African, forging a close relationship with Nyerere. His legal advice and influence were significant in shaping a number of the government's decisions on provisions in the Constitution. Roland Brown, interview with author, London, 1 June 2010. See also: Ibid., Chap. 5, 'Making of the First Constitutional Conference: Part 2', pp. 7–10.
29. McAuslan, 'The Republican', p. 502.
30. A record of the recommendations of the Constitutional Conference on the judiciary is available in: Colonial Office, *Report of the Tanganyika Constitutional Conference, 1961* (London, 1961), pp. 5–6.
31. As quoted by: C. Fundikira, 'Reorganization of the Courts in Tanganyika', *Journal of Local Administration Overseas*, 4 (1962), p. 258.
32. Tanganyika (Constitution) Order in Council 1961, s 58(3).
33. Judicature and Application of Laws Ordinance 1961, s 2(1).
34. Tanganyika (Constitution) Order in Council 1961, Part V.
35. I.G. Shivji et al., *Constitutional and Legal System of Tanzania: A Civics Sourcebook* (Dar es Salaam, 2004), p. 43.
36. Tanganyika (Constitution) Order in Council 1961, s 59(1–2).

37. Ibid., s 60(1).
38. Ibid., s 60(3).
39. The details of the process are outlined in: ibid., s 60(4–6).
40. Ibid, 58(2); s 71(3 & 5).
41. See: Judicial Service Act 1962.
42. Tanganyika (Constitution) Order in Council 1961, s 65(1).
43. A body with this name was established under British rule in 1955 and replaced in 1960, but was only 'advisory to the Governor and enjoyed no executive powers'. J.S.R. Cole and W.N. Denison, *Tanganyika: The Development of Its Laws and Constitution* (London, 1964), p. 67.
44. Tanganyika (Constitution) Order in Council 1961, 64(1).
45. Ibid., s 59(3).
46. Tanganyika (Constitution) Order in Council 1961, s 58(2).
47. As the territories under the jurisdiction of the Court of Appeal for Eastern Africa achieved independence in the early 1960s, the Court was 'reconstituted' by the Eastern Africa Court of Appeal Order in Council 1961 to allow for the independence of Tanganyika and create the framework for independent countries to send appeals to it. The Court eventually fell under the auspices of the East African Common Services Organisation. J.S. Read, 'A Century Plus of Appeal Courts in Tanzania', in C.M. Peter and H.K. Bisimba (eds.), *Law and Justice in Tanzania: Quarter of a Century of the Court of Appeal* (Dar es Salam, 2007), pp. 63–64.
48. Tanganyika (Constitution) Order in Council 1961, s 62(2). The provisions on the types of cases that could be appealed to the Court of Appeal for Eastern Africa and the Privy Council and the processes for appeals are available in: Appellate Jurisdiction Ordinance 1961, Parts II and III respectively.
49. Tanganyika (Constitution) Order in Council 1961, s 62(1).
50. McAuslan, 'The Republican', pp. 504, 505.
51. For the rationale supporting the creation of the role of executive President, see: Listowel, *The Making*, pp. 412–413.
52. Tanganyika, Government Paper Number 1 of 1962: Proposals of the Tanganyika Government for a Republic (Dar es Salaam, 1962), p. 1, as quoted in McAuslan, *The Republican*, p. 505.
53. Listowel, *The Making*, p. 412.
54. Tanganyika, Government Paper Number 1 of 1962: Proposals of the Tanganyika Government for a Republic (Dar es Salaam, 1962), p. 3, as cited in McAuslan, *The Republican*, p. 505.
55. McAuslan, *The Republican*, 543. On maintaining the rule of law, see: Ibid, pp. 542–566.
56. An Act to Declare the Constitution of Tanganyika 1962, s (respectively) 48(3), 48(1), 52(1), 47(3), 61(3&5), 46(2), 46(2).

57. Ibid., s 47(1–2).
58. Ibid., s 48(4–6).
59. Appellate Jurisdiction Act 1962, s 11(1–2). Section 12 allowed the Privy Council to rule on any appeals that were pending at the time until 8 June 1964, when it lost jurisdiction over cases from Tanganyika.
60. An Act to Declare the Constitution of Tanganyika 1962, s 51(1).
61. Pratt, *The Critical Phase*, p. 63.
62. Judicial Advisers' Conference 1956, pp. 5–6.
63. ARJ 1964, p. 1.
64. Local Courts (Amendment) Ordinance 1961, s 38(3c).
65. Ibid., s 38(3). See also: Cotran, 'Some Recent Developments', pp. 22–23.
66. Local Courts (Amendment) Ordinance 1961, s 5(3A).
67. For a description of the duties of this new office see: J.F. Lewis-Barned, 'Integration of Judicial Systems: The Recent Reform of the Local Courts Appeal System of Tanganyika', *Journal of African Law,* 7 (1963), pp. 86–92.
68. ARJ 1962, p. 1. Not all duties of provincial commissioners in relation to Local Courts were passed on to the Local Courts appeals officer. For instance, the Minister for Justice gained the power to establish Local Courts, which had been held by the provincial commissioners during colonial rule.
69. Local Courts (Amendment) Ordinance 1961, s 39(1–3).
70. Lewis-Barned, 'Integration', p. 86.
71. Ibid., p. 92.
72. Local Courts (Amendment) Ordinance 1961, s 39(D)(1); s 39(D)(3); s 39(A). Rulings by the High Court on cases appealed from Local Courts in 1962 and 1963 are available in: Tanganyika, *A Digest of Appeals from Local Courts 1962* (Dar es Salaam, 1963); Tanganyika, *A Digest of Appeals from Local Courts 1963* (Dar es Salaam, 1964).
73. McAuslan, 'The Republican', p. 550.
74. Local Courts (Minister for Justice and Regional Local Courts Officers) Act 1962, s 2(1–3).
75. ARJ 1965, p. 4.
76. ARJ 1962, p. 2.
77. Tanganyika, *A Digest of Appeals from Local Courts 1964* (Dar es Salaam, 1965), p. i.
78. Patrick Ellis, interview with author, Bishops Stortford, 9 November 2009.
79. Patrick Ellis, interview with author, Bishops Stortford, 25 March 2009.
80. ARJ 1962, p. 2.
81. The government first implemented this change in the towns and districts with large numbers of cases, such as Moshi and Rungwe. Tanner,

'Codification', p. 105. Allot asserts that in some urban areas 'a single magistrate or "stipendiary"' was appointed to be president of a Local Court after 1953. Allott, 'The Development of the East African Legal Systems', p. 375.

82. Graham, 'Indirect Rule', p. 9. On the political dynamics between chiefs and TANU in the 1950s, see: Listowel, *The Making*, pp. 312–322. On the politics surrounding chieftaincy during transition to independence in Tanganyika, see: S. Feierman, *Peasant Intellectuals: Anthropology and History in Tanzania* (London, 1990), pp. 223–232.
83. F. DuBow, 'Justice for People: Law and Politics in the Lower Courts of Tanzania', Ph.D. thesis (University of California—Berkeley, 1973), p. 15.
84. Feierman, *Peasant Intellectuals*, p. 230.
85. Ibid., p. 257.
86. Respectively, L. Weston, P.R.N. Fifoot, and P.H. Johnston. RHL, MSS Afr. s. 1461, P.H. Johnston Papers, File 2, Working Party on the Integration of the Courts Systems, 'Working Party on the Integration of the Courts Systems: Preliminary Report', p. 1.
87. A copy of the report is available in: Ibid. This three-tier structure has been roughly maintained in mainland Tanzania since 1964 and was the only major overhaul of the court system since national independence, with the exception of the creation of the national Court of Appeal in 1979, which is now the highest court sitting above the High Court. For a discussion of the present system, see: Court of Appeal, *The History*, pp. 56–67; Shivji, et al., pp. 221–232.
88. TNA (UK), Dominions Office (DO) 168/13, Acting High Commissioner of Tanganyika to the Commonwealth Relations Office, 'Tanganyika Fortnightly Summary for the period 22 November–5 December, 1963', received date 18 December 1963, p. 4.
89. Magistrates' Courts Act 1963, s 4; s 14. Hereafter MCA.
90. Ibid., s 57.
91. Ibid., s. 66(1). See: Cotran, 'Integration', p. 115.
92. MCA, s 7(1)(a). On the provision for appointment and dismissal of these magistrates, see: E. Cotran, 'Integration', p. 109.
93. African Conference on Local Courts and Customary Law, *Record of the Proceedings of the Conference Held in Dar Es Salaam, Tanganyika, 8–18 September 1963* (Dar es Salaam, 1963), p. 102.
94. ARJ 1963, p. 3.
95. Shivji et al., *Constitutional*, p. 224. MCA, s 29(1). Advocates were, however, allowed in cases from the Primary Courts being heard on appeal in the District Courts. Cotran, 'Integration', p. 113.
96. MCA, s 32.

97. Ibid., s 12(1). RHL, MSS Afr. s. 1620, P.H. Johnston Papers, 'Tanganyika, 1938–65', p. 26.
98. MCA, s 8. An amendment to the MCA in 1964 required that Primary Court magistrates sit with two assessors. Cotran, 'Integration', p. 121, fn 9.
99. MCA, s 16. On the provisions relating to the transfer of cases, see: Cotran, 'Integration', pp. 113–114.
100. MCA, s 35. For appellate and revisionary powers of District Courts, see: s 17–18 (respectively).
101. Ibid., s 5; s 7(1)(b).
102. Cotran, 'Integration', p. 114.
103. On district magistrates, see: P.T. Georges, 'The Role of Judges and Magistrates' in R.W. James and F.M. Kassam (eds.), *Law and its Administration in a One Party State: Selected Speeches of Telford Georges* (Dar es Salaam, 1973), pp. 82–83. Some of the first district magistrates went on to obtain law degrees from the Law Faculty in Dar es Salaam (examined in Chap. 7) and join the High Court Bench.
104. MCA, s 12(2).
105. Ibid., s 6; s 7(1)(c).
106. ARJ, 1965, p. 4. The regional administrative reorganisation is discussed in the following chapter in the context of the Africanisation of the civil service.
107. MCA, s 69 (1).
108. Ibid., s 21(1) & 38.
109. Ibid., s 3 & 26.
110. Ibid., s 23(1)(b).
111. Ibid., s 23(4). See also: Cotran, 'Integration', pp. 112, 115–121; A. Sawyerr, 'Customary Law in the High Court of Tanzania', *Eastern Africa Law Review* 6 (1973), pp. 265–284.
112. The Primary Court magistrates were technically under a Special Commission, which was comprised of the Chief Justice, the Puisne judge serving on the Judicial Service Commission at the time, and two other members appointed by the Minister for Justice. On the procedures relating to the supervision of the employment of Primary Court magistrates, see: McAuslan, 'The Republican', pp. 550–552; Cotran, 'Integration', p. 108.
113. ARJ 1963, p. 3.
114. ARJ 1962, p. 2.
115. R.W. James and F.M. Kassam, 'The Courts in a One Party State' in R.W. James and F.M. Kassam (eds.), *Law and its Administration in a One Party State: Selected Speeches of Telford Georges* (Dar es Salaam, 1973), pp. 16–17; RHL, MSS Afr. s. 1620, P.H. Johnston Papers, 'Tanganyika, 1938–65', p. 25.

116. ARJ 1963, p. 2.
117. ARJ 1965, p. 5.
118. On concerns over delays in the transition of the court system, see: RHL, MSS Afr. s. 1461, P.H. Johnston Papers, File 3, 'Working Party on the Integration of the Courts Systems: Annexure A', p. 2.
119. ARJ 1962, p. 1. One judge from this period recalls going on about four circuits per year by train for two to three weeks at a time, much like judges had during colonial rule. David Williams, interview with author, London, 17 March 2010.
120. ARJ 1965, p. 5.
121. Patrick Ellis, interviews with author, Bishops Stortford, 9 November 2009; 25 March 2009.
122. Patrick Ellis Personal Papers, Bishops Stortford, P. Ellis, Report on Courts System during the Early Stages of the Integration of the Courts, n.d. [c. 1963], p. 1.
123. Tanner, 'Codification', p. 108; ARJ 1965, p. 5; James and Kassam, 'The Courts in a One Party State', p. 19.
124. Patrick Ellis Personal Papers, Bishops Stortford, P. Ellis, [unpublished memoir] 'A life in the Colonial Service, Tanganyika, As Seen By Patrick J.C. Ellis, 1952–54', n.d. [accessed by author on 25 March 2009], p. 115.
125. Patrick Ellis, interview with author, Bishops Stortford, 9 November 2009.

CHAPTER 6

Colonial Judges in a Fading Empire, 1961–1965

At the beginning of 1964 the structural decolonisation of Tanganyika's colonial court systems was nearing completion, but the process of decolonising the High Court Bench was still at an early stage.[1] Ending the legacy of the exclusion of Africans from participating in the administration of justice at the highest levels was a central component of the decolonisation of the High Court as an institution. Yet, at the time of independence in 1961, the new government was faced with the challenge of beginning the process of decolonising the High Court Bench without qualified Tanganyikan Africans.[2]

During the following decade the process of decolonising the High Court Bench involved appointing former colonial officials, foreign judges from West Africa and the West Indies, an Asian advocate, and Tanganyikan Africans with legal qualifications to the High Court. This chapter examines the initial stage of this process between 1961 and 1965 when the High Court Bench remained entirely populated by former colonial officials. The next chapter examines the government's decision to invite foreign judges from the West Indies and West Africa to fill the open seats in the middle and late 1960s, and explores how the first Tanganyikan Africans entered the higher levels of the judicial service.

Colonial judges and former colonial magistrates played a key role in the process of decolonising the Bench. Shortly before independence in 1961 the government asked colonial judges, along with most other British

E.R. Feingold, *Colonial Justice and Decolonization in the High Court of Tanzania, 1920–1971*, Cambridge Imperial and Post-Colonial Studies Series, https://doi.org/10.1007/978-3-319-69691-1_6

colonial officers, to continue to serve as they had during British rule. Though it may appear that the continued presence of colonial judges on the Bench after independence was perpetuating British control of the Court, this chapter demonstrates that their continued service can be understood as an early part of the Bench's decolonisation process. By staying on, colonial judges allowed the Court to survive the transition to independence, maintaining the standards in the Constitution for appointments to the Bench while the government made efforts to help Tanganyikan Africans qualify for the posts.[3]

As Tanganyika 'Africanised' large sections of its government service during 1962 and 1963 the High Court Bench did not receive any African appointees. In 1964, however, Tanganyika transitioned to a policy of 'localisation'.[4] The process of decolonising the High Court Bench between 1961 and 1971 can therefore be more accurately characterised as one of localisation than of Africanisation. Race played an important role in shaping this process—the appointment of a majority of Tanganyikan Africans was the long-term goal—but it was not the only factor that determined who was on the Bench in the 1960s. This chapter and the next illustrate that interpersonal relationships within the government and legal community were crucial factors in determining who was appointed to the Bench and how long they served.

Immediately following independence most colonial judges continued to serve on the Bench while their administrative colleagues departed, but by the mid-1960s there was increasing and mutual discomfort between the colonial Bench and the government. This growing tension was particularly evident in relation to three key events: the closure of the Dar es Salaam Club; the enactment of the Minimum Sentences Act; and the trial of the nation's first mutineers. Shortly after these events, nearly all the judges who had been on Bench at the time of independence departed Tanganyika. Some former colonial magistrates who had remained in Tanganyika working in various government roles since 1961 stepped in to fill the open seats. Their position in Tanganyika and their careers differed from those of more senior colonial judges, as did their motivations for staying in the judiciary in Tanganyika after independence. Tanganyika's last remaining colonial judge—Justice Biron—became localised and, it is argued, can be considered the first local judge to serve on the Bench, rather than as a colonial relic.

The decolonisation of Tanganyika's High Court Bench offers a fresh perspective on national governments' responses to the staffing challenges they faced following independence. The existing studies of how governments approached staffing as colonial officers departed largely focus on the civil service and police forces, but how countries without local Bars localised their Benches remains underexplored.[5] Moreover, while it was not uncommon to invite foreign judges to join the national courts in decolonising Africa, little is known about the impact of foreign judges on national courts, or of the influence of former colonial officials who remained in post-colonial states after the end of colonial rule.[6]

What is apparent from this study is that individual motivations and interpersonal relationships—in addition to politics and policies—shaped the process of decolonising the High Court as an institution. During the colonial period, when colonial institutions were stable, individual colonial judges had little room to make a substantial impact on the High Court. The personal motivations and preferences of individual judges did not determine where they served or who else from the Colonial Legal Service was on their Court, as these decisions were made by the Colonial Office. Furthermore, individual judges could not break with colonial expectations and traditions on their own. During the independence period though, British institutions, like the Colonial Office, lost influence and were replaced with local institutions. This process created a more fluid environment with space for individual personalities, motivations, relationships, and perspectives to play a prominent role in determining who was on the Bench. The history of the decolonisation of the High Court Bench illustrates that during periods of rapid social change, as in Tanganyika in the 1960s, personal ties and preferences played a much more substantial role in shaping institutions than during periods of stability. Therefore, this and the following chapter focus on selected individuals who had a significant impact on the process of decolonising the Bench, or who represent trajectories and rationales that others on the Bench shared. With the exception of two, none of the judges discussed in these chapters have been the subject of published research to date.[7]

From Africanisation to Localisation

The replacement of colonial officials in the middle and senior ranks of government with Tanganyikan Africans was a primary goal of TANU after national independence.[8] Yet there were very few Tanganyikan Africans in a position to compete for high-level jobs with members of the expatriate and Asian communities. Most Africans in Tanganyika had had little or no access to the level of education and professional training programmes that would have prepared them to carry out the work of officers at the higher levels of the civil service. In September 1960 African employees comprised a mere 15% of the senior grade posts in the public service, with the majority of Africans working for the government in the lowest grades.[9] In the professional sectors the situation was even worse; as of 1962 Africans accounted for only 16 of the 184 physicians and one of the 84 civil engineers.[10] This posed a substantial challenge for the independence government in its efforts to hire Tanganyikan Africans for the posts from which they had previously been excluded.

Government officials considered two approaches to staffing after Tanganyika's independence. One was Africanisation, which was defined by one government official, Rashidi Kawawa, as hiring 'an African citizen of Tanganyika', thereby excluding non-Africans and non-Tanganyikans from employment. The other was localisation, which meant employing people from the local population, both African and non-African.[11] Supporters of Africanisation argued that this was necessary in order to break down the legacy of exclusion of Africans from the middle and senior ranks of the government services during British rule.[12] They also framed it as part of the realisation of independence from colonialism because it shattered the racial hierarchies that had placed expatriates above Asians, and Asians above Africans, offering Africans participation in and ownership of the government, which they had previously been denied.[13]

Nyerere did not support Africanisation as the wholesale policy for staffing, however. He expressed concern about the use of race as the primary criterion for employment because it was discriminatory.[14] Instead, he advocated giving priority to Tanganyikan Africans so that the civil service would have a 'local look' that would 'broadly reflect the racial pattern of the territory's population'.[15] This meant that the majority of employees ought to be Tanganyikan Africans, but did not exclude other local people from working in government. Nyerere offered terms other than Africanisation that he believed better captured the nature of what he supported, including 'Tanganyikanisation' and 'belongingisation'.[16] Though Nyerere resisted rapid Africanisation of the entire government service, there was growing pressure from more radical elements of TANU and the trade unions to Africanise as many posts as possible.[17]

In addition to an ideological objection to the policy, Nyerere also had the more practical concern that there were few educated and trained Tanganyikan Africans in a position to take over most of the jobs that overseas officers had performed. He knew that colonial officers were necessary to maintain stability at home and legitimacy abroad, fearing that rapid Africanisation would 'discourage expatriates' and make them want to leave before there were qualified Tanganyikan Africans to replace them.[18] Therefore, Nyerere sought to convince expatriate officers to stay and help with the transition and to keep the government running while it made efforts to educate and train Tanganyikan Africans to perform government jobs. He sent a letter to all colonial officers shortly before independence appealing to their 'sense of duty' and promising material compensation if they would agree to 'stay on' and help after the political transfer of power.[19] To keep these officers in Tanganyika until Tanganyikan Africans were prepared to replace them, Nyerere agreed to an expensive compensation scheme for officers of Her Majesty's Overseas Civil Service and officers designated under the Overseas Aid Agreement.[20] The British government was eager to keep its officers on the ground, as it hoped to retain influence over and maintain stability in Tanganyika after it became constitutionally independent.[21] Though British colonial officers began retiring in the run up to independence, approximately 70% agreed to stay on, continuing to do their work through the political transitions in 1961.[22] Some Tanganyikan Africans began to replace colonial officials in senior posts in the government and as the heads of ministries in the months around independence, but there was growing political pressure to increase the number of Tanganyikan Africans in government and thus for the process to move faster.

In 1962 Nyerere, who had been Prime Minister since independence, stepped down. Under the new Prime Minister, Kawawa, the government began to expand its Africanisation efforts, which included the formation of the Africanisation Committee, tasked with developing detailed plans for Africanising each of the government sectors, especially at the highest levels.[23] Even the Commission itself, however, acknowledged that it would not be immediately possible to move away from the use of 'foreign expertise' in technical and professional sectors.[24] The employment of Tanganyikan Africans in these ministries would take longer than in non-professional sectors and be reliant on them gaining the relevant educational qualifications.[25]

Instead, Kawawa's government targeted the police and the provincial administration.[26] These sectors were the focus of Africanisation for three reasons. First, they were the divisions where the government could make progress on Africanisation as many of the jobs in them were not seen to require a high degree of education. Second, these were politically important positions because they were perceived as symbols of and the practical means for maintaining British rule, which Africanisation promised to change.[27] Third, they were the positions through which most Africans in Tanganyika interacted with the government and would have the impact of providing visible changes to the identity of public officers.[28]

In 1962 a new national administrative structure divided the nation into regions and the remaining provincial commissioners from the era of British rule were made regional secretaries under the newly appointed African regional commissioners.[29] One officer who had heard rumours of the impending reorganisation of the entire administration before independence described it as the 'death knell of old DC [district commissioner] system'.[30] The government removed more expatriate ministers from their powerful positions, including the Commissioner of Police and hundreds of other non-African civil servants.[31] These measures strained relations between some of the remaining officers, who had agreed to stay because they believed they were needed to keep the government running, and the political leadership of the government, who were keen to Africanise as many posts as fast as possible.[32] Many younger colonial officers chose to leave during the following two years because they either did not envision a professional future in Tanganyika, hoped to start a new career outside Tanganyika, or were uncomfortable with their new positions under often less-qualified and politically active Tanganyikan Africans.[33]

By 1964 the government was awaiting the completion of training courses to fill the offices that were vacant after the departure of a large number of former colonial officers.[34] Declaring in a letter to the government bodies that 'Africanisation is dead', Nyerere, who had returned to the government as the nation's first President at the end of 1962, asserted that it was time for the nation to transition to a policy that made citizenship the main criteria for employment, rather than race.[35] Nyerere framed the Africanisation period as a stage in the process of achieving self-government that had passed and, from 1964, argued that the consideration of race was no longer necessary. Reflecting on this shift in policy he said,

> Once we had demonstrated—to ourselves and others—that being an African did not have to mean being a junior official, the nation was able to accept that in some fields we can, without shame, hire the skilled people who are needed. This had been done by January, 1964, and we were therefore able to revert to a policy of priority to citizens regardless of their racial origin.[36]

Though it was relatively short-lived, the phase of Africanisation and debate around it had a profound impact on the public services as well as playing a role in shaping race relations and the political landscape in the years following independence.[37] By 1965 Tanganyikan citizens occupied 66% of the senior- and middle-grade posts in the public service, most of whom were Tanganyikan Africans.[38] Thus, even though there was a substantial increase in the number of Africans in the higher ranks of the government, Tanganyika's phase of Africanisation was more tempered that it might have been and it had allowed a considerable number of non-Africans to remain in government service.[39]

In the lower levels of the judiciary, Tanganyikan Africans accounted for a large percentage of the new Judicial Service by 1964. Within the first two years of the Magistrates' court system, the vast majority of the district magistracy and more than a third of the resident magistracy consisted of Tanganyikan Africans.[40] The High Court Bench, however, was essentially unaffected by the progress made in other government services and in the lower courts because there were no Tanganyikan Africans with the relevant qualifications to join the Bench.

Why were so few Tanganyikan Africans qualified for legal posts? During the colonial period the only law faculty in Eastern Africa was the one at the University of Khartoum, and the colonial government of Tanganyika provided very few scholarships for Africans to attend programmes overseas.[41] The rationale offered by the British for not training Tanganyikan Africans in the law was that it was more important for the purposes of development to focus on training engineers and doctors.[42] The decision to limit access to legal education, however, may also have been a deliberate response to the significant role that colonial subjects with legal educations had played in political movements resisting British rule in India—such as Mohandas K. Gandhi—and other parts of the Empire where legal education had been accessible to colonial subjects.[43] A more locally driven explanation for the lack of legal training is that lawyers in general had a 'relatively minor role' in the colonies in East Africa.[44] Lawyers were not allowed to represent clients in the Native Courts and the Asian and European lawyers generally served the relatively small community of non-Africans who engaged the British courts that permitted lawyers. Therefore, in the early 1960s, while West African Bars had sizeable numbers of Africans on their rolls, there were only a handful of African lawyers on the East African rolls. In Tanganyika, of the 57 advocates on the roll in 1961, only two were Africans.[45]

From the early stages of planning to bring Tanganyikan Africans into the higher levels of the government, Nyerere had recognised that the dearth of Tanganyikan African lawyers presented a unique challenge and that the process of hiring Tanganyikan Africans would be different from most other sectors of government. Moreover, the constitutional requirements for appointment to the High Court Bench ensured that standards for employment could not be lowered out of a desire to see Tanganyikan Africans on the Bench for the first time. In 1960 Nyerere delivered a speech to the Legislative Council in which he raised the issue and asserted,

> Take our Judiciary. We have only two African lawyers in the country ... One of our problems is, when we have reached that constitutional stage, how to replace my hon. colleague here, the Attorney-General. The answer certainly is not going to be Africanisation, at all. *We will have to find another answer.*[46]

The 'answer' for Nyerere was a nearly decade-long process of localisation. This involved taking steps to prepare Tanganyikan Africans to join the High Court Bench in the long term. It also meant hiring foreign judges on a temporary basis and appointing non-African local officials.

In the first stage of this process, Nyerere asked colonial judges to remain on the High Court Bench to maintain the Court. Beyond being asked to stay, colonial judges had personal motivations for remaining on the Bench in the years immediately following independence, rather than departing Tanganyika with many of their administrative colleagues.

Colonial Judges in a Fading Empire

By 1961 the judges who had been on the High Court Bench during the 1950s had all departed Tanganyika, either to posts outside Tanganyika or had already entered retirement before the Colonial Office offered the compensation scheme and the date for independence was fixed. Thus, all nine High Court judges on the Bench in 1961 had been appointed in the preceding three years and almost all of them chose to remain on the Bench in Tanganyika for at least another three to four years after independence.

Two judges did, however, choose to leave around the time of independence. First, Ernest B. Simmons retired in July 1961, the very month that the Overseas Aid Scheme became available. The scheme offered compensation to those who stayed and provided it to judges between the ages of 40 and 62 for the curtailment of their careers in the colonies.[47] At the age of 48, he qualified for the scheme and it is not entirely clear whether after leaving Tanganyika he remained in retirement or went on to other employment.[48] The other judge who left around independence was David J. Williams. His retirement in July 1962 was motivated by a desire to return to England to care for his mother after the death of his father.[49]

Other than Simmons and Williams, all members of the High Court Bench remained in their posts. An examination of the judges who chose to stay on highlights their status in the early 1960s, both in Tanganyika and the fading Empire. Though there is not conclusive evidence to explain why each individual judge decided to continue to work on the Bench in Tanganyika, this study has identified three explanations for what motivated these judges to continue to serve on the Bench after independence.

The first motivating factor was an interest in helping the High Court to continue to function at the standard it had during British rule, underpinned by a commitment to seeing the common law system survive the transition to independence. Colonial judges were aware that there were few people who could replace them with hardly any new arrivals from the Colonial Office. When independence appeared imminent in 1960, Tanganyika stopped recruiting officers on permanent pensionable terms; instead anyone who came to Tanganyika to work for the government signed one- or two-tour contracts.[50] Though some new officers chose to come to Tanganyika on these terms, during this period legal recruitment in the Colonial Office plummeted as it became clear that employment with it was no longer an offer of a career, but was simply a short-term job opportunity. The Legal Adviser to the Colonial Office at the time, Kenneth Roberts-Wray, observed that the Legal Service was 'cracking from top to bottom', as vacancies at the top with the retirement of High Court judges were being filled by magistrates already in the service, whose posts would in turn remain vacant without new recruits to replace them.[51] Some of those who chose to stay may have regarded staying on as a short-term commitment until arrangements could be made to replace them.

Second, there were few changes at the High Court immediately after independence that would have made High Court judges want to leave. While the administration was facing reorganisation and Tanganyikan African ministers were taking over the top government posts, the High Court was under no such threat, and its judges were increasingly gaining power and authority that they had not enjoyed during British rule. The constitutional provisions and political rhetoric from the new government indicated that the High Court would be preserved and not impinged on by the political efforts of the new government. It appeared at the time that the political transition was not going to lessen their status or the status of the Court in Tanganyika. Moreover, colonial judges continued to enjoy the lifestyle and privileges they had become accustomed to during the 1950s, plus they had the added benefit of increased compensation for remaining in Tanganyika.

Finally, colonial judges faced limited career prospects if they chose to leave Tanganyika.[52] These judges had little hope of continuing to serve as judges back in Great Britain and faced adversity in returning to the Bar in England or the colonies. In the 1950s the Colonial Office had discouraged and tried to prevent judges from practising law or serving as directors of companies in the territories where they had served on the Bench.[53] It also wanted to prohibit judges who had served on regional appellate courts from practising law in all the territories where they had held jurisdiction by virtue of their position on the appellate Bench, as well as in any territories that fell under the jurisdiction of the appeals court after their retirement from the appellate Bench.[54] The Colonial Office was concerned that litigants might believe that by hiring a former judge they would have influence over former colleagues and friends still on the Bench and thus wanted to avoid accusations of the abuse of power by retired judges.[55] Therefore, the Tanganyika Law Society passed a resolution in 1952 prohibiting judges of the High Court and Court of Appeal from admission to the territory's Bar.[56] This act made it virtually impossible for judges to work in a lucrative role in Tanganyika outside the government.[57]

Colonial judges were not prohibited from returning to the Bar or Bench in England, but their likelihood of success was low given their age and disconnection from the English legal community. Colonial judges were still separate from the English legal community and were seen, by some, as second rate. One former magistrate remarked that a colonial judge would have been regarded by members of the English legal community as 'an interloper' and did not believe that any former judges of the High Court of Tanganyika had gone on to serve on a Bench in England after independence.[58] Former judges and legal officers could enlist the help of the Overseas Service Resettlement Bureau to place them in new jobs after leaving Tanganyika, though many of their placements were in business.[59] Some former legal officers and judges obtained legal roles, but not positions of prestige comparable to those they had enjoyed in Tanganyika. For example, Justice David Williams worked in the Lord Chancellor's Office after he left Tanganyika in 1962 until his retirement in 1979.[60] It took years for a young magistrate to make it to the High Court Bench and therefore many judges of the High Court were simply too old to start another career or life back in Great Britain. Some chose to ride out the political transition at the High Court and look for opportunities to remain as judges in other courts in the region or elsewhere in the fading Empire.

Colonial Judges in a Post-Colonial State

In the early 1960s the colonial Bench was led by two long-standing members of the Overseas Judiciary: the Chief Justice, Ralph Windham, and Justice Law. Both had joined the Colonial Legal Service in the 1940s and served in numerous territories in East Africa. Among former members of the Overseas Judiciary and Legal Service they had reputations for being fair, hard-working, and competent judges.[61] According to one member of staff, Windham had a formal style and remained 'remote' from most other members of colonial society.[62] Some of his contemporaries in the expatriate community found his style appropriate for his position as Chief Justice, but some young African lawyers found it difficult to relate to him and regarded him as being 'withdrawn'.[63] He was famous among members of the colonial judiciary for having been abducted from his Court in Tel Aviv by the Irgun while serving on the Bench in Palestine, and for developing a rapport with the men guarding him over their shared love of music during the period he was held by them.[64] Justice Law was also a leading figure of the Court during the independence period. He had been on the Bench in Kenya during the Mau Mau emergency and 'tried far more Mau Mau cases than any other member of the Bench'.[65] Perhaps in part due to their previous experiences in colonies during times of conflict, these two men appeared to be unruffled by Tanganyika's political transition, which was progressing relatively smoothly compared with what they had observed in other British territories in their previous postings.

Colonial judges and their families were able to continue their lives in Dar es Salaam much as they had under British rule in the year following independence. By late 1963, however, certain elements of the colonial lifestyle began to disappear. At that time, the new government was actively trying to break down the social and racial barriers entrenched under colonial rule. One of the government's targets was the colonial clubs that had been a central part of socialising for members of the Overseas Service.[66] The Dar es Salaam Club was the most elite and was only a short distance from the High Court. This 'sacred' colonial club had been frequented by High Court judges and was off limits to non-Europeans.[67] As a result, the Club came to symbolise the racism of colonial rule and was, according to the Attorney General, 'something of an anachronism in an independent Tanganyika'.[68]

The racism of the Club became a 'low-level political issue' in 1963.[69] In December that year Tanganyika's Parliament unanimously passed the Dar es Salaam Club (Dissolution) Act, mandating the closure of the Club.[70] The Act apparently came as a 'great shock' to the expatriate community because it was introduced and passed without warning to the Club or its members.[71] The takeover was especially unsettling for members of the judiciary, as it was perceived by some as an assault on their way of life.[72] Justice Law's widow recalled that the Club had been an important part of their lives in Dar es Salaam and connected its closure in 1963 to the end of Law's tenure in Tanganyika the following year. She said 'I think that when they [the government] took the Dar es Salaam Club that finished my husband.'[73] Moreover, after its closure, the Club's building was used by members of the new government for social events. For example, the Attorney General at the time, Roland Brown, gained permission shortly after the closure of the Club to use the building (pictured in Fig. 6.1) for his wedding reception in February 1964. He recalled that although he had invited members of the judiciary, all 'boycotted' the event because it was in the closed-down Club.[74] The closure of the club was a signal to members of the Bench that their lives would no longer continue as they had done during the late 1950s and early 1960s. Justice Harold Platt described its closing as representing that 'another bastion had crumbled'.[75]

While the drama surrounding the Club was of little practical significance to the High Court in its work, the passing of the Minimum Sentences Act in June 1963 was of much greater importance to the attitude of the judges of the High Court towards the government of Tanganyika. It may also have indicated the government's feelings towards them. The Act specified the minimum periods of incarceration and corporal punishment for anyone convicted of the crimes it designated in its list of scheduled offences, including theft from public funds, cattle theft, burglary, and violence associated with these and similar acts.[76] With increasing episodes of theft in the years following independence, Nyerere became concerned about the impact of this type of crime on the state. Observing events in Tanganyika at the time, the British High Commission connected Nyerere's

Fig. 6.1 The building that housed the Dar es Salaam Club during colonial rule and became the home of the Court of Appeal of Tanzania in 1979 (Photo by A.K. Dewar and E.R. Feingold, Dar es Salaam, December 2008. Photos taken and reprinted with the permission of the photographers and the Court of Appeal of Tanzania)

announcement of the Act specifically to his 'fury at the robbery of a retail co-operative shop in Mwanza immediately before he formally opened it'.[77] While the Act was certainly meant to curtail this type of crime, it was also an opportunity for the government to communicate to the country's African population that breaking a law was no longer a subversion of colonial law, and by extension a reaction against colonial injustices, but that it was now an offence against the post-colonial state.[78]

The Minimum Sentences Act may not only have been motivated by a concern over increasing crime of this nature and a desire to make its severity clear, however. The Attorney General at that time recalled that the Act was also,

> some indication that the Tanzanians didn't think they were being well served by expatriate judges … they thought that expatriate judges took crimes that affected Tanzanian individuals … lightly and they wanted to see something done, stark and effective. There was enormous amount of public support for doing something.[79]

The Act impacted the Bench by limiting its flexibility in sentencing and its oversight of the lower courts. Under the Act the Local Courts had the power to try the scheduled offences and the minimum sentences they handed down were not subject to confirmation by the High Court.[80] Moreover, the requirement of corporal punishment under the Act was, according to Read, 'a distinct and marked change in penal policy, representing a clear dissent by an independent nation from the policies of the former colonial power', which had moved away from corporal punishment in the later years of colonial rule in Tanganyika.[81] Some colonial judges did not agree with the Act and Justice Law was particularly vocal in his opposition.[82] Its merits were hotly debated among members of the Bench. The differences of opinion among the judges about the Act revealed tremendous ideological rifts between members of the Bench about the trajectory and policies of the new government and, according to Justice Platt, 'left a growing worry as to the stability of the judiciary'.[83]

Another indication that the government was concerned about the continued use of colonial judges was the lack of the inclusion of a Bill of Rights in the country's independence Constitution. As a substitute, the Constitution's preamble was shaped to include statements affirming the state's commitment to human rights.[84] Charles Parkinson asserts that the decision not to include a Bill of Rights was influenced, in part, by a concern that it could lead to conflict between executive and judiciary, which might damage the legal system.[85] The continued exclusion of a Bill of Rights in subsequent constitutions in 1962 and 1965, however, may also indicate a specific concern in the early 1960s over the continued role of colonial judges on the Bench, rather a general concern about avoiding conflict between executive and judiciary. The Attorney General recalled that colonial judges 'were tolerated, but not much liked' and he, as an adviser to the government, feared that if a Bill of Rights was included in the Constitution and on that basis a colonial judge still on the Bench struck down legislation passed by Parliament, 'the fragile structure of judicial independence might collapse altogether'.[86] It is notable, however, that the country did not amend its Constitution to include a Bill of Rights until 1985, almost exactly 20 years after the departure of most of the colonial Bench, and this indicates that the continued role of colonial judges in the 1960s may not have been the main rationale or purpose of its sustained exclusion.

The implementation of the Minimum Sentences Act and the closure of the Club both affected the way in which some of the remaining colonial judges felt about staying in Tanganyika.[87] The dramatic events in 1964, however, also raised concern within the government about the continued reliance on British colonial judges in the post-colonial state. After the end of the phase of Africanisation of the civil service in 1964, the colonial Bench seemed more and more out of step with the rest of the government. Though the judiciary did not experience any major episodes of political interference in the early 1960s, the difficulty of maintaining a colonial Bench in a post-colonial state came to the surface with the trial following the mutiny of January 1964.

The mutiny involved African troops in the Tanganyika Rifles seizing crucial government buildings in Dar es Salaam, including State House and police stations, as well as arresting British officers and attacking Europeans and Asians.[88] Nyerere went into hiding and the stability of the government hung in the balance over the course of approximately six days, until British troops were brought in to put down the mutiny. Tanganyika's need for help from Great Britain—the colonial power it had only recently become independent from—to end the mutiny and to restore the government was, according to Justice Platt, 'humiliating' for Nyerere.[89] To some the mutiny was 'a defining moment in the development of Tanganyika'.[90] James Brennan asserts that it 'laid bare the fragility of the post-colonial state and hastened the government's erratic drive towards eliminating formal political opposition'.[91]

The mutiny clearly had significant political ramifications, but it also had a direct effect on the judiciary and the colonial judges on the Bench. After the mutiny, the government began to detain people under its new Preventive Detention Law and although it released most prisoners, it brought charges against 19 of the 'ringleaders' of the mutiny.[92] In March of that year, Parliament passed the Special Tribunals Act, which provided for trials of members of the police force, the prisons service, and the national service charged with mutiny and related offences.[93] The Act specified that the tribunals would be comprised of three officers, one judge and two appointed officers from the relevant services, and their decisions were to be based on a majority vote and could not be appealed or reviewed by any other court.[94] Subsequently, the government established a special court to try the accused mutineers. Chief Justice Windham led the proceedings with two officials from the military.[95] The trial of the mutineers resulted in five acquittals and 14 convictions. Though amendments had been made to the law to allow the convicted mutineers to receive very severe punishments, those who were convicted received relatively short prison sentences of five to 15 years, with most receiving sentences of ten years.[96]

Given the implications of the mutiny for the state and the significance of Tanganyika having to call on the British for help, as well as the personal shame Nyerere felt, he 'publically deplored the leniency of the sentences'.[97] The trial had attracted the public's attention and newspaper editorials also expressed frustration at the sentences, asserting that the crimes the 14 were convicted of 'merit much stiffer penalties than those awarded'.[98] Nyerere, despite his disappointment in the sentences, did not intervene, emphasising the importance of judicial independence in maintaining the rule of law and arguing that 'we must not allow even our disgust with the mutineers to overcome our principles'.[99] Thus, one key impact of the trial was that it was an early test of the independence of the judiciary and became an opportunity for Nyerere to reaffirm the role of the independent judiciary in the maintenance of the state.

The trial of the mutineers, however, had another effect on the judiciary: it drew attention to Chief Justice Windham and the colonial Bench. For Nyerere one of the most difficult elements of the mutiny episode was the need for help from Great Britain. That the trial of the mutineers had been led by the British Chief Justice meant that the British had both put down the mutiny and played a central role in deciding how the mutineers would be punished for their crimes, crimes which had severely threatened the stability of the independent state of Tanganyika. This state of affairs brought out a degree of discomfort in the government with the colonial judges on the Bench and highlighted the ongoing position of authority that colonial judges occupied.[100] Ronald Aminzade argues that the mutiny allowed Nyerere and opponents of Africanisation to 'move decisively against those who continued to press for Africanisation', because those who had mutinied had done so in part out of the desire to see British officers replaced by Tanganyikan Africans.[101] In the case of the judiciary, however, the trial of the mutineers may have helped propel changes to membership of the Bench, and particularly the position of Chief Justice.

The mid-1960s were a turning point for colonial judges of the High Court. Growing and mutual discomfort among colonial judges and the government resulted in the departure of the colonial judiciary during 1964 and 1965. One magistrate, who joined the High Court after they left, surmised that those who had left during this period 'were glad to be out'.[102] Though it is not known whether Windham chose or was asked to leave, it was clear to him on his departure that his successor would not be a colonial judge. One colonial official recalled that when Chief Justice Windham was asked who was coming out from England to replace him, he reportedly replied, 'I understand there is going to be a dark outsider'.[103] Windham and Law made preparations to leave, with Law writing a note for the incoming Chief Justice that pointed out the 'salient problems being handed over' and giving an overview of the state of affairs at the Court, which had been standard practice during colonial rule for outgoing judges to do for incoming ones.[104]

By the end of 1965 every judge who had been appointed to the High Court before the date of independence, except Justice Biron, had left the High Court Bench. Two returned to England, continuing to work in law-related roles, though not on the Bench.[105] Notably, Chief Justice Windham became the Commissioner of the Foreign Compensation Commission.[106] The other three went to other benches in Africa. Justice Law and Justice John Spry joined the Bench of the Eastern Africa Court of Appeal.[107] Though independent governments in the region chose to adopt the Court of Appeal as an extension of their national legal systems after independence, the Court essentially remained in its colonial form. At the time, the Court of Appeal's Bench was mostly filled with distinguished former colonial judges who were not yet at retirement age, but were advanced in age and would finish their careers as judges. Judges' lifestyles in Nairobi resembled those of colonial judges in Tanganyika in the early 1960s. The Court visited the territories under its jurisdiction on circuit each year, as it had during British rule. In their capacity as judges of appeal, they were able to serve as judges in Tanganyika again when the Court of Appeal came on circuit, but were distanced from internal events.

The third judge to join another Bench in Africa was Justice Laurence Weston, who had arrived in Tanganyika in mid-1961. He then left in 1965 to take up the post of Chief Justice of Botswana (formerly the Bechuanaland Protectorate) while it was still under British rule.[108] Once in Botswana he remained in the post for under three years, leaving in 1968 following Botswana's independence in 1966. While colonial officials in countries transitioning to independence could move to the remaining territories under colonial rule, as more and more colonies became nations there were fewer opportunities for colonial officials, including judges, to find employment overseas.[109]

From Colonial Magistrates to Post-Colonial High Court Judges

Departures of High Court judges made room on the High Court Bench for the promotion of remaining magistrates from the Overseas Service. The practice of promoting officers from lower offices to the High Court was the approach used during colonial rule and continued to be the model as posts opened on the Bench and in other senior legal roles. These officers were ready hands and the government did not yet have many other options.

The decisions of younger officers to remain in Tanganyika involved different considerations than those of High Court judges of advanced ages. Officers who were in the beginning stages of their careers in the early 1960s had the chance to go home and start a new career. Despite offers of enhanced compensation in Tanganyika, the prospects of a legal career in Great Britain—including one that could result in an appointment to the Bench—were much better for young legal officers than their colonial superiors. Some who left were actually able to return to the English and Scottish Bars. One former Crown Counsel in Tanganyika, Norman Macleod, became a judge in Scotland. He recalled that serving in Tanganyika had actually been 'a very good training ground for my experience when I came back to Scotland' as he had had more time in court than many of his contemporaries who had stayed in Scotland, which helped him excel when he returned home.[110] Even with possibilities of this nature available to younger officers, a few who were close to reaching the High Bench remained in the country. Two experienced magistrates joined the High Court from the magistracy between 1962 and 1964, J.K. Williams and Graham J.E. Reide. They filled the empty places on the Bench, but only served for relatively short periods, departing around the same time as the senior colonial judges.[111]

Between 1964 and 1965 three other men joined Biron, the last colonial judge still on the Bench. They had been magistrates under colonial rule and worked on contract with the new government in legal roles since independence. These new judges, Platt, A.E. Otto, and Liam B. Duff, had been part of the new crop of post-war magistrates that joined the Colonial Legal Service in the 1950s. While there is insufficient data on the three colonial magistrates, who became High Court judges in the mid-1960s, to generalise about this cohort's decisions to stay, interviews with Justice Platt have offered an insight into why he continued to work in Tanganyika and joined the Court in 1965, as well as how he perceived his position in the post-colonial state and the implications of this for the process of the decolonisation of the Bench.

Platt first came to Tanganyika in 1954 as a Resident Magistrate. During his tenure he served as an Acting Judge of the High Court as well as a judge on the 'Water Court', under Ministry of Lands, Settlement and Water Development, making decisions about the control of water among farmers and other landowners.[112] In 1960, at the age of 35, he chose to sign a contract to work for the Tanganyikan government rather than return to England and seek out other employment opportunities.[113] His decision can be explained in part by his background and life experiences, which motivated him to make a life outside Great Britain and instilled in him an interest in working in Africa.

Platt was born in Bangalore in 1925 to parents of British and American backgrounds working in the service of the Methodist church at a school opened for socially outcast children. During World War II he joined the Royal Air Force and served until 1947, when he went to England to study at St Peter's College, Oxford. After completing his course he went to the Middle Temple and read in chambers until 1954, when he was called to the Bar. Immediately after he applied to join the Colonial Legal Service, motivated by a desire to leave Great Britain and return to a life abroad, as he had had during his childhood. Platt had few personal attachments to England and did not have a family awaiting his return.[114] Though he was young enough to return to England and begin a second career, the opportunity to stay in Tanganyika and work for the new government provided the lifestyle he sought.

Platt was also motivated to work for the new government because he wanted to stay in Africa after the British left. He recalled that, during his time in the Royal Air Force, he had been based in Southern Rhodesia where he observed 'racial tensions' and was told not to communicate with Africans, which was in stark contrast to his experiences as a child of missionaries in India. This experience was 'seminal' for him, making him want to experience living in Africa after the end of colonial rule. Once Tanganyika achieved independence, Platt recalled that he felt he 'was looking into Africa at last' and was 'making African friends', who encouraged him to stay. Moreover, though Platt did not have an attachment to England, his years of legal training gave him a strong desire to see that the common law system continued to thrive. Especially after the attack on the rule of law and stability of the state by the mutineers in 1964 and the departure of the colonial Bench, he also felt that he 'really couldn't leave them [the government] in the lurch' by departing when there was no one else to take his place.

Though he had first come to the territory as part of the colonial government, Platt did not see himself as a representative of Great Britain or as a Tanganyikan. He recalled that he 'shed my British government' after independence and instead his 'policy was to be, not a Tanganyikan, but a person helping Tanganyika out'.[115] He would give advice when necessary, but recollected that he would 'couch it in a careful way' feeling that as an 'employee of new government, [he] must act as that not anything else'.[116] Instead of seeing himself as a former colonial official or as a citizen of Tanganyika, Platt regarded his role as a free agent of the common law in East Africa. This is illustrated by his service on other national High Courts in countries with common law traditions between 1973 and 1995 in Kenya and Uganda.[117] Platt did not hope to make a life in Tanganyika permanently, but recalled that he stayed in part out of a desire to see the employment standards at the High Court maintained until Tanganyikan Africans with the relevant qualifications could take his place. The magistrates that became judges during this period, like Platt, were the first step away from the colonial Bench of the early 1960s, but still remained at a distance from the new state.

'A Man All by Himself': Justice Biron

The last colonial judge to remain on the Bench after all his colleagues had departed in the mid-1960s was 'a man all by himself', not only because he was the last one on the Bench from his cohort, but also because of his unique role in the history of the High Court of Tanganyika.[118] Moshe Chaim Ephraim Philip Biron, known as Philip Biron, became a transitional figure for the High Court, helping it to evolve from its colonial origins into an institution of the new state. He was significant to this process because he, arguably, can be better understood as the first localised judge of the High Court of Tanganyika after independence rather than the last colonial judge. An examination of Biron's life in Tanganyika helps to account for how he came to be regarded by many members of the legal community as a Tanzanian rather than a colonial holdover.[119] It also shows how he managed to remain on the Bench of the High Court continuously until his death in 1981—almost exactly 20 years after Tanganyika's independence and more than a decade after the government had finished replacing all the other remaining colonial legal officials.

There is little documentary evidence on Biron's tenure in Tanganyika other than his judgments in the law reports and some surviving original case files. Nearly every person interviewed for this study, however, recalled Biron. What emerged from these interviews is a picture of a judge who became indigenised. Biron's tenure on the Court both symbolised and facilitated Nyerere's vision for the post-colonial High Court Bench.

Biron first came to Tanganyika in 1949 after being appointed a magistrate of the Colonial Legal Service. His activities in Tanganyika during his first decade there were typical of a colonial legal officer. He served as a resident magistrate in various locations around the colony and became an acting judge of the High Court when a seat became vacant in 1957. By 1961 he was a justice of the High Court (pictured in Fig. 6.2) and, like most of his colleagues, he decided to remain on the Bench after independence and work for the new government. Though he was similar to the other judges on the Bench in that he was in his early fifties and would have had difficulty starting a new career at this late stage in life, he appears to have had unique personal motivations for remaining in Tanganyika, driven by his background, outlook, and personal circumstances.

Biron went to Tanganyika as a servant of the British Empire, but he did not have a British background, nor was he directly connected to the Empire before joining the Colonial Legal Service. Instead, Biron was a naturalised citizen of Great Britain. Born in Yasliska, Rymanawie, Galicia (formerly part of the Austrian Empire, now in Poland) in 1909, Biron's family immigrated to England when he was a child.[120] He was Jewish and initially studied to become a Rabbi at Manchester Talmudical College and Yeshiva, but his career as a Rabbi was relatively short-lived.[121] He went on to study at Manchester University for an LLB, graduating with honours, and was subsequently called to the Bar from Gray's Inn. In 1941, after the outbreak of World War II, he volunteered to join the Royal Air Force and served until 1946 when he was demobilised. He returned to the English Bar briefly, practising for three years before joining the Colonial Legal Service in 1949, at the age of 40, which was at the top end of the age range allowed for first appointments. His motivation for leaving the Bar and joining the Colonial Legal Service is unknown, but after his departure from England with the Colonial Legal Service, he would never return to live in England again.

Though he had some extended family in England, Biron seems to have had little personal incentive to return to England after the independence of Tanganyika. There is evidence that Biron was legally married when he

Fig. 6.2 A portrait of Justice Philip Biron hanging in the High Court of Tanzania, Dar es Salaam, as of 2008 (Photograph of picture by A.K. Dewar and E.R. Feingold, Dar es Salaam, December 2008. Photos taken and reprinted with the permission of the photographers and the Court of Appeal of Tanzania.) The National Portrait Gallery holds another professional portrait of Biron from 1961 taken by the photographer Elliot and Fry. In the photograph, Biron is seated in the foreground and a framed picture in the background appears to be of him during his time in the Royal Air Force during World War II. The image is accessible on the National Portrait Gallery's website: http://www.npg.org.uk/collections/search/portrait/mw99116/Sir-Moshe-Chaim-Efraim-PhilipBiron?LinkID=mp75064&role=sit&rNo=0

joined the Colonial Legal Service, but the marriage ended for an unknown reason.[122] During his tenure as an acting judge of the High Court he developed a relationship with Margret 'Rita' Henderson Colville, a Scottish woman working as the Matron of Tabora Hospital.[123] The relationship, from the perspective of other members of the Overseas Service at the time, was unconventional as they were of different backgrounds and he was of a more advanced age than her. Nevertheless, they reportedly shared an 'extremely happy' life together in Tanganyika, marrying in 1958.[124] Biron began to establish a personal life in Tanganyika and after the end of British rule openly expressed a desire to remain there with Rita.[125] In addition, like Platt, Biron expressed a strong commitment to seeing the common law system survive the transition to independence in Tanganyika and dedicated himself to being a part of building the new system after the end of colonial rule.[126]

By 1961 Biron had reportedly disassociated from his previous life in Britain and began to assimilate to post-colonial life. Though he had been part of the colonial government and apparently 'played the British life', Biron openly criticised colonial rule after independence.[127] One interviewee explained that Biron came 'off his colonial high horse that he may not have liked being on anyway'.[128] His non-British background further aided his ability to distance himself from colonial rule. One Asian barrister put it simply: 'He wasn't British, so he wasn't colonial.'[129] Biron also openly expressed admiration for Nyerere, who was not only the political leader, but part of the ethos of post-colonial society in the country. Though he did not always agree with Nyerere's decisions and policies, Biron indicated that Nyerere's approach to governing had been a factor in motivating him to want to remain in Tanganyika.[130] Successfully integrating himself into Tanganyika's post-colonial and anti-colonial political environment, Biron 'meshed very well into the new system' and to younger Tanganyikan Africans he became more of a 'bridge from the past' than a representation of it.[131]

Biron's ability to assimilate was also facilitated by his personality, which helped him to cross social boundaries.[132] He reportedly had an 'irrepressible sense of humour' and an 'eccentric' and affable personality that one interviewee asserted 'served him in good stead' in his life in post-colonial Tanganyika.[133] He developed personal friendships with Africans, Asians, and members of the British expatriate community after independence and did not remain remote from younger advocates and judges, like Windham and most other colonial judges had.[134] Instead he invited them into his home for meals and visits and encouraged them to discuss their lives and views with him. Some felt so personally close to him that they described him as a 'father figure', while others recalled that he viewed his relationships with young Africans and Asians as having a father–son dynamic.[135] Though this could be interpreted as the same paternalistic attitude that many colonial officials held towards Africans during colonial rule, one of the first African judges described Biron as 'surprisingly prepared to learn' from much younger Africans, unlike many other colonial officials.[136] Biron's attitude and relationships allowed him to become not only familiar with but also a part of these communities, and enabled him to be perceived as more of a local person than an expatriate.

The indigenisation of Biron was critical to the decolonisation of the High Court. While Nyerere did not want all former colonial officers to stay in Tanganyika indefinitely, he needed the leeway to include a select few with expertise and the desire to help build the Tanganyikan state to continue serving in the government. Thus Nyerere argued against the consideration of race in determining who could become a citizen of Tanganyika.[137] Moreover, just as colonial judges were leaving in 1964 and 1965, Nyerere was trying to transition away from Africanisation and towards localisation without regard to race. Within this context, Biron became a symbol of what Nyerere was advocating. Legal scholar Patrick McAuslan, who was teaching law in Dar es Salaam in the 1960s, remarked that, 'Nyerere would have been very unhappy if he [Biron] left ... he was a terribly important figure for Nyerere' as he represented both Nyerere's desire to move away from racial politics and his promise to maintain the standards protecting the independence of the judiciary and the rule of law.[138]

Beyond the political importance of Biron, there is also evidence to indicate that Biron became personally important to Nyerere. Though Biron admired Nyerere, he also was known to speak openly and freely with him. The country's first African Attorney General recalled that Biron was 'one of the few expatriates who felt free enough to go and stand up to him [Nyerere], so they became friends'.[139] Biron could be 'stubborn' and long-winded in defence of his strongly held principles and decisions, according to some interviewees, but others presented a picture of a person who could be 'open-minded'and was therefore willing and able to debate issues with Nyerere, which few expatriates could do, especially in the late 1960s.[140]

On his own initiative, Biron also became a mentor for individuals preparing for legal careers in Tanganyika. In a letter to one young former colonial officer still working in Tanganyika in 1963, he congratulated the officer on passing the Bar finals, assured him that, 'you'll feel much better with that behind you than in front', and unconditionally offered his help to the officer.[141] More relevant to the decolonisation of the Bench was Biron's mentorship of young Africans entering the judiciary in the middle and late 1960s. As Tanganyikan Africans began to obtain legal qualifications and join the government service, they had little practical experience and guidance outside the classroom and few advocates to model their work after. One African judge recalled that Biron was 'easily accessible to young lawyers' and offered on-the-job advice to new judges, facilitating the work of the Bench.[142]

Biron's acceptance into post-colonial Tanganyika, however, was not limitless. Though he was regarded by many as a part of the national community, he was not African. While Nyerere wanted Biron to stay, he also wanted to see Tanganyikan Africans take up the majority of seats on the High Court Bench once they had sufficient training and experience. When Chief Justice Windham's departure was imminent and Nyerere did not have the option to replace him with a qualified Tanganyikan African, he also chose not to ask Biron—the most senior judge on the Bench—to become the Chief Justice. Instead, Nyerere invited a judge from a former British colony to take up the post. Like Biron, this judge and the other foreign judges of the period who are examined in the following chapter, became important transitional figures in the process of decolonising the Bench. Yet they did not become indigenised in the way that Biron did. Though Biron would never become Chief Justice, by staying in Tanganyika and becoming a local judge, he was a key part of the process of decolonising the High Court Bench.

Similar to Biron, one other former colonial official who joined the High Court Bench in the 1960s made Tanganyika his home after independence. Justice O.T. Hamlyn was first appointed a colonial magistrate in 1947 but, unlike Biron, left the Overseas Service for a period and never became a judge during British rule in Tanganyika. He remained in Tanganyika, however, and developed a life outside the expatriate sphere, which involved engagement in politics in Dar es Salaam and the establishment of a partnership with an African woman named Mary Ibrahim.[143] Hamlyn joined the High Court Bench for the first time in 1967 and served for three years. He was the last former colonial officer appointed to the High Court, but, like Biron, he was seen by members of the legal community as someone who had become localised. His appointment was therefore not one of a former colonial official, but of a local man.

Conclusion

The decisions of most colonial judges and many members of the colonial magistracy to stay on after independence were in large part motivated by personal calculations and preferences. While some senior judges aimed to finish their careers in the colonies before retiring to Great Britain, several younger magistrates chose to build their careers in Tanganyika and other independent states in the region. These individuals' decisions and the relationships they forged with each other and the Tanganyikan government allowed the Court to maintain the professional standards set out in the Constitution. It also gave the government time to bring Tanganyikan Africans into the judicial service and provided role models for them. The last colonial judge, Biron, became a key transitional figure in the process of the decolonisation of the Bench as he was a mentor to younger African judges and advocates who were a part of the legal system for the first time.

The continued reliance on the colonial Bench after independence was relatively short-lived, however. Increasingly out of sync with the changing post-colonial state, by 1965 all the colonial judges, except Biron, had departed Tanganyika. Their exodus initiated the next phase in the process of decolonising the High Court Bench in which the first appointments of Tanganyikan judges took place. The departure of the colonial Bench was not, however, the end of Tanganyika's reliance on foreigners to staff its judiciary. With too few Tanganyikan Africans to fill all the open seats, Nyerere turned to former British colonies in West Africa and the West Indies to find judges to join the Bench between 1964 and 1970.

Notes

1. The 1964 merger of the Republic of Tanganyika and the Republic of Zanzibar and Pemba formed one country called the United Republic of Tanzania. Tanganyika is used preferentially in this chapter, except where quoting from primary sources, because the majority of the chapter covers the period before the union.
2. The phrase Tanganyikan Africans refers to Africans living in Tanganyika. In this and the following chapter it is used to differentiate between Africans from Tanganyika and Africans from other territories or countries who were working temporarily in Tanganyika as judges and magistrates in the 1960s. The word local is used to describe both Africans and non-African judges and magistrates who were living in Tanganyika at the time of independence.

3. The phrase staying on was used during the 1960s to refer to the decision of colonial officials to work for the post-colonial government.
4. The terms Africanisation and localisation were used at the time, and are still used in the literature, to describe the methods for replacing colonial officials. They are defined in the next section.
5. See, for example: A.H.M. Kirk-Greene, *Britain's Imperial Administrators, 1858–1966* (Basingstoke, 2000), pp. 263–273, 241–259. Unlike Tanganyika, India had a large local Bar and filled its Bench with many local appointments: G. Austin, *Working a Democratic Constitution: A History of the Indian Experience* (New York, 2003), pp. 124–135.
6. J.A. Widner, *Building the Rule of Law: Francis Nyalali and the Road to Judicial Independence in Africa*, 1st edn (New York, 2001), pp. 61, 160; S. Stockwell, 'Ends of Empire' in S.E. Stockwell (ed.), *The British Empire: Themes and Perspectives* (Malden, 2008), p. 287. Stockwell also notes (p. 282) that there is still only a small body of literature on the impact of decolonisation on Britons who lived and worked overseas or on British culture.
7. The two judges are Chief Justice P.T. Georges and Justice A. Mustafa. On Georges, see: A. Fiadjoe, G. Kodilinye, and J.C. Georges, *Telford Georges: A Legal Odyssey* (Kingston, 2008); Widner, *Building*, pp. 57, 61–62, 70–73, 106–109, 114–115. On Mustafa, see: Unknown, 'Against the Shadows', *Awaaz*, 3 (December, 2005), pp. 14–25; F. Mustafa, 'Introduction: Re-issuing the Tanganyika Way: 1961–2009' in S. Mustafa, *The Tanganyika Way*, (Toronto, 2009), pp. v–x.
8. J. Iliffe, *A Modern History of Tanganyika* (Cambridge, 1979), p. 573.
9. Data from: W. Tordoff, *Government and Politics in Tanzania: A Collection of Essays Covering the Period from September 1960 to July 1966* (Nairobi, 1967), p. 194.
10. Iliffe, *Modern History of Tanganyika*, p. 573.
11. NACP, RG 59, 2029, 778.1315-2962, American Embassy Dar es Salaam to Department of State, June 26, 1962, p. 1.
12. Tordoff, *Government and Politics*, p. 195.
13. R. Aminzade, 'The Politics of Race and Nation: Citizenship and Africanisation in Tanganyika', *Political Power and Social Theory* 14 (2000), p. 73.
14. Tordoff, *Government and Politics*, p. 195.
15. J.K. Nyerere, *Speech by the Chief Minister, Mr. Julius Nyerere, in the Address in Reply to the Legislative Council, 19th October 1960* (Dar es Salaam, 1960), pp. 1–2.
16. Ibid., p. 1.
17. On the political pressure for Nyerere to support Africanisation over a policy of employment based on citizenship, see: C. Pratt, *The Critical*

Phase in Tanzania, 1945–1968: Nyerere and the Emergence of a Socialist Strategy (Cambridge, 1976), pp. 106–108; Tordoff, *Government and Politics*, pp. 194–195.

18. TNA (UK), Dominions Office (DO) 168/10, J.K. Nyerere, 'Africanisation', [exact day unknown] November, 1961, p. 2; Tordoff, *Government and Politics*, p. 195.
19. R. Sadleir, *Tanzania, Journey to Republic* (London, 1999), p. 249. A version of the letter is available in: J. Lewis-Barned, *A Fanfare of Trumpets* (Witney, 1993), pp. 113–115.
20. On the politics of and negotiations on the compensation scheme for British colonial officers in Tanganyika see: Tordoff, *Government and Politics*, pp. 199–200; Pratt, *The Critical Phase*, pp. 98–103. On compensation schemes throughout the British Empire, see: Kirk-Greene, *Britain's Imperial Administrators*, pp. 261–262.
21. On Tanganyika's dependent relationship to Great Britain after independence, see: Pratt, *The Critical Phase*, pp. 90–91.
22. The data on civil servants in Tanganyika is from: Ibid., p. 100.
23. On Kawawa's tenure as Prime Minister during 1962, see: Ibid., pp. 121–126; Aminzade, 'The Politics', p. 75; Tanganyika Africanisation Commission, *Report of the Africanisation Commission, 1962* (Dar es Salaam, 1963).
24. Ibid., p. 2.
25. Tordoff, *Government and Politics*, p. 198.
26. Ibid., p. 196; M. Longford, *The Flags Changed at Midnight: Tanganyika's Progress Towards Independence* (Leominster, 2001), p. 433.
27. Pratt, *The Critical Phase*, p. 108.
28. Tordoff, *Government and Politics*, p. 196.
29. Area commissioners served under the regional commissioners and were in charge of the districts that had previously been the responsibility of district officers.
30. J. Parry-Wingfield, *Letters from Tanganyika: A District Officer's Life in the Run-up to Independence*, [self-published by J. Parry-Wingfield, copy obtained by the author from J. Parry-Wingfield], (2006), p. 99.
31. Aminzade, 'The Politics', p. 75; Pratt, *The Critical Phase*, p. 125.
32. It seems that it was not just the Africanisation of government jobs but also the way in which members of the new government went about letting go of British officers that had a substantial impact on the feelings of some lower British officers. It may have caused some to leave more quickly than they otherwise would have. For instance, in 1962 the government Africanised the post of Commissioner of Police. Oscar Kambona, the Minister for Home Affairs, summoned the British officer serving as Commissioner of Police, Geoffrey Wilson, and told him that in a half

hour he was going to announce the Africanisation of the post on the radio and Wilson could either resign or be retired. One British officer still serving in Tanganyika at that time heard about Kambona's treatment of Wilson and recalled that he thought it was, 'a rather disgraceful way of a new minister dealing with his most senior European officer—it just shows no consideration, no respect at all. And if that is the kind of thing that is going to go on in the independent Tanganyika government, maybe I at the age of … 30 ought to be thinking of another career.' David Le Breton, interviews with author, Tonbridge, 8 June 2008; Tonbridge, 22 March 2009.

33. David Le Breton, interview with author, Tonbridge, 8 June 2008; Tordoff, *Government and Politics*, p. 200. On discomfort with this new arrangement among former colonial officials, see: Lewis-Barned, *Fanfare*, p. 97; Longford, *The Flags*, pp. 433–434; Parry-Wingfield, p. 112.
34. Tordoff, *Government and Politics*, p. 203.
35. As quoted in: J.M.M.H. Listowel, *The Making of Tanganyika* (London, 1965), pp. 416–417; Tordoff, *Government and Politics*, pp. 195–196.
36. J.K. Nyerere, *Tanzania Ten Years After Independence* (Dar es Salaam, 1971), p. 8.
37. Aminzade, 'The Politics', p. 54.
38. Tordoff, *Government and Politics*, p. 202.
39. Aminzade, 'The Politics', p. 54.
40. ARJ 1966, p. 1.
41. W. Twining, 'Legal Education within East Africa', *British Institute of International and Comparative Law in East African Law Today*, Commonwealth Law Series No. 5 (1966), p. 116.
42. Ibid.
43. Ibid.; Twaib, *The Legal*, p. 31. See also: J. Harrington and A. Manji, 'The Emergence of African Law as an Academic Discipline', *African Affairs*, 102 (2003), p. 124.
44. Twining, 'Legal Education', pp. 116–117.
45. Pratt, *The Critical Phase*, p. 93. The situation was hardly better in Kenya, which had only six African lawyers on the roll at independence. Widner, *Building*, p. 49.
46. Nyerere, *Speech by the Chief Minister*, p. 3. Emphasis added by author.
47. TNA (UK), CO 822/1970, 'Staff Circular No. 4 of 1961: Scheme of retirement benefits', 28 April 1961.
48. His position as judge was almost certainly his last official post, as it is listed as his final post in: *Who Was Who, 1981–1990: A Companion to Who's Who Containing the Biographies of Those Who Died During the Decade 1981–1990* (London, 1991), p. 694.
49. David Williams, interview with author, London, 17 March 2010.

50. Kirk-Greene, *On Crown Service*, p. 73; TNA (UK), CO 1017/555, W.D. Sweeney, 'Recruitment Policy, Tanganyika', July 1960, p. 1.
51. TNA (UK), CO 1017/601, K. Roberts-Wray to Lord Perth, 30 January 1960.
52. On the impact of the process of decolonisation on the career trajectories and lives of British colonial administrators, see: Kirk-Greene, *Britain's Imperial Administrators*, 263–273; A.H.M. Kirk-Greene, 'Decolonization: The Ultimate Diaspora', *Journal of Contemporary History*, 36 (2001), pp. 133–151; A.H.M. Kirk-Greene, 'Towards a Retrospective Record: Part I—What Became of Us?' *The Overseas Pensioner*, 84 (2002), A.H.M. Kirk-Greene 'Towards a Retrospective Record: Part II—on Reflection and in Retrospect, the Colonial Service Mind', *The Overseas Pensioner*, 85 (2003), especially p. 21.
53. Roberts-Wray, *Commonwealth*, p. 476; TNA (UK), LCO 2/6949, Oliver Lyttleton, circular to the Officer Administering the Government of [sent to numerous colonies], 26 June 1952.
54. TNA, 205/18/8, Oliver Lyttleton, circular to the Officer Administering the Government of [sent to numerous colonies], 5 January 1953.
55. TNA (UK), LCO 2/6949, Secretary of State for Colonies Oliver Lyttleton, circular to the Officer Administering the Government of [sent to numerous colonies], 26 June 1952.
56. TNA (UK), CO 850/260/4, Tanganyika Law Society to H. Cox, 3 May 1952, p. 1.
57. Some former colonial judges did open private practices in colonies where they served, despite efforts to prevent them from doing so, but none of the High Court judges serving on Tanganyika's Bench at independence opened a private practice in Tanganyika after leaving the Bench.
58. Patrick Ellis, interview with author, Bishops Stortford, 25 March 2009. No documentary or oral evidence has indicated that any of the colonial judges from this period served on the Bench in Great Britain after their careers ended in Tanganyika.
59. For a discussion of the Overseas Service Resettlement Bureau and data on resettlement of Overseas officers, see: Kirk-Greene, *On Crown Service*, pp. 105–107.
60. David Williams, interview with author, London, 17 March 2010.
61. Numerous interviewees expressed these sentiments. For example: Patrick Ellis, interview with author, Bishops Stortford, 25 March 2009; Norman Macleod, interview with author, Loch Winnoch, 25 May 2009; Harold Platt, interview with author, Graz, 30 January 2010.
62. Rosemary McCleery, interview with author, Templecombe, 23 April 2009.
63. Bryan McCleery, interview with author, Templecombe, 23 April 2009; Mark Bomani, interview with author, Dar es Salaam, 26 November 2008.

64. J.K. Williams, *Black, Amber, White: An Autobiography* (Worthing, 1990), p. 81; Harold Platt, interview with author, Graz, 30 January 2010. The Irgun was a Zionist paramilitary organisation operating in Palestine. Unknown, 'Sir Ralph Windham Obituary', *The Times*, 11 July 1980, p. 16.
65. D. Anderson, *Histories of the Hanged: Britain's Dirty War in Kenya and the End of Empire* (London, 2005), pp. 310–311. Though Anderson asserts that the Court was part of Great Britain's brutal response to Mau Mau, Law's reputation among his peers does not appear to have been tarnished by his involvement in the Court during this period. Anderson cites evidence that Law actually expressed concern over the treatment of suspects in Court who were injured and appeared to have been abused.
66. It should be noted, however, that not all colonial official and judges were comfortable with or participated in the British club scene. For example: Trevor Jaggar, interview with author, London, 17 June 2009; David Williams, interview with author, London, 17 March 2010.
67. Sadleir, *Tanzania*, pp. 181–182.
68. Tordoff, *Government and Politics*, p. 14.
69. Roland Brown, interview with author, London, 1 June 2010.
70. TNA (UK), DO 168/13, Dar es Salaam High Commission to Commonwealth Relations Office, 6 December 1963; *Dar es Salaam Club (Dissolution) Act 1963.*
71. TNA (UK), DO 168/13, Dar es Salaam High Commission to Commonwealth Relations Office, 6 December 1963.
72. Tordoff, *Government and Politics*, p. 201
73. Patricia Law, interview with author, Canterbury, 14 May 2009.
74. Roland Brown, interview with author, London, 1 June 2010.
75. Harold Platt, interview with author, Graz, 30 January 2010.
76. Cole and Denison, *Tanganyika*, p. 311.
77. TNA (UK), DO 168/13, British High Commission Dar es Salaam to Commonwealth Relations Office, 26 April 1963, p. 2.
78. This rationale for the Act was given by Vice-President Kawawa, as quoted in: J.S. Read, 'Minimum Sentences in Tanzania', *Journal of African Law*, 9 (1965), pp. 22–23.
79. Roland Brown, interview with author, London, 1 June 2010.
80. Cole and Denison, *Tanganyika*, pp. 312–313.
81. Read, 'Minimum', p. 24.
82. Harold Platt, interview with author, Graz, 30 January 2010.
83. Ibid.
84. S.B. Pfeiffer, 'The Role of the Judiciary in the Constitutional Systems of East Africa', *The Journal of Modern African Studies*, 16 (1978), p. 35.
85. C. Parkinson, *Bills of Rights and Decolonization: The Emergence of Domestic Human Rights Instruments in Britain's Overseas Territories* (Oxford, 2007), p. 232.

86. Roland Brown Personal Papers, Copenhagen, R. Brown, untitled and unpublished memoir, [emailed to author, accessed on 4 July 2010], Chap. 5: 'Making of the First Constitutional Conference: Part 2', p. 19. Parkinson gives a similar assessment in: Parkinson, *Bills of Rights*, pp. 234–235.
87. As there was no Bill of Rights during colonial rule, the exclusion of one does not appear to have had a substantial impact on High Court judges during the early 1960s in the same way as the closure of the Club and the implementation of the Minimum Sentences Act.
88. For accounts of mutiny, see: Listowel, *The Making*, pp. 430–440; Tanzania Peoples Defence Force, *Tanganyika Rifles Mutiny, January 1964* (Dar es Salaam, 1993); T. Lawrence and C. MacRae, *The Dar Mutiny of 1964: And the Armed Intervention That Ended It* (Sussex, 2007). On motivating factors, see: Aminzade, 'The Politics', pp. 78–79.
89. Harold Platt, interview with author, Graz, 30 January 2010. See also: Aminzade, 'The Politics', p. 79.
90. Lawrence and MacRae, *The Dar Mutiny*, p. 19.
91. J. Brennan, 'The short history of political opposition and multi-party democracy in Tanganyika 1958–1964' in G. Maddox and J.L. Giblin (eds.), *In Search of a Nation: Histories of Authority & Dissidence in Tanzania* (Oxford, 2005), p. 267.
92. Aminzade, 'The Politics', p. 79; Lawrence and MacRae, *The Dar Mutiny*, p. 201.
93. Special Tribunals Act 1964. On the implications of the Act, see: McAuslan, 'The Republican', p. 572.
94. Ibid.
95. Lawrence and MacRae, *The Dar Mutiny*, p. 201.
96. Ibid.; TNA (UK), DO 185/47, British High Commission Dar es Salaam to the Dominions Office, 11 May 1964.
97. Lawrence and MacRae, *The Dar Mutiny*, p. 204.
98. Unknown, 'Quality of Mercy', *The Nationalist*, 12 May 1964, p. 4.
99. J.K. Nyerere, 'Comment on the Mutineers' Sentences' in J.K. Nyerere (ed.), *Freedom and Unity—Uhuru Na Umoja: A Selection from Writings and Speeches, 1952–65* (London, 1967), p. 299.
100. Harold Platt, interview with author, Graz, 30 January 2010.
101. Aminzade, 'The Politics', pp. 78–79.
102. Harold Platt, interview with author, Graz, 30 January 2010.
103. Personal communication with former colonial official in 2009. Interviewee requested anonymity on this point.
104. Harold Platt, interview with author, Graz, 30 January 2010. Despite extensive searching by the author, these documents or any similar notes have not been located in public or private collections.

105. Justice Richard H. Murphy taught law at the Polytechnic of Central London after leaving Tanganyika. *Who Was Who, 1991–1995: A Companion to Who's Who Containing the Biographies of Those Who Died During the Period 1991–1995* (London, 1996), p. 396. Justice Lionel P. Mosdell was the closest to the British Bench, serving on a number of tribunals in Great Britain, including the Immigration Appeals Tribunal and Pension Appeals Tribunal. *Who Was Who, 1920–2008*; online edn., Oxford University Press, 'MOSDELL, Lionel Patrick', [accessed 28 October 2011].
106. *Who Was Who, 1971–1980: A Companion to Who's Who, Containing the Biographies of Those Who Died During the Decade 1971–1980* (New York, 1981), pp. 871–872.
107. Williams, *Black*, p. 157.
108. *Who Was Who, 1971–1980*, p. 846.
109. Stockwell, 'Ends of Empire', p. 286.
110. Norman Macleod, interview with author, Loch Winnoch, 25 May 2009.
111. Both appear to have left due to personal reasons, rather than in response to the changes discussed above. Williams wrote in his memoir that he returned to England because of the failing health of his mother. Williams, *Black*, 156. Reide apparently retired after having a stroke in Tanganyika, finding his work to be a strain on his health. Ibid., pp. 78, 122.
112. ARJ 1964, p. 2.
113. Harold Platt, interview with author, Graz, 30 January 2010. All the information in the following paragraphs on Platt is generated from the first interview, unless otherwise cited.
114. Platt married an Austrian countess from the Habsburg family in 1971.
115. Harold Platt, interview with author, Graz, 31 January 2010.
116. Ibid.
117. Ibid.
118. Ibid.
119. Multiple interviewees referred to him as Tanzanian. For example: Steven Bwana, interview with author, Dar es Salaam, 31 October 2008.
120. TNA (UK), Home Office (HO) 405/16557, Home Office Reference:—G. 9086, 20 January 1939. Biron was his mother's maiden name. His father's last name was Golditch.
121. *Who Was Who, 1981–1990*, p. 66.
122. The staff lists from the period indicate that he was married when he arrived in 1949 with a lowercase letter *m* next to his name. TSL 1950, p. 55. Multiple interviewees indicated that they were aware that Biron had been married in England and that that marriage had ended. For example: Harold Platt, interview with author, Graz, 30 January 2010.

123. Longford, *The Flags*, p. 429; R.J. Muya, interview with author, Dar es Salaam, 17 December 2008.
124. Longford, *The Flags*, p. 429.
125. Lameck Mfalila, interview with author, Dar es Salaam, 12 November 2008; Barnabas Samatta, interview with author, Dar es Salaam, 3 December 2008; R.J. Muya, interview with author, Dar es Salaam, 17 December 2008.
126. R.J. Muya, interview with author, Dar es Salaam, 17 December 2008.
127. Priyavadan Majithia, interview with author, Dar es Salaam, 5 December 2008.
128. Patrick McAuslan, interview with author, London, 6 October 2009.
129. Priyavadan Majithia, interview with author, Dar es Salaam, 5 December 2008. Ismail expressed similar sentiments describing his attitude as 'anti-colonial'. Mohamed Ismail, interview with author, Dar es Salaam, 3 December 2008.
130. Mark Bomani, interview with author, Dar es Salaam, 26 November 2008.
131. Lameck Mfalila, interview with author, Dar es Salaam, 12 November 2008. Similar sentiments were expressed by: Steven Bwana, interview with author, Dar es Salaam, 31 October 2008; Patrick McAuslan, interview with author, London, 6 October 2009.
132. Priyavadan Majithia, interview with author, Dar es Salaam, 5 December 2008.
133. Norman Macleod, interview with author, Loch Winnoch, 25 May 2009. Similar sentiments expressed in: Longford, *The Flags*, p. 429; Sol Picciotto, interview with author, Leamington Spa, 8 October 2009.
134. It should be noted that Biron was not uniformly admired by everyone in the legal community. Sentiments expressed by multiple interviewees, for example: Mark Bomani, interview with author, Dar es Salaam, 26 November 2008; Priyavadan Majithia, interview with author, Dar es Salaam, 5 December 2008.
135. Priyavadan Majithia, interview with author, Dar es Salaam, 5 December 2008; R.J. Muya, interview with author, Dar es Salaam, 17 December 2008.
136. Louis Makame, interview with author, Dar es Salaam, 19 December 2008.
137. Aminzade, 'The Politics', p. 70. It has not been possible to determine whether Biron actually became a citizen of Tanganyika or, if he did, when he gained citizenship. What is significant is that many in the legal community perceived him as Tanzanian and did not query his citizenship status during the interviews.
138. Patrick McAuslan, interview with author, London, 6 October 2009.

139. Mark Bomani, interview with author, Dar es Salaam, 26 November 2008. Similar sentiments were expressed by: Augustino Ramadhani, interview with author, Dar es Salaam, 12 November 2008; Robert Kisanga, interview with author, Dar es Salaam, 28 November 2008.
140. Kantilal Jhaveri, interview with author, Dar es Salaam, 16 December 2008. Some interviewees recalled that Biron gave very long judgments. For example: Harold Platt, interview with author, Graz, 30 January 2010. One of his judgments reportedly took 13 hours to deliver. Longford, *The Flags*, p. 242. Priyavadan Majithia, interview with author, Dar es Salaam, 5 December 2008.
141. Patrick Ellis Personal Papers, Bishops Stortford, M.C.E.P. Biron to P. Ellis, 7 September 1963.
142. Steven Bwana, interview with author, Dar es Salaam, 31 October 2008.
143. Kantilal Jhaveri, interview with author, Dar es Salaam, 16 December 2008; Shyanisingh Jadeja, interview with author, Dar es Salaam, 15 December 2008; Urmila Jhaveri, interview with author, Dar es Salaam, 16 December 2008.

CHAPTER 7

Foreign Judges and the Emergence of a Tanzanian Judiciary, 1964–1971

Beginning in 1964, the Tanzanian government began to fill the open seats on the High Court Bench with a combination of local and foreign judges.[1] Unable to appoint Tanganyikan Africans to all the openings, it filled a large proportion of the vacancies between 1964 and 1971 with black foreign judges from other former British colonies.[2] This chapter examines this phase in the process of decolonising the Bench and argues that the foreign judges served as a stepping stone between a colonial and a localised Bench.

There were numerous local Asian advocates who were qualified to fill the open posts in the judiciary, but only one joined the High Court Bench in the 1960s. This chapter assesses the government's decision to rely instead on foreign barristers to staff its judiciary. The government first used this approach in 1961, when colonial magistrates were departing and the government urgently needed to fill the open seats. Nyerere looked to West Africa for assistance and appointed Nigerians to the magistracy. Though he succeeded in hiring qualified barristers to fill the posts, the appointments often proved problematic because the Nigerians had difficulty adjusting to their duties and lifestyles in Tanganyika. Therefore, in 1964, when the colonial judges began to leave the Bench, Nyerere instead sought to hire judges from the West Indies, and filled a substantial portion of the open seats on the High Court Bench, including the post of Chief Justice, with West Indian judges. These appointments provided a visible

E.R. Feingold, *Colonial Justice and Decolonization in the High Court of Tanzania, 1920–1971*, Cambridge Imperial and Post-Colonial Studies Series, https://doi.org/10.1007/978-3-319-69691-1_7

change from the exclusively colonial Bench before 1964. Though the foreign judges were intended to be a temporary solution, they had a substantial impact on the Bench during their tenure and successfully resisted some of the early episodes of executive encroachment on the judiciary. Oral history accounts of the foreign judges—and especially Chief Justice Telford Georges—reveal the deep gratitude that many Tanganyikan and British officials felt towards this cohort. The celebratory or reverential tone of their remarks herein should be interpreted as both a reflection of their appreciation and as nostalgia for the collegial relationships they established with the foreign judges, rather than a verdict on the judges' service on the Bench or a value judgement about the decision to hire them.

Since 1960 the government had actively worked to give Tanganyikan Africans the training and experience required so that eventually the majority of the High Court Bench would be populated by them. It sent Tanganyikan Africans abroad for legal education and made efforts to bring the handful of qualified Africans into the magistracy and other government roles. This chapter explores the motivations of the first Tanganyikan African barristers to study the law and how they were able to gain legal qualifications. These men were brought into the magistracy and were promoted quickly through the ranks of the judiciary, with the first two reaching the High Court in 1964 and the third in 1969. One of the government's long-term goals, however, was to train its own lawyers in Tanganyika, allowing it to be self-sufficient and therefore no longer dependent on other countries to educate its citizens. Thus, a crucial element of decolonising the High Court Bench was the establishment of East Africa's first Faculty of Law in 1961 in Dar es Salaam and the employment of its graduates in the judicial service upon graduation in the middle and late 1960s. By the end of 1971 the government's efforts to bring Tanganyikan Africans into the judiciary resulted in a High Court Bench with a majority of Tanganyikan Africans, as well as other local judges, and the appointment of the first Tanganyikan African Chief Justice.

Asian Advocates and High Court Appointments

As seats became vacant on the High Court Bench in the mid-1960s following the departure of colonial judges, there were still too few Tanganyikan Africans with the qualifications to replace them. There were, however, Asian advocates with the necessary legal qualifications who could have been called on to join the judiciary. Nevertheless, Nyerere decided to invite barristers from other former British colonies to join the judiciary temporarily and fill the posts until more Tanganyikan Africans became qualified to join the Bench. Before examining the role of these foreign judges and the implications of this decision for the High Court, it is first necessary to explain why all, except one, of the experienced local Asian barristers with the relevant qualifications did not join the judiciary during the period when the government's approach to staffing was localisation.

There are three explanations. First, the relationship between the Asian and African communities was tenuous. There was a perception among some Africans that Asians had benefitted from the colonial policies that discriminated against Africans and, after the end of British rule, that the small Asian community wielded a disproportionate amount of power through their role in the economy.[3] McAuslan, who taught law in Tanganyika in the early 1960s, recalled that he observed 'a lot of undercover animosity about Asians' among Africans.[4] The Attorney General in the early 1960s, Roland Brown, recollected that 'Asian lawyers in Tanganyika were seen, perhaps quite wrongly, as an extension of the Asian commercial sector and accordingly not natural participants in the legal and political business connected with major constitutional changes.'[5] Moreover, Asian advocates were typically disconnected from African village life outside the main towns and, for this reason, McAuslan asserted that, 'average members of the party would not be happy with these people judging Africans'.[6]

Second, though there were a relatively large number of Asian advocates, few were 'outstanding' as the most successful advocates often worked in Nairobi, which 'dominated the law profession in East Africa'.[7] Third, it is not clear that many Asians would have wanted to join the Bench if they had been asked. Some of these advocates may have seen it as inappropriate given the political climate or, more practically, regarded the posts as undesirable because of the pay.[8] Local judges signing contracts directly with the government in the mid- to late-1960s had substantially lower salaries than those received by colonial judges during colonial rule and continued to receive immediately after independence due to the overseas additions on their basic salaries.[9] For those Asian advocates with profitable private practices, joining the government would probably have reduced their salaries and required them to leave or sell their practices.[10] Consequently, government work was likely regarded as undesirable for successful Asian advocates because it would have created financial difficulties for their families whose livelihoods depended on their income.

There was one Asian barrister, however, who was appointed to the High Court Bench in the mid-1960s. Abdulla Mustafa became the first judge of the High Court appointed from within the local legal community in Tanganyika, though he was not born in the colony. Mustafa was born in Hong Kong in 1916; his mother was a Chinese Muslim and his father was an Indian colonial civil servant.[11] As a young man he moved to Lahore and then colonial India to attend the Government College there.[12] From there he moved to East Africa, first living and working in Nairobi, before going to London to qualify for the English Bar at Lincoln's Inn.[13] When he returned to Nairobi he began his career as an advocate, but then in 1948 decided to move to Tanganyika where he opened a legal practice in Arusha called 'Mustafa and Zaffer Ali, Advocates'.[14]

During the decade that followed Mustafa worked outside of government service and politics, but in 1958 became known to Nyerere through his wife, Sophia Mustafa, after she entered national politics.[15] An elected member of the Tanganyika Legislative Council from the Northern Province, Sophia Mustafa's candidacy was supported by TANU and she and her family became politically and personally close to Nyerere during her years as an elected official. Through this connection, Abdulla Mustafa became a 'very respected adviser' to Nyerere, recalled one judge from the period.[16] His close relationship with Nyerere made him exceptional among the Asian Bar. Before his appointment as a High Court judge, Mustafa had already shown his willingness to offer his legal skills to the government when he served as the Secretary of the Presidential Commission on a One-Party State in 1964.[17] The Commission made recommendations for building a democratic one-party state, which were subsequently enshrined in the Interim Constitution of 1965.[18] Though Mustafa did not necessarily endorse all of TANU's political agenda—he was known for being fiercely independent from political influence on the Bench—he was able to maintain a working relationship with Nyerere.[19] Ultimately, Mustafa agreed to join the High Court in 1965 and once on the Bench, like Justice Biron, he became central to the work of the Court as well as to the advancement of younger judges, who regarded him as a mentor.[20]

Mustafa's appointment was in line with Nyerere's ideas about localisation and a multi-racial as well as multi-religious society. The appointment also illustrated Nyerere's willingness to bring Asians into government who were willing to work with TANU. His appointment was an important step in the decolonisation of the Bench. It was an exception, however, and did not precipitate the appointment of any other Asian advocates to the High Court Bench at the time. Instead, Nyerere looked outside of Tanzania to fill the vacancies in the judiciary.

Foreign Magistrates: The Nigerian 'Experiment'

Nyerere's strategy of inviting barristers from outside the country to join the judiciary on a contractual basis began with the magistracy when colonial magistrates started to depart in 1961. He initially sought help from West African nations that had previously been under British rule. Nigeria boasted relatively large numbers of African barristers in the early 1960s since Nigerian Africans had had greater access to law faculties in the region and in Great Britain than East Africans had experienced. Nyerere's decision to employ these men may reflect his commitment to pan-Africanist ideals and a belief that West African barristers could identify with Africans in Tanganyika by virtue of their shared experiences as Africans under British colonial rule. The arrival of the Nigerian magistrates during the phase of Africanisation was also motivated, according to Attorney General Brown, by the desire to 'have some black faces sitting on the Bench dealing with criminal cases'.[21] Thus the use of Nigerian magistrates was a type of Africanisation, but did not realise the inclusion of Tanganyikan Africans in the judiciary that the government sought. Nevertheless, their role in the administration of justice was a milestone because it broke with the colonial legacy of excluding Africans from professional legal roles. It also filled the growing void in the magistracy, thereby preventing it from grinding to a complete halt.

In 1962 the American Embassy in Dar es Salaam noted with interest that three 'experienced African resident magistrates are to be seconded to Tanganyika by the Nigerian government'.[22] The following year the Tanganyikan government appointed 14 more Nigerian magistrates and subsequently placed Nigerians in other legal positions, such as registrar and even acting judge when faced with vacancies on the High Court Bench.[23] For joining Tanganyika's legal system at a time of need the Nigerian barristers had generous contracts for their service, though this does not mean they were uniformly appreciated.[24]

After only a short period in Tanganyika the Nigerian magistracy came under attack by other legal officers. There was a growing sense among those in the higher ranks of the judiciary that the quality of these magistrates was low and 'that Nigeria was dumping either third rate or discredited people on Tanzania'.[25] The Attorney General recalled that the use of Nigerian Magistrates had been 'a disaster' for Tanganyika's judiciary.[26] One magistrate wrote about his observations of the Nigerian magistracy at the time asserting that

> the experiment [of using Nigerian Magistrates in Tanganyika] has not so far been a success. These men and their families have a sophistication which makes it difficult for them to find friends among Tanganyikans of whose backwardness and low standard of living they are openly despicable. The Nigerians insist on appointment to larger towns where they cling to the hope they may find some of the High-Life to which they are accustomed back home. With two notable exceptions their dissatisfaction with their conditions (despite their salaries being a cause of envy to their more experienced European and Tanganyikan colleagues) affected their work. Advice and guidance from these colleagues is not taken, nor is any serious attempt made to study the basic statutes which they are applying. This is shown by the tiring frequency with which their judgments and sentences in criminal cases are being set aside of revisional or appellate proceedings before the High Court.[27]

Despite problems with the use of Nigerian magistrates, many of these men remained in Tanzania for years. Then, in 1967, when the Republic of Biafra seceded from Nigeria, the Nigerian government decided it would no longer loan magistrates to Tanzania. In 1968 it recalled its magistrates from Tanzania with only a week's notice, creating a crisis for Tanzania's courts.[28] Furthermore, the Nigerian magistrates who identified with the new Biafran state were caught in the middle of the conflict. Tanzania was one of the few countries to recognise Biafra, and Nyerere disputed Nigeria's ability to summon these magistrates, arguing that although they had come to Tanzania in the early 1960s as Nigerians, 'they are now "Biafrans" and there could be no question of the Nigerian government recalling them'.[29] Nevertheless, most of the Nigerians did leave Tanzania in the year following their recall.[30]

Though the Nigerian 'experiment' had not lived up to Nyerere's hopes, he still brought in a select few West African judges to the High Court. The first was E.A.L. Bannerman from Ghana in 1964. Then, in 1970, G.C.M. Onyiuke from Nigeria was appointed to the High Court. There is little evidence available on Onyiuke's service in Tanzania, but there are some indications that he was a somewhat well-established legal figure before his arrival in Tanzania. He had served as chair of an important government commission investigating the massacre of 'persons of Eastern Nigerian origin in Northern Nigeria'.[31] Members of the legal community in Tanzania recalled that he was 'very able' and turned out to be the 'brightest of all judges that had come to us' from West Africa.[32]

The use of Nigerians in Tanzania's magistracy and High Court Bench succeeded in filling open posts in the magistracy until Tanganyikan Africans could take them over. The poor reputation of the Nigerian magistrates in early 1960s, however, may have motivated Nyerere to look to the British West Indies when he needed to fill the post of Chief Justice and other seats on the Bench in the middle and late 1960s, rather than relying solely on West Africa.[33] The islands were already a source for judges in other East African territories and from 1964 Tanzania began to fill open positions on the Bench with West Indians.[34]

Foreign Judges: Chief Justice Georges and the West Indians

Foreign judges from the British West Indies were crucial to the process of decolonising the High Court Bench because they filled the gap during the transition between the departure of the colonial judiciary and the appointment of a majority of Tanganyikan Africans. These judges overcame the colonial legacy of black barristers being excluded from the High Court Bench by occupying the Court's highest post of Chief Justice and more than a third of the Court's open seats between the middle and late 1960s. In these positions, the West Indian judges exerted a much greater influence over the development of the Court than the West Africans, especially Georges, who led the Court in the wake of the departure of the last colonial Chief Justice.

In a sense, foreign judges were like the colonial judges from the Colonial Legal Service. Most had served in other newly independent countries before coming to Tanzania or would go on to other countries after leaving Tanzania. One important difference, however, was that they were individual agents and did not enter Tanzania as part of an 'entrenched governing elite' as colonial judges had.[35] Instead, they had to navigate the political and social challenges they faced on their own.

Georges was the first judge to join Tanzania's High Court Bench from the West Indies and became the country's first non-white and non-colonial Chief Justice upon taking up his appointment in early 1965. He was the 'dark outsider' Windham had predicted and became a key transitional figure in the process of decolonising the Bench because he replaced Windham and served until the first Tanganyikan African judge became Chief Justice in 1971. Georges was born in Dominica in 1923 and earned a BA in Law in Canada in the early 1940s, avoiding England because of the outbreak of World War II.[36] After the end of World War II, Georges moved to England where he studied for the Bar finals, passing in 1949.[37] Georges then went to Trinidad, which would become his adopted home country, and practised law there for 13 years.[38] During his years at the Bar he came to the notice of Trinidad's Chief Justice who offered him his first judicial appointment as a judge of the Supreme Court in Port of Spain in 1962.[39] Only two years later, however, he left Trinidad's Supreme Court, accepting an invitation from Nyerere to become Tanzania's Chief Justice.

Georges was invited to join the High Court after meetings between Nyerere and the Prime Minister and Chief Justice of Trinidad. Nyerere asked if they had any judges that would be willing to come to Tanzania to replace Windham as Chief Justice, and Trinidad's leadership was enthusiastic about filling the post with one of its judges.[40] Thus, shortly after the meeting, the Tanzanian Solicitor General, Mark Bomani, travelled to Port of Spain to search for a judge. Georges' biographers assert that he was the last choice as he was the most junior.[41] Though Tanganyikan lawyer Leopold Kalunga speculated that the Prime Minister of Trinidad had specifically suggested Georges for the role because Georges had an interest in politics and the Prime Minister feared that if he became restless on the Bench in Trinidad he might become a politician.[42] Georges accepted Tanzania's invitation as he was apparently becoming 'bored' with court work and was able to bring his family with him to Tanzania.[43] Moreover, the position was an opportunity to move quickly to the top of a court. It was also a chance to leave Trinidad. McAuslan surmised that the country had become 'too small' for Georges and that he sought a 'slightly wider canvas'.[44]

The appointment of Georges 'was greatly lauded across the country' in Tanzania, but was received 'in silence' by the judiciary, as its members had never heard of Georges and did not know how he would react to the colonial Bench.[45] Upon his arrival, though, Georges was quickly welcomed into the legal community. Bomani recalled that he was 'just the right person, he settled down very easily and very quickly' and members of the Bar and Bench asserted that his intelligence and geniality facilitated his ability to develop friendships and loyalty among members of the Bench in a short period of time.[46]

Though Georges was welcomed to Tanzania, it was clear from the beginning that his position there was temporary. His biographers assert that when Georges first met Nyerere he 'asked the question whether, if he settled in Tanzania for many years and learnt to speak Swahili like a native, he would be regarded as a Tanzanian. The President replied unhesitatingly that he would not, because he was not a Tanzanian'.[47] Nevertheless, during his time in Tanzania Georges made efforts to relate to Tanzanians and learn about the country.[48] He studied Kiswahili, even though it was not the language of the High Court, so that he could converse directly with Tanzanians who did not speak English, rather than through interpreters.[49] Widner claims that he became so immersed in Tanzania that some described him as 'more Tanzanian than Tanzanians themselves'.[50] Georges (pictured in Fig. 7.1) succeeded at becoming accepted in a way his predecessor Windham had not been in post-colonial Tanzania, and although his acceptance was not complete, it gave him the personal and political capital to make some innovations to the Court.

One of Georges' most impactful innovations related to the process of decolonising the Bench was his initiation of meetings for members of the judiciary called the Judges' and Magistrates' Conferences.[51] The first of their kind in Tanzania, these conferences were an opportunity for members of the judiciary to 'reflect on their roles in the developing State in which they were no longer servants of the Crown and part of a larger colonial legal service'.[52] The conferences were also a forum for addressing problems in the magistracy and lower courts, and to monitor and enhance the quality of the work of the High Court. Moreover, judges working outside Dar es Salaam at High Court stations could become very isolated and disconnected from the rest of the Bench who interacted on a daily basis in Dar es Salaam. One foreign judge who was based in Mwanza recalled that one of the biggest challenges he faced was that 'you never see another judge'.[53] Therefore, these conferences offered an opportunity for members of the judiciary to meet one another, especially as there were new arrivals as well as departures each year.[54]

Georges was the only West Indian on the Bench in the mid-1960s until Philip L.U. Cross, known by his middle name Ulric, joined him in 1967. Cross was originally from Trinidad and had come to England to serve in the Royal Air Force during World War II. After being demobilised he

Fig. 7.1 A portrait of Chief Justice Philip Telford Georges hanging in the High Court of Tanzania, Dar es Salaam, as of 2008 (Photograph of picture by A.K. Dewar and E.R. Feingold, Dar es Salaam, December 2008. Photos taken and reprinted with the permission of the photographers and the Court of Appeal of Tanzania)

remained in England and was called to the Bar in 1949. Before coming to Tanzania, he had served in other African nations, holding legal roles in Ghana and West Cameroon.[55] Brown recalled that he was not only 'highly competent', but also 'very sensitive to how to handle difficult political situations'.[56]

Following the perceived success of the appointments of Georges and Cross, the government then appointed two more West Indians: Cecil Bramble and Earle E. Seaton. Though Seaton was from the West Indies, he had actually worked in Tanganyika as early as the 1950s. During those years, Seaton provided legal representation to Africans when they were engaged in high-level disputes that left the realm of the Local Courts and were handled in the magistrates' courts and High Court. Seaton was involved in a number of notable high-profile cases in Tanganyika. For instance, he represented the Wa-Meru community in their efforts to get the UN General Assembly to adopt a resolution recommending that 'the British return the Wa-Meru lands which have been taken away from them'.[57] In this case he was the intermediary between the African population and external legal and political institutions, which were difficult for Africans to gain access to during the colonial period.

Seaton's role in Tanganyika in the 1950s also had a direct impact on the decolonisation of the Bench: he became a role model for one man who would later become the third Tanganyikan African to join the High Court Bench. Louis Makame recalled being inspired by Seaton after observing him advocate for Makame's community in court. Seaton was able to win compensation for Makame's community in a lawsuit against a group of Europeans they accused of intentionally causing a bus accident that harmed several Africans. He recalled that Seaton's success in court 'made a very strong impression on me, *that lawyers could do things*'.[58] Seaton's advocacy for Africans in the British courts illustrated to Africans under colonial rule that it could be beneficial to engage in the British legal system, if they could obtain a legal education or the assistance of someone with the qualification.

The Position of Foreign Judges in Tanzania and Their Responses to Early Executive Encroachment on the Judiciary

The role of foreign judges on the Tanzanian Bench created an exception to the measures protecting the security of tenure of High Court judges provided for in the Constitution. This was briefly an issue of concern in relation to colonial judges on contracts during the phase of Africanisation between 1961 and 1964.[59] The appointments of non-local judges, however, were made with the understanding that they would serve briefly and only until local people were able to take up the posts. Therefore, the foreign judges who joined the Bench served on a contractual basis and both the judges and the government had the option to terminate the contract with six months' notice.[60]

There is no evidence, however, to indicate that any of the foreign judges who worked on contract in Tanzania had their contracts terminated prematurely and it seems that they felt they enjoyed security during their tenures. On this topic Georges himself said that there was 'nothing to indicate that overseas Judges feel that the possibility of their appointments being terminated is in any way a threat'.[61] Perhaps one explanation for this is that foreign judges were invited to Tanzania because the government needed them. The government stood to lose more than the judge if a foreign judge left, as he could return to his home country and rejoin the Bench or private practice, while the government would have been left without qualified officials to serve on the Bench. Widner asserts that foreign judges on African courts were generally 'more cautious than others' due to the contractual nature of their employment and their position as expatriates.[62] Yet a closer look at Georges' responses to early episodes of executive encroachment on the judiciary indicates that he was bold in dealing with Nyerere's actions that threatened the judiciary.

Georges served in Tanzania at a time of tremendous economic and political change. He arrived shortly after the transition to a one-party state in the 1965 Constitution and was Chief Justice when Nyerere read the Arusha Declaration in 1967, declaring Tanzania a socialist state.[63] The 1965 Constitution maintained the main provisions in the 1962 Constitution in relation to the independence of the High Court and judiciary, and the Arusha Declaration of 1967 did not have an immediate impact on the judiciary.[64] Yet the late 1960s was a period in which TANU and Nyerere consolidated their power in Tanzania. Thus, during Georges' tenure the judiciary was faced with some of the first instances of the executive threatening the independence of the judiciary and the rule of law in Tanzania.

Though Georges was a strong advocate for the independence of the judiciary and rule of law in Tanzania, he did not believe that required him to remain remote from Tanzanian society or the government's initiatives.[65] Rather distancing himself from the policies the government was pursuing, Georges was generally supportive of the government's initiatives, so long as they did not violate the role and independence of the judiciary. R.W. James and F.M. Kassam assert that Georges attempted to, 'forge a completely new relationship between the Bench, Bar, Society and Government—a relationship of inter-dependence … Mr. Georges attended most government and party functions and encouraged other members of the judiciary to follow suit'.[66] He also developed a rapport with Nyerere, on which he would increasingly rely in the late 1960s.[67]

As a foreign judge Georges was able to stand up to Nyerere during two of the earliest instances of executive encroachment after independence, and protected the judiciary from severe intrusions during his tenure.[68] First, Georges challenged Nyerere's actions in one instance in 1969 when his behaviour threatened to damage the independence of the judiciary through executive interference. In 1969 a Member of Parliament, Kasella Bantu, was arrested and accused of inciting a group of men in Tabora to attack a group of men they believed were stealing cattle.[69] Four men were killed during the attack and Kasella Bantu and others involved in the attack were arrested and brought before the magistrate's court in the area.[70] The magistrate released the accused on bail and the regional commissioner reported the situation to Nyerere. Nyerere, apparently furious at the magistrate's release of the accused on bail because of the severity of the crime, subsequently decided to detain the magistrate for not keeping the accused in detention. Georges learnt about the detention and confronted Nyerere, warning that he could not keep the magistrate in detention or punish him for the granting of bail. This was a violation of the procedures established in the Constitution and acts of Parliament, which protected judicial officers from this type of intervention by members of the executive. Nyerere ultimately agreed to release the magistrate as a result of Georges' intervention. The story of the detained magistrate in Tabora was retold by numerous interviewees not only as an example of some of the earliest instances in which Nyerere threatened the independence of the judiciary, but also as an example of how Georges was able and willing to successfully challenge Nyerere.[71] For this Georges was widely admired among members of the Tanzanian judiciary.

A second example of executive encroachment on the judiciary that Georges challenged during his tenure in Tanzania is the government's use of preventive detention.[72] Preventive detention, in essence, allows an executive or agents of an executive to detain people it perceives to have already committed or believes are likely to commit a crime without bringing charges against them in a court of law. In 1962 Tanganyika's Parliament passed the Preventive Detention Act, though laws had been in place during British rule allowing the colonial government to detain people without trial.[73] In the late 1960s and early 1970s the government began to progressively rely on preventive detention as a means of law enforcement. Its use became a point of contention between Nyerere and Georges in late 1969 and early 1970, when Nyerere attempted to justify law enforcement's use of preventive detention for a variety of crimes.[74] For instance, the government had used preventive detention in 1969 to hold 39 people it suspected were involved in a passport forgery ring.[75]

Georges openly objected to Nyerere's rhetoric on the use of preventive detention fearing that it could be used to fundamentally undermine the rule of law and the role of the courts in maintaining the rule of law. Georges asserted that 'the use of the Preventive Detention Act as a normal method of criminal law enforcement would run contrary to the ideals set out in the preamble to the constitution of the United Republic' and damage the judicial system in the country.[76] Georges was most concerned, however, that the government's use of preventive detention would 'set up alternative procedures, the exact nature of which would not be known beforehand'.[77] These could be contrasted with the procedures used in the Courts for dealing with this type of crime, which were already established and known.

Georges went further and commented more broadly on the state of law enforcement in Tanzania. He said it was necessary for Tanzanian police to 'learn more sophisticated methods of investigation and be more careful and thorough in their work'.[78] He believed that by increasing the sophistication of the police 'the argument for some other method of law enforcement [referring to preventive detention] would then disappear'.[79] In this debate Georges expressed his concerns as Chief Justice, but he also moved out of the judicial sphere to comment more broadly on the challenges facing the administration of justice in Tanzania.

When challenged by Georges about preventive detention, Nyerere tempered what he had previously said about the need for preventive detention in Tanzania, asserting that he was only advocating the use of the measure in a 'crisis situation'. Georges publicly accepted Nyerere's comments.[80] However, American embassy staff observing the debate later commented that it had been clear that Nyerere and Georges did not see 'eye to eye' on the matter.[81]

The debate between them is another example of Georges resisting Nyerere's use of measures outside those provided for under the law and reflects his growing concern that Nyerere was increasingly operating outside the law and interfering with the judiciary. These two issues also illustrate that Georges, as a foreign judge, felt that he was in a position to confront executive encroachment on the judiciary and also was successful in abating the impact of Nyerere's actions on the judiciary during his tenure.

The First Tanganyikan African Judges

Though 1964 was noteworthy due to the appointment of Georges, the arrival of the first two Tanganyikan Africans at the High Court that same year was an even more significant milestone in the process of decolonising the Bench. Their appointments marked the end of the exclusion of Tanganyikan Africans from the High Court Bench and made progress towards a Bench that reflected and relied upon the local population. These men were among the very small number of Africans who were able to leave Tanganyika and gain legal qualifications abroad during the late colonial era and early independence period. In the 1960s nearly all of those in Tanganyika with legal qualifications were brought into government service, some of whom would quickly become the first Tanganyikan Africans to join the High Court Bench.

The first Tanganyikan African judges of the High Court were a relatively homogenous group.[82] Nearly all the Africans educated in the law in Tanganyika before and shortly after independence came from three secondary schools in Tanganyika, the most famous of which was the St. Mary's Tabora Government School.[83] Opened in 1925, it was modelled on a British public school and was created to educate future chiefs.[84] By 1935, though, candidates for the school gained entrance though an exam, which was open to 'gifted commoners' and was no longer only for the sons of chiefs and headmen.[85] The two other schools that the members of this group came from were St. Francis School in Pugu, a Catholic school, and Minaki (also known as St. Andrews College), an Anglican school. Tanganyika's first lawyers were talented students who were first educated at mission or government primary schools and then attended these secondary schools in the late 1940s and 1950s. During their time at these boarding schools, the students from this cohort developed close relationships with one another and with other classmates who would enter political leadership roles in Tanganyika during the transition to independence.[86] The programmes at these secondary schools enabled students to compete for places at Makerere in Kampala, Uganda, and other programmes abroad, making them part of an educational elite in the region.

Students' attendance at these schools was not only linked to their intellectual abilities, but also somewhat to their religion. As Christian mission schools provided a large share of primary education in Tanganyika and two of the secondary schools discussed above were Christian institutions, the relationship between higher education and religion in colonial

Tanganyika created a narrow path towards the possibility of the legal education that was a prerequisite for joining the Bench after independence.[87] Though Christians made up less than one third of the population of Tanganyika in the 1960s, the first three Tanganyikan African judges to join the Bench were Christians, as were the majority of those who would join in the 1970s.[88] Though not all from privileged backgrounds, the boys that attended these schools can be understood as 'elites' or individuals with agency who, as a social group, helped shape the process of decolonisation.[89]

The first Tanganyikan African barristers chose to pursue a legal education over other academic paths more readily available to them. Justice Makame was motivated to become a lawyer out of concern for the inability of Africans to advocate for themselves and their communities. He recalled another childhood incident involving the destruction of his father's farm by a timber company in which he remembered thinking to himself: 'maybe if I become a lawyer … I might be able to help'.[90] Others simply found the law to be the subject most appealing to them, or developed a desire to study law while they were students.[91] Some were encouraged by representatives of TANU to study the law when they visited educational institutions in order to motivate gifted students to obtain degrees and use their education to help build the future independent state of Tanganyika.[92]

Those who wanted to gain a legal education had to be extremely committed to it over other, more accessible, educational paths. The attitude among some British officials and educators that Africans could not become lawyers initially discouraged Robert H. Kisanga, who became a judge in 1970, from studying law for his first degree. While he was studying for his A-levels at Makerere in the late 1950s, a faculty member told Kisanga that he 'wouldn't think of being represented by an African' in Court when Kisanga expressed an interest in leaving Makerere for an institution that offered a programme in law.[93] As a result, instead of leaving Makerere Kisanga spent more than three years there studying economics. It was not until 1961, when representatives from the Tanganyika government visited Makerere and offered scholarships to Tanganyikans who wanted to study law abroad, that he sought and was awarded a scholarship to study for his LLB in Birmingham. He was later called to the Bar at the Middle Temple in London before returning to Tanganyika in 1965.[94] Thus the Tanganyikan Africans that were able to join the Bench in the 1960s had had to fight for access to legal education. Only those who were highly committed and prepared to assert that they were capable of becoming lawyers, in some cases in the face of cynicism and discouragement, were able to manoeuvre through the barriers and find their way to law programmes abroad.

Those students who were able to go abroad to study the law went to either England or India. To finance their education they relied on scholarships from a variety of sources, as virtually no Tanganyikan African families had the resources to finance their children's education abroad. There were a small number of scholarships from local organisations, while others received scholarships from the Indian government, which offered educational funding to some countries in Africa as part of their development aid. There were also a small number of scholarships from the British government in the years preceding independence. Finally, as shown in the description of Kisanga's background, around the time of independence the Tanganyikan government began to offer scholarships to Tanganyikan Africans enabling them to study law abroad.

India received a relatively large number of African students from Tanganyika in a variety of disciplines in the 1950s. John Malecela, a Tanganyikan politician who studied in India in the late 1950s, recalled that many in the community of African students in India shared aspirations to use their skills to support their countries as they emerged from colonial rule.[95] Augustino B. Saidi, also called by the name Augustine, who was one of the first two Tanganyikan Africans on the Bench and the first to become Chief Justice of the High Court, also obtained his degrees in India. He was born near Mount Kilimanjaro in 1929, and after completing his secondary education received funding from the Kilimanjaro Native Cooperative Union to support his education in India.[96] Though Saidi was a practising Catholic, he earned his BA, LLB, and MA at Aligarh Muslim University.[97] Saidi was, according to one of his contemporaries in India, 'a very serious student' and his professors at Aligarh considered him to be an exceptional student.[98] One professor in the Department of Law at Aligarh described him as 'a brilliant and industrious student keenly devoted to his studies and possessing considerable legal acumen'.[99] A professor from the Department of Political Science who taught him proclaimed that he was 'one of the very best students ... during my thirty-five years' service at this University'.[100] His high level of education and achievement made him a desirable candidate for the Bench. He returned to Tanganyika in 1957 after a short period in chambers in India, and in 1961, after briefly working as an advocate in Moshi, he joined the magistracy. A newspaper interview with Saidi credits his relationship with national leaders as motivating him to join the magistracy, becoming one of the first Tanganyikan Africans to hold the post of resident magistrate.[101]

Not all of the Tanganyikan Africans with legal qualifications would join the Bench or go directly into government service, however. Some went into private practice or worked for the government of Tanganyika in other roles. Neither of the two African advocates on the roll at independence, Juma Mawalla and Humphrey Noel Z. Mkondya, known as Noel Mkonyda in Tanganyika, would become High Court judges.[102] Mkondya studied in India, earning his LLB at the same time and university as Saidi.[103] He completed his studies in 1957 and went back to Dar es Salaam, but after difficulty finding an advocate to train him in Tanganyika, Mkondya went to India once more to prepare for a career as an advocate. In 1959 he returned to Tanganyika to look for work and was employed in various clerkship roles in Dar es Salaam. Shortly before independence he enrolled as an advocate, but then went back to work for the government as a deputy town clerk. He would go on to spend most of his career as a lawyer in government agencies, but not become a member of the Bench.

Though Saidi never went to England for legal training, a majority of Tanganyikan Africans who joined the High Court Bench in the 1960s and early 1970s had attended British institutions. For example, Mark P.K. Kimicha and Makame, who joined the Bench in 1964 and 1969 respectively, both qualified for the British Bar. Tanganyikan Africans who studied in England also filled the top executive legal positions in the Tanganyikan government. Most of those who studied at British universities earned LLBs and then were affiliated with one of the Inns of Court, before qualifying as British barristers. Bomani qualified for the Bar from Lincoln's Inn in 1962 and had a short career in private practice in Tanganyika before joining the government, first as Solicitor General and then as the first African Attorney General in 1965.[104] Though the opportunity to join the Inns of Court was a rare privilege for Africans from East Africa, the time spent in England preparing for the Bar presented its own difficulties. Notably, there were few East Africans at the Inns of Court. One former colonial officer who continued to work with Tanganyika on developing scholarship schemes recalled observing 'how lonely life could be for a young African student far from home in a strange land and cold climate, in every sense of the word'.[105] After completing the requisite dinners and exams at the Inns, Kimicha and Makame returned to Tanganyika and worked in the magistracy. Makame recalled that when he entered the magistracy there were so few Tanganyikan Africans working as resident magistrates that people assumed he was Nigerian because 'most people had never seen a Tanzanian professional lawyer'.[106] These barristers were quickly promoted and found themselves in relatively senior roles at young ages and within a few years of beginning to work for the government.

The two Tanganyikan Africans who reached the High Court in 1964, Saidi and Kimicha, were given the title Associate Judge, a new position created under the Magistrates' Courts Act. The purpose of this 'hybrid' position was to hear appeals generating from the newly created Primary Courts, but with the powers of a regular High Court judge.[107] The role was only in use for a short time and was abolished only months after Saidi and Kimicha filled it, and both associate judges became the Court's first Tanganyikan African judges. Saidi's appointment, which was roughly simultaneous with Kimicha's initial appointment to the Bench, was considered the first appointment of an African 'to the higher Bench in both East and Central Africa'.[108] Their appointments broke down the barrier to the High Court Bench that had been in place since it began its work in 1921.

The rapid promotion of these men was part of the process of decolonising the Bench. The government was anxious to see Tanganyikan Africans on the High Court Bench for the first time, so it promoted Saidi and Kimicha to the High Court as soon as they had gained some experience at the senior levels of the magistracy. Yet the government also wanted these young judges to help the country by linking the court system in the mainland to the courts in Zanzibar after the Union in 1964. Therefore, both Saidi and Kimicha were sent to serve on the Bench in Zanzibar for relatively short periods between 1965 and 1971; Saidi served as Acting Chief Justice of Zanzibar, a role that would prepare him for his appointment as Chief Justice of the High Court in 1971. The alternating transfers of Saidi and Kimicha usually left the High Court with only one Tanganyikan African judge at a time until 1969, when the government appointed Makame, making him the third Tanganyikan African member of the Bench.

Localisation Through Legal Education: The Faculty of Law, Dar es Salaam

In addition to bringing the first Tanganyikan African barristers educated abroad into government service, the Tanganyikan government sought to train its own lawyers who could serve in the various legal roles in the government, including on the High Court Bench. The establishment of a college, with a Faculty of Law, was part of Nyerere's vision for a post-colonial Tanganyika that would become self-sufficient, no longer needing to rely on the former colonial power or any other non-African country to educate the people it needed to run its government.[109] The opening of the Faculty of Law in 1961, the first faculty in the country, was one of the government's earliest measures towards decolonising the Bench. It would not be until almost a decade later, however, that lawyers trained at Tanganyika's Faculty of Law would join the High Court Bench, and then eventually come to lead it.

The idea of opening a Faculty of Law in Tanganyika is typically traced to a British committee, under the leadership of Lord Denning, established to examine legal education for students from Africa in 1960.[110] One of the Committee's recommendations in its report to Parliament, published in January 1961, was that a Faculty of Law should be set up in Tanganyika.[111] The intention was to give Africans greater access to legal education in Africa, and to develop law programmes that would be more relevant to the African context than the programmes in England. Within weeks of the publication of the Committee's recommendations Tanganyika established a Provisional Council for a University College of the University of London to be set up in Dar es Salaam.[112] The government planned to eventually have multiple faculties and affiliate its University College with the colleges in Kenya and Uganda to form a federated University of East Africa, but it was not slated to operate until 1963/4. Nyerere wanted to open multiple faculties in Tanganyika, but the limited resources in the region prevented the duplication of programmes with the colleges in Kenya and Uganda, so Dar es Salaam started with only the Faculty of Law.[113] Therefore, the government intended the Faculty of Law to serve not only Tanganyika, but the whole of East Africa, and possibly Central Africa as well.[114]

William Twining, one of the Faculty of Law's first lecturers, recalled that 'everything was done at a terrific rate', as the Tanganyikan government scrambled to find a location for the College, hire lecturers to teach in the law programme, and make arrangements for its first students.[115] The Faculty started with three members: an Australian Dean, A.B. Weston, and two young British lecturers, Twining and McAuslan.[116] The three men met each other for the first time and held the Faculty's initial meeting on a park bench in Russell Square in London in the summer of 1961.[117] Twining recalled that although the degree programme was under the supervision of the University of London, it gave the Faculty of Law a lot of freedom to develop a syllabus appropriate to the East African context.[118] As they built the programme from scratch (a three-year LLB), they had the dual responsibility of preparing students to pass the London law exams and to serve in their national governments after completing their degrees, rather than open private practices.[119] The faculty members set about developing courses and collecting materials while simultaneously conducting original research into the legal systems of East Africa that their students had been living under and would work in after completing their degrees.[120] Described by one of their academic contemporaries, Terrance Ranger, as a 'very bright young bunch', these lecturers and the lecturers who joined them in the years that followed would produce some of the seminal legal and historical research on the legal systems of East Africa that remain the foundational texts in the field today.[121]

The College held its opening ceremony in October 1961, within ten months of the Denning Committee's recommendation for its establishment, and less than two months before independence. At the ceremony Nyerere said that the College had 'started in a rush';[122] one visible result of which was that the College did not have its own accommodation. Instead, it operated out of a TANU building on Lumumba Street in central Dar es Salaam.[123] For his role in the founding of the Faculty of Law, Denning became 'almost every law student's role model', according to Justice Cross, who would later become Dean, and the students named the college's law journal and law society in his honour.[124] In 1964 the College moved to a new site, University Hill, outside central Dar es Salaam, where the University of Dar es Salaam, founded in 1970, currently stands.[125]

The first class in 1961 had only 14 students, seven from Tanganyika, four from Kenya, and three from Uganda.[126] Like the Africans who had studied the law abroad, the law students in Dar es Salaam were gifted—the 'crème de la crème'.[127] McAuslan recalled that despite their different backgrounds, the students had a sense of camaraderie and 'realised they were pioneers', as the first African law students in the region.[128]

Upon graduation the law students entered government service in Tanzania, drastically increasing the number of Tanganyikan Africans working in the judiciary and in legal roles in the executive. Though they were required to work for the government, they were given some choice in their roles. Most chose to join the magistracy or became state attorneys in the Attorney General's chambers.[129] As with the Tanganyikan African barristers educated abroad, these graduates were promoted rapidly, despite having little experience outside the classroom.[130] Two students from the first intake who graduated in 1964, Musa H.H. Kwikima and Z.N. El-Kindy, became the first students of the Law Faculty to join the

High Court Bench in 1970, less than seven years after graduating. Another notable member of the first class was Julie Manning. She became the first female judge of the High Court Bench in 1974, only a decade after graduating.[131] Manning's appointment was an important milestone in the history of the judiciary and it reflects the historic exclusion of women from legal education and employment in Great Britain and former British colonies, as well as the gender imbalance of Tanzania's nationalist project of the 1960s and 1970s.

Though many of the Faculty's graduates would become important figures on the Bench, in government, and at the Bar in Tanzania and throughout East Africa, one of the Faculty's students had the distinction of being the first African educated at home to be appointed Chief Justice in Tanzania. Barnabas A. Samatta was in the third intake of law students in 1963 and was identified early by his lecturers as 'one of the brightest'.[132] After he graduated in 1967, he worked as a state attorney and was promoted to become Director of Public Prosecutions in 1972.[133] He was appointed to the High Court Bench in 1976 and in 2000, after nearly a quarter of a century on the Bench he became the third Tanganyikan African Chief Justice, after Saidi and Francis L. Nyalali.[134]

By the early 1970s the graduates from the Faculty of Law began to dominate the legal community. Since these students had studied together, they established close relationships with each other and had networks of classmates. This new network created a division between the Tanganyikan African judges who were educated abroad and were first in the government, and those who come from the locally celebrated Law Faculty. One of the first Tanganyikan African High Court judges, who was educated in England, Kisanga, recalled that he and members of his cohort were

> at a disadvantage in that we were out of touch with the bulk of the rest of our colleagues ... We suffered because unlike people who were trained here, when we went to an office ... you found that you were contemporaries but were not in the same place, so you were strange. You couldn't expect friendship and cordiality from them ... I personally suffered from them. I think I continued to suffer throughout my career in public service.[135]

The division between Africans trained in the law abroad and at home indicates the significance of the founding of the Faculty of Law for the decolonisation of the Bench. The entrance of the Dar es Salaam students into the legal system was the realisation not only of Tanganyikan Africans' participation in the administration of justice at the highest level, but also of Tanzania's ability to maintain its Bench without any external assistance, particularly from British institutions. As McAuslan put it in 1980, 'the legal establishment then is not just Africanised ... but Dar es Salaamised'.[136]

The Dynamics of a Diverse Bench

Between 1964 and 1969 the Bench was approximately one third former colonial judges and magistrates, one third foreign judges, and one third local Asian and African judges (as shown in Fig. 7.2). The diversity of the High Court Bench during this period made it different from other government institutions in the post-colonial state, which were staffed almost exclusively by Tanganyikan Africans by the late 1960s.

The combination of local and foreign judges brought together individuals of wide-ranging backgrounds with a variety of experiences and perspectives. Yet the differences in background did not prevent the

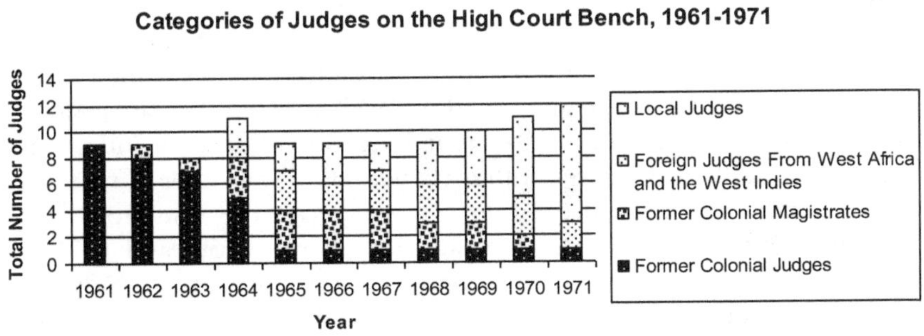

Fig. 7.2 Chart showing categories of judges on the High Court Bench, 1961–1971. (Data compiled from: ARJ 1961–1967 & 1970–1971, TSL 1961–1964, and the Law Reports from the Court of Appeal for Eastern Africa from 1961 to 1971. The numbers of judges are approximate because some served for parts of a year due to their date of appointment or retirement and some magistrates became acting judges temporarily to fill vacancies. The judge with the full appointment for the majority year is counted here where it was possible to determine, even if another judge from another category served as an acting judge in his place temporarily. It should also be noted that the increased number of judges on the Bench in 1964 resulted from the appointment of two Tanganyikan African judges as associate judges. This is only relevant for 1964, as the post was abolished within the year and the two associate judges became full judges of the High Court.)

development of close, though complex, relationships between individual judges. What bound them together was that they were all trained in the British common law tradition, having qualified as barristers, most at the Inns of Court in London. When asked whether he felt there were differences among the judges on the Bench, Cross, a foreign judge, asserted 'we were all English lawyers', and whatever differences in background existed, their shared legal backgrounds mattered most in their interactions.[137] Georges similarly stated that there was a 'brotherhood of professionalism' not just among judges but also among magistrates in the lower courts.[138] Moreover, the judges of the 1960s were all committed to seeing the common law system survive. Though more than half of these judges had been colonial subjects, they did not regard the common law as simply a tool of British rule, but as a legal system that could be a central feature of an independent democratic state. Therefore, the close relationships between some of these judges can be best understood through the lens of lawyerly culture and the camaraderie of a professional community, rather than as representative of the prevailing race relations of the period.

As indicated above, some of the older and more experienced judges, like Biron, Mustafa, and Georges, became mentors for younger and less experienced judges, like Cross and Makame, among others. One Tanganyikan African judge appointed in 1973 asserted that 'in a way we owe them a lot of gratitude … we relied very much on their judgments, and even ethically … so to speak they trained us'.[139] This type of reverence for the senior members of the Bench was expressed in numerous interviews with African magistrates and judges from the 1960s and 1970s.[140] Though there was a large range of age and experience among judges on the Bench, oral evidence also indicates that the relationships between younger and older judges were not as hierarchical as one might expect. Justice Platt recalled that, at times, judges from different age groups worked together to reason cases.[141]

The dynamics of this diverse Bench, however cordial and cooperative they were at times, were not without tensions.[142] Yet the schisms in relationships between members of the Bench did not generate from their varied backgrounds per se, but more from their differing views on new government policies, the role of the judiciary in the developing state, and its responses to challenges it began to face in the late 1960s. A noteworthy difference between Tanganyikan African judges and foreign judges was that the foreign judges, like Georges, were able to remain outside the political fray and TANU affiliation, perhaps making it easier for them to confront Nyerere and other politicians who attempted to encroach on the independence of the judiciary in the late 1960s, as examined above. This was a more daunting challenge for some of the first Tanganyikan African judges, particularly Saidi, who was close to national leaders and was tasked with leading the Court in the early 1970s, when the executive and its policies were increasingly encroaching on the judiciary.

The Appointment of Chief Justice Saidi

Between 1970 and 1971, the localisation of the Bench dramatically accelerated. The government's efforts to train Tanzanian lawyers and bring those with training into government had resulted in the appointment of many more local judges on the Bench. In 1971 the Bench was 75% Tanzanian, most of whom were Africans. The judges appointed during 1970 and 1971 expanded the size of the Bench and filled the seats of some of the key figures who had led the judiciary during the 1960s.[143] Many of the departing judges moved on to other roles in the region; Mustafa was promoted to represent Tanzania on the Court of Appeal for Eastern Africa in 1969, Cross became the Dean of the Faculty of Law in 1970, and Platt briefly worked in the Attorney General's chambers between 1970 and 1972, before joining the Bench in Kenya in 1973. The only foreign and colonial judges remaining on the Bench in 1971 were Onyiuke, Bramble, and Biron. Onyiuke was the final foreign judge to join the Bench in 1970 and would only stay for approximately four years, departing in 1974 with Bramble. Biron would spend the rest of his career in Tanzania as a member of the High Court Bench.

The most significant departure was the retirement of Chief Justice Georges, however, who returned to the Bench in Trinidad in 1971.[144] Having served as Chief Justice since 1965, he had become a central figure in the Tanzanian government and a stalwart of the Bench, not only defending it from executive encroachment, but also engaging with Nyerere and his government's policies rather than remaining remote, as shown above. An American embassy staff member observed that Georges' departure was a bittersweet occasion for Tanzania:

> Tanzanians are undoubtedly pleased and proud to have one of their own as Chief Justice. Many, however, regretted Chief Justice Georges' departure. He was widely respected in Tanzania for his hard work, fairness and dedication to the ideals of the nation. Georges leaves behind in Tanzania an outstanding reputation as a jurist.[145]

In preparation for his departure, Georges apparently attempted to secure the appointment of another foreign judge, Seaton, in order to give the Tanganyikan Africans on the Bench time to gain more experience and the government a larger pool of candidates to eventually select a Chief Justice from.[146] Georges was unsuccessful in convincing Nyerere to choose a non-Tanzanian, however. The country was preparing to mark a decade since the end of British rule and Nyerere was anxious to see a Tanzanian Chief Justice leading the Bench.

The choice of Saidi out of the small pool of Tanzanian judges to succeed Georges was somewhat clear-cut for Nyerere because Saidi was the most senior Tanganyikan African on the Bench.[147] He was also personally known to Nyerere, who had taught Saidi when he was a student at secondary school in Tabora.[148] Saidi's appointment was celebrated in Tanzania because it was the first time a Tanzanian had occupied the highest post in the judiciary.[149]

Saidi's selection for the post, however, caused concern among members of the Bench. Widner asserts that his appointment was 'met with a very cool reception from the Bench whose members felt Saidi lacked the ability to stand up to authority in defence of his judges' in the way that Georges had.[150] Numerous interviewees expressed similar sentiments to this, while some also emphasised that Saidi 'tried his best', but had a 'less bold' personality than Georges and was thrust into a position of leadership without enough experience as a result of Nyerere's rush to see a Tanzanian lead the Court.[151] Thus Saidi's position can perhaps be best understood in the context of the process of decolonising the Bench. Nevertheless, Saidi's appointment was a defining moment in the history of the High Court Bench and marked the end of its process of decolonisation.

Conclusion: A Tanzanian Institution

The process of decolonising Tanzania's Bench between 1961 and 1971 involved former colonial judges and magistrates, an Asian advocate, foreign judges, and Tanganyikan African advocates trained abroad, and, later, at home. The foreign judges played a particularly important role in this process, providing a bridge between the period before 1964, when the Bench was entirely populated by colonial judges, and after 1970, when it was dominated by Tanzanian judges. The year 1971 witnessed the final steps in the process of decolonising the Bench. At that time, Saidi took leadership of an almost completely localised High Court

Bench, atop a single and unified court system, thereby finally breaking down the last colonial barrier to Tanganyikan Africans accessing and participating in the administration of justice at the highest level. Therefore, in 1971 not only was the process of decolonising the Bench complete, but the process of decolonising the High Court as an institution also reached its conclusion.

As the Court was reaching the end of this process, it removed one of the strongest symbols of its British heritage: the wigs.[152] Wigs had been in use by colonial judges continuously since the opening of the Court in 1921. These wigs were one of the last prominent features of the Court's British heritage, and by hanging up their wigs the members of the Bench no longer looked like colonial or foreign commonwealth judges but became more visibly Tanzanian judges.[153]

In the early 1970s a new chapter in the history of the High Court was beginning. Rather than undergoing changes in reaction to its colonial past, as it had during the 1960s, the High Court was increasingly reacting to its position in the Tanzanian state and to challenges from the Tanzanian executive. During the 1970s the Court was engaged with fulfilling its role in the state and responding to actions of the Tanzanian government as a Tanzanian institution. The process of decolonising the High Court had come to an end.

Notes

1. Tanzania is used in this chapter to refer to the country from 1964, when Tanganyika and Zanzibar merged, whereas Tanganyika is used where reference is made to the period before the union. It should be noted that the legal systems of Tanganyika and Zanzibar remained separate and the focus here remains on the Bench of the High Court for the mainland, which changed its title from the High Court of Tanganyika to the High Court of Tanzania.
2. The term black is used sparingly in this chapter as a means to refer to people who were categorised as being of the same race as Tanganyikan Africans, but were from West Africa and the West Indies, where the issue under discussion is race not nationality.
3. R. Aminzade, 'The Politics of Race and Nation: Citizenship and Africanisation in Tanganyika', *Political Power and Social Theory* 14 (2000), p. 67. On relations between Asians and Africans during colonial rule and the transition to independence, see also: R. Nagar, 'The South Asian Diaspora in Tanzania: A History Retold', *Comparative Studies of*

South Asia, Africa, and the Middle East, 16 (1996), pp. 64–65; J. Brennan, 'South Asian Nationalism in an East African Context: The Case of Tanganyika, 1914–1954', *Comparative Studies of South Asia, Africa, and the Middle East*, 19 (1999), pp. 24–39; Aminzade, 'The Politics', pp. 57–61 and 67.

4. Patrick McAuslan, interview with author, London, 6 October 2009.
5. Roland Brown Personal Papers, Copenhagen, R. Brown, untitled and unpublished memoir, [emailed to author, accessed on 4 July 2010], Chap. 4, 'Making of the First Constitutional Conference: Part 1', p. 4.
6. Patrick McAuslan, interview with author, London, 6 October 2009.
7. William Twining, interview with author, Oxford, 26 October 2009.
8. Sol Picciotto, interview with author, Leamington Spa, 8 October 2009.
9. In 1964 the overseas addition for Justice Biron was £1250 (50 % of his basic salary, which was £2500). In comparison, Saidi, an African associate judge, had the same basic salary, but only a £200 addition. TSL 1964, p. 230.
10. Fawzia Mustafa, correspondence with author, 4 September 2009.
11. F. Mustafa, 'Introduction: Re-issuing the Tanganyika Way: 1961–2009' in S. Mustafa, *The Tanganyika Way*, (Toronto, 2009), p. vii.
12. Ibid.
13. Ibid.
14. Kemal Mustafa, correspondence with author, 15 October 2009.
15. For her firsthand account of her entrée into politics and her political career: S. Mustafa, *The Tanganyika Way* (London, 1962). Her political career is also described in: J.M.M.H. Listowel, *The Making of Tanganyika* (London, 1965), p. 345; Unknown, 'Against the Shadows', *Awaaz*, 3 (December, 2005).
16. Harold Platt, interview with author, Graz, 30 January 2010.
17. Mustafa, 'Introduction: Re-issuing the Tanganyika Way', p. vi.
18. On the Commission and 1965 Constitution, see: P.W.B. McAuslan and Y.P. Ghai, 'Constitutional Innovation and Political Stability in Tanzania: A Preliminary Assessment', *Journal Of Modern African Studies*, 4 (1966); C. Pratt, *The Critical Phase in Tanzania, 1945–1968: Nyerere and the Emergence of a Socialist Strategy* (Cambridge, 1976), pp. 201–206; J.S. Read, 'Human Rights in Tanzania' in C. Legum and G. Mmari (eds.), *Mwalimu the Influence of Nyerere* (London, 1995), pp. 130–131.
19. R. Rweyemamu, 'Judge Clocks 42 Years of Stardom', *Business Times* [Tanzania], 9 June 1989. Multiple interviewees expressed these sentiments, for example: Ulric Cross, interview with author, by telephone from Port of Spain, 28 February 2010.
20. Ulric Cross, interview with author, by telephone from Port of Spain, 28 February 2010.

21. Roland Brown, interview with author, London, 1 June 2010.
22. NACP, RG 59, 2029, 778.2/10-160, American Embassy Dar es Salaam to Department of State, 24 May 1962.
23. ARJ 1963, p. 1.
24. W. Tordoff, *Government and Politics in Tanzania: A Collection of Essays Covering the Period from September 1960 to July 1966* (Nairobi, 1967), p. 203.
25. Patrick Ellis, interview with author, Bishops Stortford, 9 November 2009. Similar sentiments expressed by additional interviewees, for example: Louis Makame, interview with author, Dar es Salaam, 19 December 2008; Roland Brown, interview with author, London, 1 June 2010. Some Nigerian magistrates were also well-regarded by members of the judiciary. For example, Justice Williams offers a favourable view of at least one Nigerian magistrate in: J.K. Williams, *Black, Amber, White: An Autobiography* (Worthing, 1990), p. 115.
26. Roland Brown, interview with author, London, 1 June 2010.
27. Patrick Ellis Personal Papers, Bishops Stortford, P. Ellis, Report on Court System during the Early Stages of the Integration of the Courts, n.d. [c. 1963], p. 2.
28. NACP, RG 59, 2516, POL 15-2 Tanzan, American Embassy Dar es Salaam to Secretary of State, 23 April 1968.
29. Ibid.
30. Louis Makame, interview with author, Dar es Salaam, 19 December 2008.
31. Report of the Justice G.C.M. Onyiuke Tribunal, *Massacre of Ndi Igbo in 1966* (Lagos, 1968), p. 7.
32. Damien Lubuva, interview with author, Dar es Salaam, 27 November 2008; Leopold Kalunga, interview with author, Dar es Salaam, 31 October 2008.
33. A. Fiadjoe, G. Kodilinye, and J.C. Georges, *Telford Georges: A Legal Odyssey* (Kingston, 2008), p. 28.
34. J.S. Read, 'A Century Plus of Appeal Courts in Tanzania', in C.M. Peter and H.K. Bisimba (eds.), *Law and Justice in Tanzania: Quarter of a Century of the Court of Appeal* (Dar es Salaam, 2007), p. 64.
35. Fiadjoe, Kodilinye, and Georges, *Telford Georges*, p. 30.
36. Ibid., pp. 1, 10, 13.
37. Ibid., pp. 14–15.
38. Ibid., p. 18.
39. Ibid., p. 24.
40. Ibid., pp. 28–29.
41. Ibid., p. 29.
42. Leopold Kalunga, interview with author, Dar es Salaam, 31 October 2008.

43. Fiadjoe, Kodilinye, and Georges, *Telford Georges*, pp. 27 and 29.
44. Patrick McAuslan, interview with author, London, 6 October 2009.
45. Harold Platt, interview with author, Graz, 30 January 2010.
46. Numerous interviewees expressed these sentiments, for example: Steven Bwana, interview with author, Dar es Salaam, 31 October 2008; Leopold Kalunga, interview with author, Dar es Salaam, 31 October 2008; Lameck Mfalila, interview with author, Dar es Salaam, 12 November 2008; Mark Bomani, interview with author, Dar es Salaam, 26 November 2008; Harold Platt, interview with author, Graz, 30 January 2010.
47. Fiadjoe, Kodilinye, and Georges, *Telford Georges*, p. 41.
48. At Georges' farewell dinner Nyerere praised him for having, 'joined with the people in their political, economic, and social activities—both large and small'. J.K. Nyerere, 'Socialism and Law' in J.K. Nyerere (ed.), *Freedom and Development—Uhuru na Maendeleo: A Selection from Writings and Speeches 1968–1973* (London, 1973), p. 260.
49. Widner, *Building*, p. 57.
50. Ibid., p. 62. Similar sentiments expressed by: Steven Bwana, interview with author, Dar es Salaam, 31 October 2008.
51. His speech at the first conference in 1965 in Dar es Salaam is available in: P.T. Georges, 'The Role of Judges and Magistrates' in R.W. James and F.M. Kassam (eds.), *Law and its Administration in a One Party State: Selected Speeches of Telford Georges* (Dar es Salaam, 1973), pp. 69–82. See also: P.T. Georges, 'Report on Judges' and Magistrates' Conference', *Eastern Africa Law Review*, 1 (1968), pp. 167–174.
52. Fiadjoe, Kodilinye, and Georges, *Telford Georges*, p. 34.
53. Ulric Cross, interview with author, by telephone from Port of Spain, 28 February 2010.
54. Ibid.
55. Ibid. On Cross, see: Fiadjoe, Kodilinye, and Georges, *Telford Georges*, pp. 44–45.
56. Roland Brown, interview with author, London, 1 June 2010.
57. NACP, RG 59, 4035, [file untitled], American Embassy Dar es Salaam to Department of State, October 30, p. 1. On the Wa-Meru land case, see: Listowel, *The Making*, pp. 209–217; Pratt, *The Critical Phase*, pp. 119–120; K. Japhet and E. Seaton, *The Meru Land Case* (Nairobi, 1967).
58. Louis Makame, interview with author, Dar es Salaam, 19 December 2008. Emphasis added by author.
59. On the phase of Africanisation and the security of tenure of the colonial Bench, see: McAuslan, 'The Republican', pp. 546–549.
60. James and Kassam, 'The Courts in a One Party State', pp. 25–26.
61. Ibid.
62. Widner, *Building*, p. 61.

63. TANU, *The Arusha Declaration and TANU's Policy on Socialism and Self-Reliance* (Dar es Salaam, 1967).
64. McAuslan and Ghai, 'Constitutional Innovation', pp. 487, 507. The Declaration did, however, raise questions at the Court about whether socialist policies in the future would translate into cases being filed in which litigants may attempt to use the Court as a source of protection from the executive. On Georges' fear of this, see: Fiadjoe, Kodilinye, and Georges, *Telford Georges*, p. 45.
65. Numerous interviewees expressed these sentiments, for example: Steven Bwana, interview with author, Dar es Salaam, 31 October 2008; Lameck Mfalila, interview with author, Dar es Salaam, 12 November 2008; Joseph Warioba, interview with author, Dar es Salaam, 25 November 2008; William Twining, interview with author, Oxford, 16 June 2009.
66. R.W. James and F.M. Kassam, 'Introduction' in R.W. James and F.M. Kassam (eds.), *Law and Its Administration in a One Party State: Selected Speeches of Telford Georges* (Dar es Salaam, 1973), p. 4.
67. Augustino Ramadhani, interview with author, Dar es Salaam, 12 November 2008; Patrick McAuslan, interview with author, London, 6 October 2009, Roland Brown, interview with author, London, 1 June 2010.
68. On the rule of law and personal freedom in Tanzania under socialist policies, see: R. Martin, *Personal Freedom and Law in Tanzania: A Study of Socialist State Administration* (Nairobi, 1974).
69. The situation is described in greater detail in: Fiadjoe, Kodilinye, and Georges, *Telford Georges*, pp. 51–52.
70. The case was ultimately tried by Georges himself at the High Court. Bierwagen and Peter cite the following case resulting from this incident as: 1969 H.C.D. [High Court Digest] 170. R.M. Bierwagen and C.M. Peter, 'Administration of Justice in Tanzania and Zanzibar: A Comparison of Two Judicial Systems in One Country', *The International and Comparative Law Quarterly*, 38 (1989), p. 410.
71. The story was retold in interviews with many Tanganyikan African lawyers and judges, for example: Augustino Ramadhani, interview with author, Dar es Salaam, 12 November 2008; Lameck Mfalila, interview with author, Dar es Salaam, 12 November 2008; Joseph Warioba, interview with author, Dar es Salaam, 25 November 2008; William Maina, interview with author, Dar es Salaam, 16 December 2008.
72. On preventive detention in Tanzania, see, for example: Pratt, *The Critical Phase*, pp. 184–189; C.M. Peter, 'Tanzania' in A. Harding and J. Hatchard (eds.), *Preventive Detention and Security Law: A Comparative Survey* (Dordrecht, 1993), pp. 247–257; Read, 'Human Rights', pp. 136–141; C.M. Peter, 'Incarcerating the Innocent: Preventive Detention in

Tanzania', *Human Rights Quarterly*, 19 (1997), pp. 113–135; Widner, *Building*, pp. 117–122.

73. Preventive Detention Act 1962. See: Read, 'Human Rights', p. 137; Peter, 'Incarcerating', pp. 115–118.
74. Martin, *Personal Freedom*, pp. 92–93. He had previously justified its use in his speech at the opening of the new University College campus in 1964, see: J.K. Nyerere, 'Opening of the University College Campus' in J.K. Nyerere (ed.), *Freedom and Unity—Uhuru Na Umoja: A Selection from Writings and Speeches, 1952–65* (London, 1967), pp. 312–313.
75. Martin, *Personal Freedom*, pp. 92–93; NACP, RG 59, 2618, POL 15-2 Tanzan, American Embassy Dar es Salaam to Department of State, 13 February 1970.
76. Unknown, 'Georges on independence of Judiciary', *The Nationalist*, 11 February, 1970, p. 1; NACP, RG 59, 2618, POL 15-2 Tanzan, American Embassy Dar es Salaam to Department of State, 13 February 1970.
77. Unknown, 'Georges on independence of Judiciary', p. 1.
78. NACP, RG 59, 2618, POL 15-2 Tanzan, American Embassy Dar es Salaam to Department of State, 13 February 1970.
79. Unknown, 'Georges on independence of Judiciary', p. 1.
80. Ibid.
81. NACP, RG 59, 2618, POL 15-2 Tanzan, American Embassy Dar es Salaam to Department of State, 13 February 1970.
82. Widner's assessment of Chief Justice Nyalali's background as, 'typical of the first generation of African judges' concurs with evidence collected by the author on judges appointed to the Bench in the 1960s and early 1970s. Widner, *Building*, pp. 45–49.
83. Ibid., p. 47. On Tabora Government School, see: Listowel, *The Making*, pp. 85–104; J. Iliffe, *A Modern History of Tanganyika* (Cambridge, 1979), pp. 328, 338–339, 341, 446, 553. See also: A. Eckert, *Herrschen Und Verwalten : Afrikanische Büokraten, Staatliche Ordnung Und Politik in Tanzania*, 1920–1970 (Munich, 2007), pp. 63–79.
84. Listowel, *The Making*, pp. 85 and 89.
85. Ibid., p. 93.
86. Widner, *Building*, p. 47. For example, Nyerere attended Tabora Government School.
87. On educational disparity among Christians and Muslims in Tanzania and the implications for the entrance of Africans into government service, see: F. Mkenda, 'Tensions, Threats, and a Nation's Weakest Link: Muslim-Christian Relations and the Future of Peace in Tanzania', unpublished paper (Campion Hall, Oxford, 2011), pp. 2, 11, 15.
88. The United Republic of Tanzania, *1967 Population Census, Volume 3: Demographic Statistics*, (Dar es Salaam, 1971), pp. 249–251.

89. J. Duffler and M. Frey, 'Introduction', in J. Duffler and M. Fry (eds.), *Elites and Decolonization in the Twentieth Century* (Basingstoke, 2011), p. 2.
90. Louis Makame, interview with author, Dar es Salaam, 19 December 2008.
91. Noel Mkondya, interview with author, Dar es Salaam, 8 November 2008; Robert Kisanga, interview with author, Dar es Salaam, 28 November 2008.
92. Widner, *Building*, p. 48.
93. Robert Kisanga, interview with author, Dar es Salaam, 28 November 2008.
94. Ibid.
95. John Malecela, interview with author, Dar es Salaam, 22 November 2008.
96. Daniel Augustino Saidi (with Elizabeth Kilasara [Saidi]), Dar es Salaam, 18 December 2008.
97. R. Rweyemamu, 'How Mwalimu's Former Pupil Rose to be Tanzania's Chief Justice', *The Standard*, 18 May 1971, p. 4. Though the University was and continues to be a Muslim university, it is open to all students regardless of religious affiliation. It was founded under British rule in 1875 and is in modern day Uttar Pradesh, India.
98. John Malecela, interview with author, Dar es Salaam, 22 November 2008.
99. Augustine Saidi Personal Papers, Dar es Salaam, Letter of reference for A. Saidi by M.I. Khowaja, 30 July 1957.
100. Augustine Saidi Personal Papers, Dar es Salaam, Letter of reference for A. Saidi by M. Habib, 30 July 1957.
101. Rweyemamu, 'How Mwalimu's Former Pupil', p. 4.
102. Mawalla went to the Inns of Court in England after completing his studies in India and was called to the Bar. Mark Bomani, interview with author, Dar es Salaam, 26 November 2008.
103. Noel Mkondya, interview with author, Dar es Salaam, 8 November 2008.
104. Mark Bomani, interview with author, Dar es Salaam, 26 November 2008.
105. R. Sadleir, *Tanzania, Journey to Republic* (London, 1999), p. 238.
106. Louis Makame, interview with author, Dar es Salaam, 19 December 2008.
107. Mark Bomani, interview with author, Dar es Salaam, 26 November 2008; MCA, s 23(1–2).
108. Rweyemamu, 'How Mwalimu's Former Pupil', p. 4.
109. J.K. Nyerere, 'Education and Law' in J.K. Nyerere (ed.), *Freedom and Unity—Uhuru Na Umoja: A Selection from Writings and Speeches, 1952–65* (London, 1967), p. 130.

110. On the Denning Committee, see: W. Twining, 'Legal Education within East Africa', *British Institute of International and Comparative Law in East African Law Today*, Commonwealth Law Series No. 5 (1966), pp. 119–120; Y. Ghai, 'Law, Development and African Scholarship', *The Modern Law Review*, 50 (1987), pp. 752–755; Widner, *Building*, pp. 54–55; J. Harrington and A. Manji, "Mind with Mind, Spirit with Spirit": Lord Denning and African Legal Education', *Journal of Law and Society*, 30 (2003), pp. 279–383; J. Harrington and A. Manji, 'The Emergence of African Law as an Academic Discipline', *African Affairs*, 102 (2003), pp. 125–127.
111. Great Britain, *Report of the Committee on Legal Education for Students from Africa* (London, 1961), p. 28, as cited in: Twining, 'Legal Education', p. 120. For a discussion of the recommendations in the Denning Report, see: Harrington and Manji, 'Mind', pp. 383–385.
112. University College, Dar es Salaam (Provisional Council) Ordinance 1961.
113. A.B. Weston, 'Tanganyika', *Journal of African Law*, 6 (1962), p. 151.
114. Ibid., p. 152.
115. William Twining, interview with author, Oxford, 16 June 2009; Twining, 'Legal Education', p. 120.
116. I.N. Kimambo, 'Establishment of Teaching Programmes' in I.N. Kimambo; B.B.B. Mapunda, and Y.Q. Lawi (eds.), *In Search of Relevance: A History of the University of Dar Es Salaam* (Dar es Salaam, 2008), pp. 108–109.
117. William Twining, interview with author, Oxford, 16 June 2009.
118. Ibid.
119. This played a role in the decision to develop a three-year rather than a four-year degree programme, see: Weston, 'Tanganyika', p. 153. For a description of the curriculum, see: Widner, *Building*, p. 153.
120. Ghai, 'Law', pp. 755–760; Patrick McAuslan, interview with author, London, 6 October 2009.
121. Terence Ranger, interview with author, Oxford, 30 April 2009. The two foundational texts were authored by McAuslan, one of the original faculty members, and two men who joined the faculty in the 1960s: Y.P. Ghai and J.S. Read. In 1970 Ghai and McAuslan published *Public Law and Political Change in Kenya*, and in 1972 Read (with H.F. Morris) published *Indirect Rule and the Search for Justice*. Twining, another one of the original three faculty members, became one of the pioneers of the 'law in context' perspective on the discipline of law, see: W. Twining, *Law in Context: Enlarging a Discipline* (Oxford, 1997), pp. 23–25. For an overview of the subsequent careers and publications of faculty members and students, see: Widner, *Building*, pp. 52–53, fn 18.
122. Nyerere, 'Education and Law', p. 130.

123. B.B.B. Mapunda, 'Infrastructure', in I.N. Kimambo, B.B.B. Mapunda, and Y.Q. Lawi (eds.), *In Search of Relevance: A History of the University of Dar Es Salaam* (Dar es Salaam, 2008), p. 62.
124. Ulric Cross, interview with author, by telephone from Port of Spain, 28 February 2010. Named *The Denning Law Journal* and the Denning Law Society. Widner, *Building*, p. 55.
125. On the physical infrastructure of the College, see: Mapunda, 'Infrastructure', pp. 61–67.
126. Weston, 'Tanganyika', p. 152.
127. Terence Ranger, interview with author, Oxford, 30 April 2009. Similar sentiments expressed by: Gerald Ndika, interview with author, Dar es Salaam, 6 November 2008. Class lists from the first year until the 1980 intake on are available in: S.E.A. Mvungi (ed.), *Forty Years of the Faculty of Law University of Dar Es Salaam 1961–2001* (Dar es Salaam 2002), pp. 151–159. For Faculty members' memories of teaching law in Dar, see: I.G. Shivji, *Limits of Legal Radicalism: Reflections on Teaching Law at the University of Dar Es Salaam* (Dar es Salaam, 1986).
128. Patrick McAuslan, interview with author, London, 6 October 2009.
129. Edward Mwesiumo, interview with author, Dar es Salaam, 7 November 2008.
130. The cohort of Tanganyikans in the judiciary (and other branches of government) who were able to move up quickly due to the vacancies after independence can be compared to young ICS officials in India who received 'usually rapid promotion' as British officers left during India's transition to independence. J.M. Brown, *Windows into the Past: Life Histories and the Historian of South Asia* (Notre Dame, 2009), p. 27.
131. J.L. Mwalusanya, *The Judiciary in Tanzania* (Dar es Salaam, 1988), p. 34.
132. Sol Picciotto, interview with author, Leamington Spa, 8 October 2009. Similar sentiments expressed by: Patrick McAuslan, interview with author, London, 6 October 2009.
133. Barnabas Samatta, interview with author, Dar es Salaam, 3 December 2008.
134. Ibid. The Tanzanian government loaned Samatta to Zimbabwe's Bench between 1983 and 1987.
135. Robert Kisanga, interview with author, Dar es Salaam, 28 November 2008.
136. RHL, MSS. Afr. s. 1830, Proceedings of a symposium on the Administration of Law in British Africa, 1–2 July 1980, P. McAuslan, 'The Training of Legal Personnel: Reflections from an East African Perspective', p. 7.

137. Ulric Cross, interview with author, by telephone from Port of Spain, 28 February 2010.
138. Georges, 'The Role of Judges', pp. 62–63.
139. Edward Mwesiumo, interview with author, Dar es Salaam, 7 November 2008.
140. For example: Lameck Mfalila, interview with author, Dar es Salaam, 12 November 2008; William Maina, interview with author, Dar es Salaam, 16 December 2008.
141. Harold Platt, interview with author, Graz, 30 January 2010.
142. Harold Platt, interview with author, Graz, 30 January 2010; Ulric Cross, interview with author, by telephone from Port of Spain, 28 February 2010.
143. The new judges on the Bench were Justices Kisanga, N.S. Mzavas, J.M.M. Mwakasendo, J.B. Patel, and P.M. Jonathan, who had earned their law degrees abroad, and El-Kindy and Kwikima, from the first class of the Faculty of Law in Dar es Salaam.
144. Widner, *Building*, pp. 114–115; Fiadjoe, Kodilinye, and Georges, *Telford Georges*, p. 56.
145. NACP, RG 59, 2618, POL 15-2 Tanzan, American Embassy Dar es Salaam to Department of State, 8 April 1971.
146. Fiadjoe, Kodilinye, and Georges, *Telford Georges*, pp. 51–52.
147. Augustino Ramadhani, interview with author, Dar es Salaam, 12 November 2008.
148. Rweyemamu, 'How Mwalimu's Former Pupil'.
149. Ibid.
150. Widner, *Building*, p. 115. Georges' biographers assert that Georges did not think Saidi, 'had the character necessary for the job'. Fiadjoe, Kodilinye, and Georges, *Telford Georges*, p. 52
151. Patrick McAuslan, interview with author, London, 6 October 2009; Joseph Warioba, interview with author, Dar es Salaam, 25 November 2008; Robert Kisanga, interview with author, Dar es Salaam, 28 November 2008.
152. Shivji mentioned the removal of the wigs as a symbol of the court moving on from its colonial past in: Issa Shivji, interview with author, Dar es Salaam, 20 November 2008.
153. Louis Makame, interview with author, Dar es Salaam, 19 December 2008. The robes were also replaced around this time, reportedly on Georges' request. Widner, *Building*, pp. 61–62; Louis Makame, interview with author, Dar es Salaam, 19 December 2008.

CHAPTER 8

Conclusion

By the early 1970s nearly all the colonial high courts that had been in operation across the British Empire had become part of post-colonial states. Each transfer of political power from Great Britain to a new nation initiated or hastened a locally driven process of change and presented an opportunity for the new nation to determine how the courts would function in the new political structure and post-colonial legal culture.

In Tanzania the colonial structures that were dismantled during the process of decolonising the High Court can be traced back to the colonial justice system created during the first decade of indirect rule. The severing of the Court's relationship with the African population and Native Courts in the 1920s was formative for it as a colonial institution and for indirect rule in the territory. The Court lost appellate jurisdiction over the Native Courts for the remainder of British rule and thus played a very limited role, relative to administrators, in the administration of justice for Africans, except in the most serious cases. While the Court's jurisdiction over and interaction with Africans was very restricted after the Native Courts Ordinance of 1929, the Court was still crucial to the colonial state because it facilitated British rule both practically and symbolically. In the heated debates in the late 1920s about the size of the High Court and its relationship to the Native Courts system, and in the 1930s about magisterial powers that the colonial government had bestowed on administrators, the underlying matter of dispute was how a professional judiciary should fit

E.R. Feingold, *Colonial Justice and Decolonization in the High Court of Tanzania, 1920–1971*, Cambridge Imperial and Post-Colonial Studies Series, https://doi.org/10.1007/978-3-319-69691-1_8

into the indirect rule system. At stake in these debates was not just the position of the Court, but also the nature of indirect rule in the territory and region, as well as the extent of administrative authority over Africans and other state institutions.

The effect of the creation of the Colonial Legal Service and related policies on the careers of colonial judges was contemporaneous with these debates in East Africa in the 1930s. These Colonial Office policies united colonial legal officers into a single Empire-wide service that would make transfer of legal personnel between colonies easier. One significant outcome of the creation of these polices, however, was that colonial judges became more disconnected from the specific places they served. The prevailing attitude towards colonial judges in the Colonial Office and in the colonial government of Tanganyika was that they should adapt to local circumstances only when necessary, but not play a role in moulding them.

After World War II British rule in the territory shifted in relation to the Colonial Office's new emphasis on reconstruction and development of the Empire. The judiciary became a part of the Tanganyikan administration's conception of 'colonial development' and the size and jurisdiction of the professional judiciary grew. As the wind of change gathered speed in Tanganyika in the late 1950s, the British also used the Court in its efforts to contain TANU's, and particularly Nyerere's, activities. In the same way the Court had been invoked as a symbol of British 'civilisation' and the righteousness of British rule during the interwar period, the British colonial government used the Court to help manage its image at the end, pointing to the institution as the foremost legacy of the 40 years of British rule of Tanganyika.

While the High Court of Tanganyika has been in continuous operation since 1921, it was only in the 1950s that colonial administrators accepted the need for more than a handful of colonial judges and professional magistrates. Though the most substantial changes to the Court occurred between 1961 and 1971, the roots of the decolonisation of the High Court were in the 1950s. It was then that the initial links between the High Court and Local Courts were made and the use of both professional magistrates and the first non-professional African magistrates began to diminish the reliance on administrators to administer justice. Thus, this book has argued that while the process of decolonising the Court was connected to the transfer of power in 1961, it began before and continued long after, ending approximately a decade following independence. The history of the High Court of Tanganyika illustrates the importance of studying the decolonisation of colonial institutions as a process originating prior to independence—rather than merely at the moment of the transfer of power or at other specific moments in its history.

In the decade following independence the post-colonial government altered the High Court of Tanganyika in reaction to the ways in which the Court's position relative to the administration and African population reinforced colonial administrative authority. The changes, divided into the two categories of structure and personnel utilised throughout this book, reflected the priorities and ideology of the new national government.

The first category concerned the structural relationships between the High Court and other institutions. The unification of the dual court systems into a single system restored the jurisdiction the Court lost in 1929 and made it an institution that was, by law, equally accessible to everyone in the territory. The colonial practice of using race as the determining factor for access to colonial courts, which dated back to the era of German rule, was finally ended by law through the Magistrates Courts Act of 1963, and in practice in the years that followed the Act with the implementation of the new three-tier court system. The government also abolished the colonial practice of granting judicial power to administrative officers, which the Bushe Commission had argued for in principle 30 years earlier, but unhappily accepted as impractical at the time. In addition to changes within the court system and government of Tanganyika, the structural decolonisation of the Court also involved severing the High Court of Tanganyika's long-standing relationship with the Privy Council, and therefore with the other high courts of the Empire. This placed the Court within the confines of state authority, but with constitutional provisions intended to protect the independence of the judiciary from executive encroachment and to establish an appellate relationship with the Eastern Africa Court of Appeal.[1]

The second category of change the post-colonial government made to the High Court concerned its personnel. The government sought to replace colonial judges with local ones, but the process of localising Tanganyika's Bench was much slower than in other government sectors because of the need for judges to have legal qualifications. The history of the High Court illustrates that the extent to which local populations had access to education and professional training under British rule shaped how post-colonial states approached replacing colonial officials in different parts of government, resulting in uneven processes among state institutions.

Since the legal profession in Tanganyika had only two African members at independence, colonial judges continued to populate the Bench in the years following independence. In the context of decolonisation in the mid-twentieth century, colonial judges throughout the Empire found themselves in a difficult position as they had enjoyed job security in the colonies, but had become estranged from the legal community in Great Britain. Tanganyika's colonial judges responded to decolonisation in one of two ways; they either sought to finish out their careers on a Bench in the colonies or former colonies, or returned to Great Britain and took up a job off the Bench until retirement. Yet the end of British rule did not lead to the curtailment of all colonial judges and magistrates' careers in Tanganyika. Indeed, one colonial judge, Justice Biron, and colonial magistrates like Justice Platt, regarded the end of British rule as an opportunity and chose to make or further their careers in Tanganyika.

As colonial judges largely departed Tanganyika in the mid-1960s, the government invited foreign judges from former British colonies to join the Bench until Tanganyikan Africans acquired the necessary qualifications for appointment. The use of foreign judges indicates that decolonisation, even on an institutional level, can be a transnational project. Like the struggles for independence in some countries, the process can require and be shaped by outside assistance and intervention. Moreover, Tanganyika's reliance on West Indian and West African barristers in the 1960s was possible because of their shared colonial foundations that linked legal systems and legal professionals to one another. This transnational group of common law barristers helped colonial legal institutions survive national political transitions from being a colony to being an independent state by moving between benches and legal positions in the new states.

The post-independence government's efforts to decolonise the Bench were ultimately aimed at giving Tanganyikan Africans a sizeable majority on the Bench and placing them in leadership roles. Of the staffing difficulties that faced the Tanganyikan government after independence, this was arguably its most difficult challenge. It also presented unparalleled opportunities for the few young Tanganyikan African advocates who had gained a legal education during British rule and in the period around independence. This cohort, and the one that emerged from the Faculty of Law in Dar es Salaam in the late 1960s, were promoted very quickly and enjoyed long careers on the Bench as a result. Nevertheless, these new judges also faced the challenge of carrying out roles that had been filled previously by experienced judges of advanced ages without many avenues for mentorship or apprenticeship.

The appointment of Chief Justice Saidi in 1971 marked the end of the phase of decolonisation of the High Court and the beginning of the next stage in the Court's history. Widner refers to the 1970s as 'the nadir' in the history of judicial independence in Tanzania, arguing that judicial legitimacy and the morale of the Court dwindled during Saidi's term as Chief Justice.[2] The 1970s were undoubtedly a very difficult decade for Saidi and the Court when the Bench was increasingly faced with strained relations with the executive as the government implemented its socialist, *Ujamaa* policies.[3] Saidi, who was supportive of TANU and whose relationship with its members had convinced him to join the judiciary in the first place, would prove to be a stark contrast to Chief Justice Georges who had confronted Nyerere during episodes of executive encroachment in the late 1960s.

There are direct parallels between the 1920s and the 1960s in the way in which the relationship between the High Court and executive in Tanganyika changed. For nearly a decade after the Court was first established in Tanganyika, it had appellate jurisdiction over cases generating from the Native Courts. Though administrators had magisterial powers, the High Court was the foremost body in the administration of justice. As the colonial administration began to entrench and consolidate its power in the late 1920s, it restricted the jurisdiction and role of the High Court in the sphere of colonial justice. Similarly, in the period following independence in 1961, the Court gained a greater degree of independence from the executive and enjoyed a more authoritative position in the court systems than it had had during colonial rule, as executive power and institutions were still developing. By the late 1960s, though, the country's political leadership increasingly challenged the independence of the judiciary and the rule of law as it consolidated its power. This parallel indicates that after a period of establishment, colonial and post-colonial executive institutions attempted to limit the ability of the judiciary to interfere in its efforts to govern according to its political priorities. Thus the conclusion of the process of decolonising the High Court of Tanganyika coincided with the consolidation of executive power in the country; in the early 1970s the High Court began to face the same challenges that judiciaries often face as executive power grows. This is not a challenge that was unique to post-colonial Tanganyika or necessarily a product of the way in which the government decolonised the Court.

While there are many similarities between the High Court of Tanganyika and colonial high courts in East and West Africa and beyond, key aspects of the process of decolonisation in Tanganyika—for example, its relatively peaceful transfer of power as compared with Kenya and the absence of an African Bar as compared to Ghana and Nigeria—limit the utility of generalising this book's specific findings about the decolonisation of the Court. However, this book has presented key themes for consideration and an approach that could be effectively applied to other colonial high courts. It demonstrates that it is crucial to examine a court's institutional relationships, as well as its practical and symbolic roles, to assess how post-colonial executive authorities perceived them during and after national independence. The structural relationships to other courts and the personnel on the Bench are key characteristics for investigating the decolonisation of any high court. More studies of colonial high courts and the process of decolonisation are needed to provide insights into how these enduring institutions functioned as part of colonial rule and were integrated into post-colonial states. Comparative studies with British colonies that had larger local Bars, such as those in West Africa, and dissimilar court systems would provide a deeper understanding of how local circumstances affected the ways in which post-colonial governments reshaped these institutions. Such studies would also reveal whether the process of decolonisation of the High Court of Tanganyika was indeed similar to that of other British colonies in the twentieth century, or was driven by the dual court system and exclusive use of colonial judges through the independence process. A further step would be to examine the supreme courts of colonies under the administration of other European imperial powers in the twentieth century and consider whether the processes that occurred in common law courts were similar to or differed from those that were part of legal systems following the civil law tradition. Expanding knowledge of the decolonisation of colonial high courts would support a more historically grounded understanding of the role of these institutions in post-colonial states and the roots of the challenges courts face in upholding the rule of law and maintaining independence from executive authority.

In the space of a decade, the High Court transformed from an institution of the colonial state staffed by colonial judges to one that had a predominantly African Bench, whose judges enjoyed a greater degree of protection by the Constitution than their forerunners, unrestricted jurisdiction over the population in the country, and supervision over a completely professionalised judiciary. While decolonisation is often described as a process of rapid change—and the High Court certainly underwent significant, and at times, quick changes—the transition to independence, both before and after 1961, was also facilitated by the endurance of the High Court. The history of colonial justice and decolonisation in the High Court of Tanzania is a powerful reminder of the crucial roles played by common law courts in the operation and legitimisation of both colonial and post-colonial states.

Notes

1. The dynamics of the highly politicised debate surrounding whether Commonwealth countries should continue to allow their citizens to appeal decisions from their highest national courts to the Privy Council is covered in detail in: D.B. Swinfen, *Imperial Appeal: The Debate on the Appeal to the Privy Council, 1833–1986* (Manchester, 1987).
2. J.A. Widner, *Building the Rule of Law: Francis Nyalali and the Road to Judicial Independence in Africa*, 1st edn (New York, 2001), pp. 114–115.
3. *Ujamaa* is a Kiswahili word that roughly translates to familyhood or togetherness. Here it refers to the political ideology underlying the African socialist policies introduced in the late 1960s and 1970s.

Bibliography

Interviews and Correspondence

Interviews

Note: Individuals whose testimony is not cited in the text are indicated with an asterisk. Their names are listed here because the oral testimony they provided contributed to the author's understanding and analysis of the history of the High Court of Tanganyika.

Abedi, Gallus, Dar es Salaam, 28 October 2008.*
Barton, Don, Oxford, 11 July 2008.*
Bomani, Mark, Dar es Salaam, 26 November 2008.
Brown, Roland, London, 1 June 2010.
Bwana, Steven, Dar es Salaam, 31 October and 3 November 2008.
Cross, Ulric, by telephone from Port of Spain, 28 February 2010 and 21 May 2010.
Cross, Ulric, London, 17 August 2010.
Ellis, Patrick, Bishops Stortford, 25 March and 9 November 2009.
Hardwick, Simon, Taunton, 21 July 2008.
Ismail, Mohamed, Dar es Salaam, 3 December 2008.
Jaggar, Trevor, London, 17 June 2009.
Jadeja, Shyansingh, Dar es Saalam, 15 December 2008.
Jhaveri, Kantilal, Dar es Salaam, 16 December 2008.
Jhaveri, Urmila, Dar es Salaam, 16 December 2008.
Kalunga, Leopold, Dar es Salaam, 31 October 2008.

E.R. Feingold, *Colonial Justice and Decolonization in the High Court of Tanzania, 1920–1971*, Cambridge Imperial and Post-Colonial Studies Series, https://doi.org/10.1007/978-3-319-69691-1

Kanywanyi, Josephat, Dar es Salaam, 28 November 2008.*
Kisanga, Robert, Dar es Salaam, 28 November 2008.
Law, Patricia, Canterbury, 13 May 2009.
Le Breton, David, Tonbridge, 8 June 2008 and 22 March 2009.
Lubuva, Damien, Dar es Salaam, 27 November 2008.
Macleod, Norman, Loch Winnoch, 25 May 2009.
Maina, William, Dar es Salaam, 16 December 2008.
Majithia, Priyavadan, Dar es Salaam, 5 December 2008.
Makame, Louis, Dar es Salaam, 19 December 2008.
Malecela, John, Dar es Salaam, 22 November 2008.
McAuslan, Patrick, London, 6 October 2009.
McCleery, Rosemary, Templecombe, 23 April 2009.
McCleery, Bryan, Templecombe, 23 April 2009.
Mfalila, Lameck, Dar es Salaam, 12 November 2008.
Mkondya, Noel, Dar es Salaam, 8 November 2008.
Muya, R. J., Dar es Salaam, 17 December 2008.
Mwesiumo, Edward, Dar es Salaam, 7 November 2008.
Ndika, Gerald, Dar es Salaam, 6 November 2008.*
Nsekela, Harold, Dar es Salaam, 11 November 2008.*
Picciotto, Sol, Leamington Spa, 8 October 2009.
Platt, Harold, Graz, 30 and 31 January 2010.
Richardson, John, Aldeburgh, 7 August 2008.*
Ranger, Terrance, Oxford, 30 April 2009.
Ramadhani, Augustino, Dar es Salaam, 12 November 2008.
Rwechungura, Charles, Dar es Salaam, 22 November 2008.*
Sadleir, Randal, London, 11 June 2009.*
Saidi, Daniel Augustino (with Elizabeth Kilasara [Saidi]), Dar es Salaam, 18 December 2008.
Samatta, Barnabas, Dar es Salaam, 3 December 2008.
Shivji, Issa, Dar es Salaam, 20 November 2008.
Snoxall, Derek, London, 28 March 2009.*
Tawney, Tim, Oxford, 11 March 2009.*
Thomas, Mark, Oxford, 29 July 2008.
Twining, William, Oxford, 16 June, 3 September, and 26 October 2009.
Warioba, Joseph, Dar es Salaam, 25 November 2008.
Williams, David, London, 17 March 2010.
Wise, Robert, Oxford, 29 July 2008.*

Correspondence

Johnson, Mary, correspondence with author, 14 July 2008.
Mustafa, Fawzia, correspondence with author, 4 September 2009.
Mustafa, Kemal, correspondence with author, 15 October 2009.

Archival Sources

Archives

Bodleian Library of Commonwealth and African Studies at Rhodes House, Oxford (RHL)

MSS. Afr. s. 505; 'Digest of Appeals, Mbulu District'.
MSS. Afr. s. 592; Mark Wilson Papers.
MSS Afr. s. 1461; P.H. Johnston Papers.
MSS Afr. s. 1620; P.H. Johnston Papers.
MSS. Afr. s. 1830; Proceedings of a symposium on the Administration of Law in British Africa, 1–2 July 1980.
MSS. Brit. Emp. s. 307; David Edwards Papers.
MSS. Brit. Emp. s. 415; Ralph Furse Papers.

Bodleian Law Library, Oxford

Cw Gen 510 A258.4a; *Africa in the Colonial Period Conference, Symposium Number Five: The Administration of Law in British Africa* University College, Oxford, 1–2 July 1980.

London School of Economics and Political Science Archive, London (LSE)

Pritt_1.35; D.N. Pritt Papers.

National Archives of the United States of America, College Park, MD (NACP)

RG 59, General Records of the Department of State, Decimal File Series
Box 2029; 1960–63, from 778.001/7-1761 to 778.5MSP/2-276.
Box 4036; 1950–54, from 778.001/2-2451 to 778.5612/2-2851.
Box 4035; 1950–54, from 777.03/7-251 to 778.00/12-154.
Box 3698; 1955–59, from 778.0019-359 to 779.001/8-1059.
Box 2618; 1970–73, [subject numeric files] Political and Defense.

Tanzania National Archives, Dar es Salaam (TNA)

205-78; Vol. II; High Court Circuits (1956–1958).
205/18/8; Law and Judicial Officers (1953–1959).

10201; Assizes (1927).
11648; African Staff Judicial Department (1928–1935).
23509; Court Interpreters (1933).
25586; Appointments to the Colonial Service – Procedure (1945).
38775; Buildings for the High Court and Its Staff in Mwanza (1949).
41755; Judicial Powers of African Administrative Assistants (1951).
43474; Expansion of Judicial Department (1953).
AB.66; Judicial Department Annual Reports (1923).
AB.67; Legal Department Annual Report (1924).
AB.461; Legal Department (1921–1922).
AB.480; Judicial Department (1925).
AB.497; Judicial Department (1926).
AB.538; Judicial Department Report by Chief Justice (1920).

The National Archives of the United Kingdom, Kew (TNA (UK))

CO 323: Colonies, General: Original Correspondence.
CO 691; Colonial Office: Tanganyika, Original Correspondence.
CO 822; Colonial Office: East Africa, Original Correspondence.
CO 850; Colonial Office: Personnel, Original Correspondence.
CO 877; Colonial Office: Appointments Department.
CO 1017; Colonial Office and Successors: Colonial Service Division, Later Overseas Service Division.
CO 1026; Colonial Office: Legal Department.
DO 168; Dominions Office and Commonwealth Relations Office: East and General Africa.
DO 185; Commonwealth Relations Office and Successors: High Commission, Tanganyika.
HO 405; Home Office: Aliens Department and Successors: Aliens Personal Files, Applications for Naturalisation.
LCO 2; Lord Chancellor's Office and Lord Chancellor's Department: Registered Files.

Private Papers and Photograph Collections

Augustine Saidi Personal Papers, Dar es Salaam

Correspondence.

Charles Law Personal Papers, Canterbury

Newspaper Clippings of Articles on Justice Law in Tanganyika.

Patrick Ellis Personal Papers, Bishops Stortford

Reports and Correspondence.
P. Ellis, Unpublished Memoir, 'A Life in the Colonial Service, Tanganyika, As Seen by Patrick J. C. Ellis, 1952–54'.

Roland Brown Personal Papers, Copenhagen

Unpublished and untitled memoir [emailed to author, accessed on 4 July 2010].

Printed Primary Sources

Acts and Ordinances

Tanganyika Order in Council 1920.
Special Tribunal Ordinance 1920.
Eastern African Court of Appeal Order in Council 1921.
Native Authority Ordinance 1921.
Appeals to the Court of Appeal Ordinance 1922.
Native Authority Ordinance 1923.
Native Courts Proclamation 1925.
Native Courts Rules 1925.
Native Authority Ordinance 1926.
Native Courts Ordinance 1929.
The Courts Ordinance 1930.
Native Courts (Appeals) (Amendment) Ordinance 1940.
The Courts Ordinance 1941.
Local Courts Ordinance 1951.
Advocates Ordinance 1954.
Tanganyika Law Society Ordinance 1954.
University College, Dar es Salaam (Provisional Council) Ordinance 1961.
Appellate Jurisdiction Ordinance 1961.
Eastern Africa Court of Appeal Order in Council 1961.
Tanganyika (Constitution) Order in Council 1961.
Judicature and Application of Laws Ordinance 1961.
Local Courts (Amendment) Ordinance 1961.
Appellate Jurisdiction Act 1962.

Judicial Service Act 1962.
Local Courts (Minister for Justice and Regional Local Courts Officers) Act 1962.
Preventive Detention Act 1962.
An Act to Declare the Constitution of Tanganyika 1962.
Dar es Salaam Club (Dissolution) Act 1963.
Magistrates' Courts Act 1963.
Special Tribunals Act 1964.

Official Series

Colonial Office, *Colonial Office List* [also Titled: The Dominions Office and Colonial Office List], (London, [1919–1940, 1946, 1948–1949, 1951–1961]).

Tanganyika, *Annual Report of the Judiciary of Tanganyika/Tanzania* (Dar es Salaam, [1936–1939, 1945–1967, 1970–1971]).

Tanganyika, *Tanganyika/Tanzania Staff List* (Dar es Salaam, [1942–1944, 1946–1961, 1963–1964]).

Tanganyika, *Law Reports of the Cases Determined by the High Court of Tanganyika and on Appeal for Eastern Africa: 1921–1952*, Vol. 1 (revised), (Dar es Salaam, 1955).

Tanganyika, *Law Reports of the Cases Determined by the High Court of Tanganyika and on Appeal for Eastern Africa and the Privy Council: 1953–1957*, Vol. 2 (revised), (Dar es Salaam, 1959).

Official Publications

African Conference on Local Courts and Customary Law, *Record of the Proceedings of the Conference Held in Dar Es Salaam, Tanganyika, 8–18 September 1963* (Dar es Salaam, 1963).

Colonial Office, *The Colonial Service: Legal Appointments* (London, 1931).

Colonial Office, *Report of the Tanganyika Constitutional Conference, 1961* (London, 1961).

The Future of Law in Africa: Record of Proceedings of the London Conference, 28 December 1959–8 January 1960 (London, 1960).

Great Britain, *Commission of Inquiry into the Administration of Justice in Kenya, Uganda, and the Tanganyika Territory in Criminal Matters, Minutes of Evidence and Memoranda Submitted to the Commission* (London, 1934).

Great Britain, *Report of the Commission of Inquiry into the Administration of Justice in Kenya, Uganda and the Tanganyika Territory in Criminal Matters, May, 1933, and Correspondence Arising Out of the Report* (London, 1934).

Great Britain, *Report of the Committee on Legal Education for Students from Africa* (London, 1961).

Great Britain Colonial Office, *Appointments in Her Majesty's Overseas Civil Service, and Other Appointments in Colonial and Overseas Territories* (London, 1957).

Nyerere, J. K., *Tanzania Ten Years After Independence* (Dar es Salaam, 1971).
Report of the Justice G.C.M. Onyiuke Tribunal, *Massacre of Ndi Igbo in 1966* (Lagos, 1968).
Russell, A., *Handbook for Magistrates*, 2nd edn (London, 1928).
Secretary of State for the Colonies, 'Judicial Advisers' Conference 1953', *Journal of African Administration*, Special Supplement (1953).
Secretary of State for the Colonies, 'Judicial Advisers' Conference 1956', *Journal of African Administration*, Special Supplement (1957).
Tanganyika, *Digest of Appeals from Local Courts* (Dar es Salaam, 1953).
Tanganyika, *A Digest of Appeals from Local Courts 1962* (Dar es Salaam, 1963).
Tanganyika, *A Digest of Appeals from Local Courts 1963* (Dar es Salaam, 1964).
Tanganyika, *A Digest of Appeals from Local Courts 1964* (Dar es Salaam, 1965).
Tanganyika Africanisation Commission, *Report of the Africanisation Commission, 1962* (Dar es Salaam, 1963).
Tanganyika Public Relations Department, *Official Opening of New High Court at Dar Es Salaam, on 17th May 1958* (Dar es Salaam, 1958).
Tanganyika Territory, *Census of the Native Population 1931* (Dar es Salaam 1932).
Tanganyika Territory, *Report on the Non-Native Census 1931* (Dar es Salaam, 1932).
Tanganyika Territory, *Tanganyika Territory Blue Book 1923* (Dar es Salaam, 1924).
TANU, *The Arusha Declaration and TANU's Policy on Socialism and Self-Reliance* (Dar es Salaam, 1967).
The United Republic of Tanzania, *1967 Population Census, Volume 3: Demographic Statistics* (Dar es Salaam, 1971).

Periodicals

Business Times [Tanzania].
The Irish Law Times and Solicitor's Journal [Ireland].
The Nationalist [Tanzania].
The Overseas Pensioner [United Kingdom].
The Standard [Tanzania].
Sunday News [Tanzania].
Tanganyika Gazette [Tanganyika].
Tanganyika Notes and Records [Tanzania].
The Times [United Kingdom].

Speeches

Fundikira, C., 'Reorganization of the Courts in Tanganyika', *Journal of Local Administration Overseas*, 4 (1962), pp. 257–258.
Macmillan, H., 'Wind of Change', Speech in the Cape Town Parliament [South Africa], 3 February 1960.

Nyerere, J. K., 'Comment on the Mutineers' Sentences' in Nyerere, J. K. (ed.), *Freedom and Unity – Uhuru Na Umoja: A Selection from Writings and Speeches, 1952–65* (London, 1967), pp. 298–299.

Nyerere, J. K., 'Education and Law' in Nyerere, J. K. (ed.), *Freedom and Unity – Uhuru Na Umoja: A Selection from Writings and Speeches, 1952–65* (London, 1967), pp. 130–132.

Nyerere, J. K., 'Opening of the University College Campus' in Nyerere, J. K. (ed.), *Freedom and Unity – Uhuru Na Umoja: A Selection from Writings and Speeches, 1952–65* (London, 1967), pp. 305–315.

Nyerere, J. K., 'Socialism and Law' in Nyerere, J. K. (ed.), *Freedom and Development – Uhuru na Maendeleo: A Selection from Writings and Speeches 1968–1973* (London, 1973), pp. 259–261.

Nyerere, J. K., *Speech by the Chief Minister, Mr. Julius Nyerere, in the Address in Reply to the Legislative Council, 19th October 1960* (Dar es Salaam, 1960).

Memoirs

Alexander, G. G., *From the Middle Temple to the South Seas*, 1st edn (London, 1927).

Alexander, G. G., *Tanganyika Memories: A Judge in the Red Kanzu* (London, 1936).

Furse, R., *Aucuparius: Recollections of a Recruiting Officer* (London, 1962).

Jhaveri, K. L., *Marching with Nyerere: Africanisation of Asians* (Delhi, 1999).

Longford, M., *The Flags Changed at Midnight: Tanganyika's Progress Towards Independence* (Leominster, 2001).

Parry-Wingfield, J., *Letters from Tanganyika: A District Officer's Life in the Run-up to Independence*, [self-published by J. Parry-Wingfield, copy obtained by the author from J. Parry-Wingfield], (2006).

Sadleir, R., *Tanzania, Journey to Republic* (London, 1999).

Williams, J. K., *Black, Amber, White: An Autobiography* (Worthing, 1990).

Printed Secondary Works

'Against the Shadows', *Awaaz*, 3 (December, 2005), pp. 14–25.

Abel, R. L., *The Legal Profession in England and Wales* (Oxford, 1988).

Adewoye, O., *The Judicial System in Southern Nigeria, 1854–1954: Law and Justice in a Dependency* (London, 1977).

Adewoye, O., *The Legal Profession in Nigeria, 1865–1962* (Ikeja, 1977).

African Studies Branch, 'A Digest of the Tanganyika Local Courts Ordinance 1951', *Journal of African Administration*, IV (1952), pp. 22–25.

Allott, A. N., 'Customary Law in East Africa', *Africa Spectrum*, 4 [Law in East Africa edition] (1969), pp. 16–22.

Allott, A. N., 'The Development of the East African Legal Systems During the Colonial Period' in Low, D. A., and Smith, A. (eds.), *History of East Africa* (3 vols., Oxford, 1976), pp. 348–382.

Allott, A. N., *Essays in African Law: With Special Reference to the Law of Ghana* (London, 1960).

Allott, A. N., 'The Judicial Ascertainment of Customary Law in British Africa', *The Modern Law Review*, 20 (1957), pp. 244–263.

Allott, A. N., *Judicial and Legal Systems in Africa* (London, 1962).

Allott, A. N., *New Essays in African Law* (London, 1970).

Allott, A. N., 'Towards the Unification of Laws in Africa', *International and Comparative Law Quarterly*, 14 (1965), pp. 866–889.

Aminzade, R., 'The Politics of Race and Nation: Citizenship and Africanisation in Tanganyika', *Political Power and Social Theory*, 14 (2000), pp. 53–90.

Andersen, C., *British Engineers and Africa, 1875–1914* (London, 2011).

Anderson, D., *Histories of the Hanged: Britain's Dirty War in Kenya and the End of Empire* (London, 2005).

Anderson, D., 'Kenya, 1895–1939: Registration and Rough Justice' in Hay, D., and Craven, P. (eds.), *Masters, Servants, and Magistrates in Britain and the Empire, 1562–1955* (London, 2004), pp. 498–528.

Anderson, D., 'Policing, Prosecution and the Law in Colonial Kenya, c. 1905–39' in Anderson, D., and Killingray, D., (eds.), *Policing the Empire: Government, Authority and Control, 1830–1940* (Manchester, 1991), pp. 183–200.

Anderson, D., and Killingray, D., *Policing and Decolonisation: Politics, Nationalism and the Police, 1917–65* (Manchester, 1992).

Anderson, J. N. D., *Islamic Law in Africa*, 1st edn (London, 1970).

Austen, R. A., 'The Official Mind of Indirect Rule: British Policy in Tanganyika, 1916–1939' in Gifford, P., and Louis, W. R. (eds.), *Britain and Germany in Africa: Imperial Rivalry and Colonial Rule* (London, 1967), pp. 577–606.

Austin, G., *Working a Democratic Constitution: A History of the Indian Experience* (New York, 2003).

Barringer, T., *Administering Empire: An Annotated Checklist of Personal Memoirs and Related Studies* (London, 2004).

Bates, D., *A Gust of Plumes: A Biography of Lord Twining of Godalming and Tanganyika* (London, 1972).

Bates, M. L., 'Tanganyika: The Development of a Trust Territory', *International Organization*, IX (1955), pp. 32–51.

Benton, L., 'Colonial Law and Culture Difference: Jurisdictional Politics and the Formation of the Colonial State', *Comparative Studies in Society and History*, 41 (1999), pp. 563–588.

Benton, L. A., *Law and Colonial Cultures: Legal Regimes in World History, 1400–1900* (Cambridge, 2002).

Bierwagen, R. M., and Peter, C. M., 'Administration of Justice in Tanzania and Zanzibar: A Comparison of Two Judicial Systems in One Country', *The International and Comparative Law Quarterly*, 38 (1989), pp. 395–412.

Bjerk, P., *Building a Peaceful Nation: Julius Nyerere and the Establishment of Sovereignty in Tanzania, 1960–1964* (Rochester, 2015).

Blom-Cooper, L. J., Drewry, G., and Dickson, B., *The Judicial House of Lords: 1876–2009* (Oxford, 2009).

Brennan, J., 'The Short History of Political Opposition and Multi-Party Democracy in Tanganyika 1958–1964' in Maddox, G., and Giblin, J. L., (eds.), *In Search of a Nation: Histories of Authority & Dissidence in Tanzania* (Oxford, 2005), pp. 250–276.

Brennan, J., 'South Asian Nationalism in an East African Context: The Case of Tanganyika, 1914–1954', *Comparative Studies of South Asia, Africa, and the Middle East*, 19 (1999), pp. 24–39.

Brereton, B., *Law, Justice, and Empire: The Colonial Career of John Gorrie, 1829–1892* (Kingston, 1997).

Brown, J. M., *Windows into the Past: Life Histories and the Historian of South Asia* (Notre Dame, 2009).

Buettner, E., *Empire Families: Britons and Late Imperial India* (Oxford, 2004).

Bushe, H. G., 'Criminal Justice in East Africa', *Journal of the Royal African Society*, 34 (1935), pp. 117–128.

Butler, L. J., *Copper Empire: Mining and the Colonial State in Northern Rhodesia, c. 1930–64* (Basingstoke, 2007).

Butler, L. J., and Stockwell, S. (eds.), *The Wind of Change: Harold Macmillan and British Decolonization* (London, 2013).

Byatt, H., 'Tanganyika', *Journal of the African Society*, 24 (1924), pp. 1–9.

Cabatingan, L., 'Time and Transcendence: Narrating Higher Authority at the CCJ', *Law and Society Review*, 50 (2016), pp. 674–702.

Cain, P. J., and Hopkins, A. G., *British Imperialism: Crisis and Deconstruction, 1914–1990* (London, 1993).

Cameron, D., and Heussler, R., *My Tanganyika Service and Some Nigeria*, 2nd edn (Washington, D.C, 1982).

Cameron, D. C., *Recent Progress in Tanganyika* (London, 1931).

Cell, J., 'Who Ran the British Empire' in Louis, W. R. (ed.), *More Adventures with Britannia. Personalities, Politics, and Culture in Britain* (Austin, 1998), pp. 303–317.

Chamberlain, M. E., *The Scramble for Africa*, 3rd edn (Harlow, 2010).

Chanock, M., *Law, Custom, and Social Order: The Colonial Experience in Malawi and Zambia* (Cambridge, 1985).

Chandrachud, A., *An Independent, Colonial Judiciary: A History of the Bombay High Court During the British Raj, 1861–1947* (New Delhi, 2015).

Chanock, M., *The Making of South African Legal Culture, 1902–1936: Fear, Favour and Prejudice* (Cambridge, 2001).

Chidzero, B. T. G., and Royal Institute of International Affairs, *Tanganyika and International Trusteeship* (Oxford, 1961).

Cole, J. S. R., and Denison, W. N., *Tanganyika: The Development of Its Laws and Constitution* (London, 1964).

Collins, R., 'The Sudan Political Service: A Portrait of "Imperialists"', *African Affairs*, 71 (1972), pp. 293–303.

Comaroff, J., 'Colonialism, Culture, and the Law: A Foreward', *Law & Social Inquiry*, 26 (2001), pp. 305–314.

Cooke, J., *One White Man in Black Africa: From Kilimanjaro to Kalahari 1951–1991* (Thornhill, 1991).

Cory, H., *Sukuma Law and Custom* (London, 1953).

Cory, H., and Hartnoll, M. M., *Customary Law of the Haya Tribe, Tanganyika Territory* (London, 1971).

Cotran, E., 'Some Recent Developments in the Tanganyika Judicial System', *Journal of African Law*, Spring (1962), pp. 19–28.

Cotran, E., 'The Unification of Laws in East Africa', *Journal of Modern African Studies*, 1 (1963), pp. 209–220.

Cotran, E., 'Integration of Courts and Application of Customary Law in Tanganyika', *East African Law Journal*, 1 (1965), pp. 108–123.

Cotran, E., 'Tanzania' in Allott, A. N. (ed.), *Judicial and Legal Systems in Africa* (London, 1970), pp. 145–169.

Coulson, A., *Tanzania: A Political Economy* (Oxford, 1982).

Court of Appeal of Tanzania, *The History of the Administration of Justice in Tanzania* (Dar es Salaam, 2004).

Crozier, A., *Practising Colonial Medicine: The Colonial Medical Service in British East Africa* (London, 2007).

Darwin, J., *Britain and Decolonisation: The Retreat from Empire in the Post-War World* (Basingstoke, 1988).

Darwin, J., *The End of the British Empire: The Historical Debate* (Oxford, 1991).

Darwin, J., 'Decolonization and the End of Empire' in Winks, R. W. (ed.), *Oxford History of the British Empire* (5 vols., Oxford, 1999), v, pp. 541–557.

Darwin, J., *The Empire Project: The Rise and Fall of the British World-System, 1830–1970* (Cambridge, 2009).

de Smith, S. A., 'Tenure of Office by Colonial Judges', *The Modern Law Review*, 16 (1953), pp. 502–506.

Deutsch, J.-G., 'Celebrating Power in Everyday Life: The Administration of Law and the Public Sphere in Colonial Tanzania, 1890–1914', *Journal of African Cultural Studies*, 15 (2002), pp. 93–103.

Dorsett, S., and McLaren, J. (eds.), *Legal Histories of the British Empire: Laws, Engagements, and Legacies* (New York, 2014).

Duffler, J., and Frey, M., 'Introduction', in Duffler, J., and Fry, M. (eds.), *Elites and Decolonization in the Twentieth Century* (Basingstoke, 2011), pp. 1–10.

Duman, D., *The English and Colonial Bars in the Nineteenth Century* (London, 1983).

Dupont, J., *The Common Law Abroad: Constitutional and Legal Legacy of the British Empire* (Littleton, 2000).

Eckert, A., 'Cultural Commuters: African Employees in Late Colonial Tanzania' in Lawrance, B. N., Osborn, E. L., and Roberts, R. L. (eds.), *Intermediaries, Interpreters, and Clerks: African Employees in the Making of Colonial Africa* (Madison, 2006), pp. 248–272.

Eckert, A., *Herrschen Und Verwalten: Afrikanische Büokraten, Staatliche Ordnung Und Politik in Tanzania*, 1920–1970 (Munich, 2007).

Elias, T. O., *The Nigerian Legal System* (London, 1963).

Engle Merry, S., 'From Law and Colonialism to Law and Globalization', *Law and Social Inquiry*, 28 (2003), pp. 560–590.

Faidjoe, A., Kodilinye, G., and Georges, J. C. G., *Telford Georges: A Legal Odyssey* (Kingston, 2008).

Feierman, S., *Peasant Intellectuals: Anthropology and History in Tanzania* (London, 1990).

Fisch, J., 'Law as a Means and as an End: Some Remarks on the Function of European and Non-European Law in the Process of European Expansion' in Mommsen, W. J., and De Moor, J. A. (eds.), *European Expansion and Law: The Encounter of European and Indigenous Law in 19th- and 20th-Century Africa and Asia* (Oxford, 1992), pp. 15–38.

Gailey, H. A., *Sir Donald Cameron, Colonial Governor* (Stanford, 1974).

Gallagher, J., and Robinson, R., 'The Imperialism of Free Trade', *The Economic History Review*, 6 (1953), pp. 1–15.

Gann, L. H., and Duignan, P., *African Proconsuls: European Governors in Africa* (London, 1978).

Gann, L. H., and Duignan, P., *The Rulers of British Africa, 1870–1914* (London, 1978).

Garner, B. A., and Black, H. C., *Black's Law Dictionary*, 9th edn (St. Paul, 2009).

Geiger, S., *TANU Women: Gender and Culture in the Making of Tanganyikan Nationalism, 1955–1965* (Oxford, 1997).

Georges, P. T., 'Report on Judges' and Magistrates' Conference', *Eastern Africa Law Review*, 1 (1968).

Georges, P. T., 'The Role of Judges and Magistrates' in James, R. W., and Kassam, F. M. (eds.), *Law and Its Administration in a One Party State: Selected Speeches of Telford Georges* (Dar es Salaam, 1973), pp. 69–93.

Ghai, Y., 'Constitution Making and Decolonisation' in Ghai, Y. (ed.), *Law, Government and Politics in the Pacific Island States* (Suva, Fiji, 1988), pp. 1–53.

Ghai, Y., 'Law, Development and African Scholarship', *The Modern Law Review*, 50 (1987), pp. 750–776.

Ghai, Y. P., and McAuslan, P., *Public Law and Political Change in Kenya: A Study of the Legal Framework of Government from Colonial Times to the Present* (Nairobi, 1970).

Goldsworthy, D., *Colonial Issues in British Politics 1945–1961: From Colonial Development to Wind of Change* (Oxford, 1971).

Goldsworthy, D., and University of London Institute of Commonwealth Studies, *The Conservative Government and the End of Empire, 1951–1957* (3 vols., London, 1994).

Gordon, J., 'African Law and the Historian', *The Journal of African History*, 8 (1967), pp. 335–340.

Gower, L. C. B., *Independent Africa: The Challenge to the Legal Profession* (London, 1967).

Graham, J. D., 'Indirect Rule: The Establishment of Chiefs and Tribes in Cameron's Tanganyika', *Tanzania Notes and Records*, 77 (1976), pp. 1–11.

Gray, J., 'Opinions of Assessors in Criminal Trials in East Africa as to Native Custom', *Journal of African Law*, 2 (1958), pp. 5–18.

Grimal, H., *Decolonization: The British, French, Dutch and Belgian Empires 1919–1963* (London, 1978).

Hailey, W. M. H., and the Royal Institute of International Affairs, *An African Survey: A Study of Problems Arising in Africa South of the Sahara*, 2nd edn (Oxford, 1945).

Hamilton, R., 'Criminal Justice in East Africa', *Journal of the Royal African Society*, 34 (1935), pp. 7–26.

Hargreaves, J. D., *Decolonization in Africa*, 2nd edn (London, 1996).

Harrington, J., and Manji, A., '"Mind with Mind, Spirit with Spirit": Lord Denning and African Legal Education', *Journal of Law and Society*, 30 (2003), pp. 376–399.

Harrington, J., and Manji, A., 'The Emergence of African Law as an Academic Discipline', *African Affairs*, 102 (2003), pp. 109–134.

Haydon, A. P., *Sir Matthew Nathan: British Colonial Governor and Civil Servant* (St. Lucia, 1976).

Heussler, R., *Yesterday's Rulers: The Making of the British Colonial Service* (Syracuse, 1963).

Heussler, R., *British Tanganyika: An Essay and Documents on District Administration* (Durham, 1971).

Holland, R. F., *Emergencies and Disorder in the European Empires after 1945* (London, 1994).

Holland, R. F., *European Decolonization, 1918–1981: An Introductory Survey* (Basingstoke, 1985).

Hollander, B., *Colonial Justice: The Unique Achievement of the Privy Council's Committee of Judges* (London, 1961).

Hone, H. R., 'The Native of Uganda and the Criminal Law', *Journal of Comparative Legislation and International Law*, 21 (1939), pp. 179–197.

Hyam, R., and University of London Institute of Commonwealth Studies, *The Labour Government and the End of Empire, 1945–1951* (4 vols., London, 1992).

Hyam, R., Louis, W. R., and University of London Institute of Commonwealth Studies, *The Conservative Government and the End of Empire, 1957–1964* (2 vols., London, 2000).

Ibhawoh, B., 'Asserting Judicial Sovereignty: The Debate Over the Abolition of Privy Council Jurisdiction in British Africa' in Dorsett, S., and McLaren, J. (eds.), *Legal Histories of the British Empire: Laws, Engagements, and Legacies* (New York, 2014), pp. 30–44.

Ibhawoh, B., 'Historical Globalization and Colonial Legal Culture: African Assessors, Customary Law, and Criminal Justice in British Africa', *Journal of Global History*, 4 (2009), pp. 429–451.

Ibhawoh, B., *Imperial Justice: Africans in Empire's Court* (New York, 2013).

Ilbert, C., *The Government of India: Being a Digest of the Statute Law Relating Thereto*, 2nd edn (Oxford, 1907).

Iliffe, J., *A Modern History of Tanganyika* (Cambridge, 1979).

Iliffe, J., 'Breaking the Chain at Its Weakest Link: TANU and the Colonial Office' in Maddox, G., and Giblin, J. L. (eds.), *In Search of a Nation: Histories of Authority & Dissidence in Tanzania* (Oxford, 2005), pp. 168–197.

Inns of Court Conservative and Unionist Society, *British Colonial Judges: Their Appointment and Tenure of Office* (London, 1956).

James, R. W., and Kassam, F. M., 'Introduction' in James, R. W., and Kassam, F. M. (eds.), *Law and Its Administration in a One Party State: Selected Speeches of Telford Georges* (Dar es Salaam, 1973), pp. 1–6.

James, R. W., and Kassam, F. M., 'The Courts in the Tanzania One Party State' in James, R. W., and Kassam, F. M. (eds.), *Law and Its Administration in a One Party State: Selected Speeches of Telford Georges* (Dar es Salaam, 1973), pp. 9–32.

Japhet, K., and Seaton, E., *The Meru Land Case* (Nairobi, 1967).

Jearey, J. H., 'The Structure, Composition and Jurisdiction of Courts and Authorities Enforcing the Criminal Law in British African Territories', *The International and Comparative Law Quarterly*, 9 (1960), pp. 396–414.

Jearey, J. H., 'Trial by Jury and Trial with the Aid of Assessors in the Superior Courts of British African Territories: I', *Journal of African Law*, 4 (1960), pp. 133–146.

Jearey, J. H., 'Trial by Jury and Trial with the Aid of Assessors in the Superior Courts of British African Territories: II', *Journal of African Law*, 5 (1961), pp. 36–47.

Jearey, J. H., 'Trial by Jury and Trial with the Aid of Assessors in the Superior Courts of British African Territories: III', *Journal of African Law*, 5 (1961), pp. 82–98.

Jeffries, C. J., *The Colonial Empire and Its Civil Service* (Cambridge, 1938).

Killingray, D., 'The Maintenance of Law and Order in British Colonial Africa', *African Affairs*, 85 (1986), pp. 411–437.

Kimambo, I. N., 'Establishment of Teaching Programmes', in Kimambo, I. N., Mapunda, B. B. B., and Lawi, Y. Q. (eds.), *In Search of Relevance: A History of the University of Dar Es Salaam* (Dar es Salaam, 2008), pp. 152–169.

Kirk-Greene, A. H. M., *Britain's Imperial Administrators, 1858–1966* (Basingstoke, 2000).

Kirk-Greene, A. H. M., 'Decolonization: The Ultimate Diaspora', *Journal of Contemporary History*, 36 (2001), pp. 133–151.

Kirk-Greene, A. H. M., *On Crown Service: A History of Hm Colonial and Overseas Civil Service, 1837–1997* (London, 1999).

Kirk-Greene, A. H. M., 'Scholastic Attainment and Scholarly Achievement in Britain's Imperial Civil Services: The Case of the African Governors', *Oxford Review of Education*, 7 (1981), pp. 11–22.

Kirk-Greene, A. H. M., *Symbol of Authority: The British District Officer in Africa* (London, 2006).

Kirk-Greene, A. H. M., 'The Thin White Line: The Size of the British Colonial Service in Africa', *African Affairs*, 79 (1980), pp. 25–44.

Kirk-Greene, A. H. M., 'Towards a Retrospective Record: Part I – What Became of Us?', *The Overseas Pensioner*, 84 (2002).

Kirk-Greene, A. H. M., 'Towards a Retrospective Record: Part II – on Reflection and in Retrospect, the Colonial Service Mind', *The Overseas Pensioner*, 85 (2003).

Knox-Mawer, R., 'The Jury System in British Colonial Africa', *Journal of African Law*, 2 (1958), pp. 160–163.

Lawrence, T., and MacRae, C., *The Dar Mutiny of 1964: And the Armed Intervention That Ended It* (Sussex, 2007).

Lawrance, B. N., Osborn, E. L. and Roberts, R. L., 'African Intermediaries and the "Bargain" of Collaboration' in Lawrance, B. N., Osborn, E. L., and Roberts, R. L. (eds.), *Intermediaries, Interpreters, and Clerks: African Employees in the Making of Colonial Africa* (Madison, 2006), pp. 3–34.

Lester, A., 'Imperial Circuits and Networks: Geographies of the British Empire', *History Compass*, 4 (2006) pp. 124–141.

Lester, A., *Imperial Networks: Creating Identities in Nineteenth Century South Africa and Britain* (London, 2001).

Lewis-Barned, J., *A Fanfare of Trumpets* (Witney, 1993).

Lewis-Barned, J. F., 'Integration of Judicial Systems: The Recent Reform of the Local Courts Appeal System of Tanganyika', *Journal of African Law*, 7 (1963).

Liebenow, J. G., *Colonial Rule and Political Development in Tanzania: The Case of the Makonde* (Evanston, 1971).

Listowel, J. M.-M. H., *The Making of Tanganyika* (London, 1965).

Louis, W. R., *Imperialism at Bay, 1941–1945: The United States and the Decolonization of the British Empire* (Oxford, 1977).

Louis, W. R., and Robinson, R., 'The Imperialism of Decolonization', *Journal of Imperial and Commonwealth History*, 22 (1994), pp. 462–511.

Louis, W. R., and Robinson, R., 'The United States and the Liquidation of British Empire in Tropical Africa, 1941–1951' in Gifford, P., and Louis, W. R. (eds.), *The Transfer of Power in Africa, Decolonization 1940–1960* (London, 1982), pp. 31–56.

Loveridge, A. J., 'The Future of Native Courts', *Journal of African Administration*, 1 (1949), pp. 7–18.

Low, D. A., *Eclipse of Empire* (Cambridge, 1991).

Lugard, F. J. D., *The Dual Mandate in British Tropical Africa*, 5th edn (London, 1965).

Lumley, E. K., *Forgotten Mandate: A British District Officer in Tanganyika* (London, 1976).

Madden, A. F., and Darwin, J., *The Dependent Empire, 1900–1948: Colonies, Protectorates, and Mandates* (London, 1994).

Mamdani, M., *Citizen and Subject: Contemporary Africa and the Legacy of Late Colonialism* (Princeton, 1996).

Mann, K., and Roberts, A. D., 'Law in Colonial Africa' in Mann, K., and Roberts, A. D. (eds.), *Law in Colonial Africa* (London, 1991), pp. 3–60.

Mapunda, B. B. B., 'Infrastructure' in Kimambo, I. N., Mapunda, B. B. B., and Lawi, Y. Q. (eds.), *In Search of Relevance: A History of the University of Dar Es Salaam* (Dar es Salaam, 2008), pp. 60–82.

Martin, R., *Personal Freedom and Law in Tanzania: A Study of Socialist State Administration* (Nairobi, 1974).

Mason, P., *The Men Who Ruled India* (2 vols., London, 1963).

Maxwell, D., 'Decolonisation' in Etherington, N. (ed.), *Missions and Empire, the Oxford History of the British Empire Companion Series* (Oxford, 2005), pp. 285–306

McAuslan, J. P. W. B., 'The Republican Constitution of Tanganyika', *The International and Comparative Law Quarterly*, 13 (1964), pp. 502–573.

McAuslan, J. P. W. B., and Ghai, Y. P., 'Constitutional Innovation and Political Stability in Tanzania: A Preliminary Assessment', *Journal Of Modern African Studies*, 4 (1966), pp. 479–515.

McLaren, J., *Dewigged, Bothered, and Bewildered: British Colonial Judges on Trial, 1800–1900* (Toronto, 2011).

McLaren, J., 'Navigating the Scylla of Imperial Politico-Legal Aspirations and Charybdis of Colonial Micro-Politics in the British Empire', in Dorsett, S., and McLaren, J. (eds.), *Legal Histories of the British Empire: Laws, Engagements, and Legacies* (New York, 2014), pp. 15–29.

Moffett, J. P., 'Native Courts in Tanganyika: A History of the Development of Native Courts from German Times', *Journal of African Administration*, 4 (1952), pp. 17–21.

Moisey, R. W., 'The Role of Assessors in the Courts of Tanzania', *East African Law Journal*, 3 (1967), pp. 348–353.

Mommsen, W. J., 'Introduction' in Mommsen, W. J., and De Moor, J. A. (eds.), *European Expansion and Law: The Encounter of European and Indigenous Law in 19th- and 20th-Century Africa and Asia* (Oxford, 1992), pp. 1–14.

Moore, S. F., *Social Facts and Fabrications: "Customary" Law on Kilimanjaro, 1880–1980* (Cambridge, 1986).

Moore, S. F., 'Treating Law as Knowledge: Telling Colonial Officers What to Say to Africans About Running "Their Own" Native Courts', *Law & Society Review*, 26 (1992), pp. 11–46.

Morris, H. F., *Some Perspectives of East African Legal History* (Uppsala, 1970).

Morris, H. F., 'English Law in East Africa: A Hardy Plant in an Alien Soil' in Morris, H. F., and Read, J. S. (eds.), *Indirect Rule and the Search for Justice: Essays in East African Legal History* (Oxford, 1972), pp. 73–108.

Morris, H. F., 'The Framework of Indirect Rule in East Africa' in Morris, H. F., and Read, J. S. (eds.), *Indirect Rule and the Search for Justice: Essays in East African Legal History* (Oxford, 1972), pp. 3–40.

Morris, H. F., 'A History of the Adoption of Codes of Criminal Law and Procedure in British Colonial Africa, 1876–1935', *Journal of African Law*, 18 (1974), pp. 6–23.

Morris, H. F., 'Native Courts: A Corner-Stone of Indirect Rule' in Morris, H. F., and Read, J. S. (eds.), *Indirect Rule and the Search for Justice: Essays in East African Legal History* (Oxford, 1972), pp. 131–166.

Morris, H. F., 'Protection or Annexation? Some Constitutional Anomalies of Colonial Rule' in Morris, H. F., and Read, J. S. (eds.), *Indirect Rule and the Search for Justice: Essays in East African Legal History* (Oxford, 1972), pp. 41–72.

Morris, H. F., 'The Reception and Rejection of Indian Law' in Morris, H. F., and Read, J. S. (eds.), *Indirect Rule and the Search for Justice: Essays in East African Legal History* (Oxford, 1972), pp. 109–130.

Morris, H. F., and Read, J. S., *Indirect Rule and the Search for Justice: Essays in East African Legal History* (Oxford, 1972).

Murphy, P., *Party Politics and Decolonization: The Conservative Party and British Colonial Policy in Tropical Africa, 1951–1964* (Oxford, 1995).

Mustafa, F., 'Re-Issuing the Tanganyika Way: 1961–*2009*' in Mustafa, S., *The Tanganyika Way* (Tornoto, 2009).

Mustafa, S., *The Tanganyika Way* (London, 1962).

Mvungi, S. E. A. (ed.), *Forty Years of the Faculty of Law University of Dar Es Salaam 1961–2001* (Dar es Salaam, 2002).

Mwakikagile, G., *Life in Tanganyika in the Fifties* (Pretoria, 2009).
Mwalusanya, J. L., *The Judiciary in Tanzania* (Dar es Salaam, 1988).
Nagar, R., 'The South Asian Diaspora in Tanzania: A History Retold', *Comparative Studies of South Asia, Africa, and the Middle East*, XVI (1996), pp. 62–80.
Ngh'waya, S., *Kesi ya Julius Kambarage Nyerere, rais wa Tanganyika African National Union, kwa "kashfa" dhidi ya maDC wa kikoloni wawili 1958* (Dar es Salaam, 1990).
Nicholson, M. E. R., 'Change Without Conflict: A Case Study of Legal Change in Tanzania', *Law and Society Review*, 4 (1973), pp. 747–766.
O'Malley, L. S. S., *The Indian Civil Service, 1601–1930*, 2nd edn (London, 1965).
Parkinson, C., *Bills of Rights and Decolonization: The Emergence of Domestic Human Rights Instruments in Britain's Overseas Territories* (Oxford, 2007).
Pesek, M., 'Cued Speeches: The Emergence of Shauri as Colonial Praxis in German East Africa, 1850–1903', *History in Africa*, 33 (2006), pp. 395–312.
Peter, C. M., 'Incarcerating the Innocent: Preventive Detention in Tanzania', *Human Rights Quarterly*, 19 (1997), pp. 113–135.
Peter, C. M., 'Tanzania' in Harding, A., and Hatchard, J. (eds.), *Preventive Detention and Security Law: A Comparative Survey* (Dordrecht, 1993), pp. 247–257.
Pfeiffer, S. B., 'The Role of the Judiciary in the Constitutional Systems of East Africa', *The Journal of Modern African Studies*, 16 (1978), pp. 33–66.
Potter, D. C., *India's Political Administrators: From ICS to IAS*, 1st Indian edn (Delhi, 1996).
Pratt, C., *The Critical Phase in Tanzania, 1945–1968: Nyerere and the Emergence of a Socialist Strategy* (Cambridge, 1976).
Ranger, T. O., 'The Invention of Tradition in Colonial Africa' in Hobsbawm, E. J., and Ranger, T. O. (eds.), *The Invention of Tradition* (Cambridge, 1983), pp. 211–263.
Ranger, T. O., 'The Invention of Tradition Revisited: The Case of Colonial Africa', in Ranger, T. O., and Vaughan, O. (eds.), *Legitimacy and the State in Twentieth Century Africa. Essays in Honour of A. M. H. Kirk-Greene* (London, 1993), pp. 62–111.
Read, J. S., 'A Century Plus of Appeal Courts in Tanzania' in Peter, C. M., and Bisimba, H. K. (eds.), *Law and Justice in Tanzania: Quarter of a Century of the Court of Appeal* (Dar es Salam, 2007), pp. 55–80.
Read, J. S., 'Crime and Punishment in East Africa: The Twilight of Customary Law', *Howard Law Journal*, 10 (1964), pp. 164–186.
Read, J. S., 'Customary Law Under Colonial Rule' in Morris, H. F., and Read, J. S. (eds.), *Indirect Rule and the Search for Justice: Essays in East African Legal History* (Oxford, 1972), pp. 167–212.
Read, J. S., 'Human Rights in Tanzania' in Legum, C., and Mmari, G. (eds.), *Mwalimu the Influence of Nyerere* (London, 1995), pp. 125–145.

Read, J. S., 'Minimum Sentences in Tanzania', *Journal of African Law*, 9 (1965), pp. 20–39.

Read, J. S., 'Patterns of Indirect Rule in East Africa' in Morris, H. F., and Read, J. S. (eds.), *Indirect Rule and the Search for Justice: Essays in East African Legal History* (Oxford, 1972), pp. 253–286.

Read, J. S., 'The Search for Justice' in Morris, H. F., and Read, J. S. (eds.), *Indirect Rule and the Search for Justice: Essays in East African Legal History* (Oxford, 1972), pp. 287–331.

Roberts-Wray, K., *Commonwealth and Colonial Law* (London, 1966).

Roberts, C. C., Nicholson, R. P., and Orde-Browne, G. S. J., *Tangled Justice: Some Reasons for a Change of Policy in Africa* (London, 1937).

Russell, A., 'The Administration of Justice in East Africa', *Journal of Comparative Legislation and International Law*, 17 (1935), pp. 1–11.

Sawyerr, A., 'Customary Law in the High Court of Tanzania', *Eastern Africa Law Review*, 6 (1973), pp. 265–284.

Schmitthener, S., 'A Sketch of the Development of the Legal Profession in India', *Law and Society Review*, 3 (1969), pp. 337–382.

Schneider, L., 'The Tanzania National Archives', *History in Africa*, 30 (2003), pp. 447–454.

Schneider, L., 'Colonial Legacies and Postcolonial Authoritarianism in Tanzania: Connects and Disconnects', *African Studies Review*, 49 (2006), pp. 93–118.

Shadle, B., 'African Court Elders in Nyanza Province, Kenya, C. 1930–1960: From "Traditional" to "Modern"' in Lawrance, B. N., Osborn, E. L., and Roberts, R. L. (eds.), *Intermediaries, Interpreters, and Clerks: African Employees in the Making of Colonial Africa* (Madison, 2006), pp. 180–201.

Shivji, I. G., *Limits of Legal Radicalism: Reflections on Teaching Law at the University of Dar Es Salaam* (Dar es Salaam, 1986).

Shivji, I. G., Majamba, H. I., Makaramba, R. V., and Peter, C. M., *Constitutional and Legal System of Tanzania: A Civics Sourcebook* (Dar es Salaam, 2004).

Simpson, A. W. B., 'The Devlin Commission (1959): Colonialism, Emergencies, and the Rule of Law', *Oxford Journal of Legal Studies*, 22 (2002), pp. 17–52.

Sinclair, G., *At the End of the Line: Colonial Policing and the Imperial Endgame 1945–1980* (Manchester, 2006).

Stanley B., and Low, A. M., *Missions, Nationalism, and the End of Empire* (Grand Rapids, 2003).

Stockwell, S., 'Exporting Britishness: Decolonization in Africa, the British Sate, and Its Clients' in Jeronimo, M. B., and Pinto, A. C., (eds.), *The Ends of European Colonial Empires: Cases and Comparisons* (London, 2015), pp. 148–177.

Stockwell, S., and Butler, L. J., 'Introduction', in Butler, L. J., and Stockwell, S. (eds.), *The Wind of Change: Harold Macmillan and British Decolonization* (London, 2013), pp. 1–19.

Stockwell, S. E., 'Ends of Empire' in Stockwell, S. E. (ed.), *The British Empire: Themes and Perspectives* (Malden, 2008), pp. 267–293.

Stockwell, S. E., '"Splendidly Leading the Way"?: Archbishop Fisher and Decolonisation in British Colonial Africa' in Holland, R., and Stockwell, S. E. (eds.), *Ambiguities of Empire: Essays in Honour of Andrew Porter* (New York, 2009), pp. 199–218.

Stockwell, S. E., *The Business of Decolonization: British Business Strategies in the Gold Coast* (Oxford, 2000).

Swanepeol, P., 'Judicial Choice During the Mau Mau Rebellion in Kenya, 1952–1960', *Fundamina*, 18 (2012), pp. 145–161.

Swanepeol, P., 'Kenya's Colonial Judges: The Advocates' Perspective', *Journal of Asian and African Studies*, 50 (2015), pp. 41–57.

Swanepeol, P., 'Transient Justice: Colonial Judges on the Circuit in Interwar Tanganyika', *Stichproben: Vienna Journal of African Studies*, 24 (2013), pp. 65–91.

Swinfen, D. B., *Imperial Appeal: The Debate on the Appeal to the Privy Council, 1833–1986* (Manchester, 1987).

Tanner, R. E. S., 'The Codification of Customary Law in Tanzania', *East African Law Journal*, 2 (1966), pp. 105–116.

Tanzania Peoples Defence Force, *Tanganyika Rifles Mutiny, January 1964* (Dar es Salaam, 1993).

Taylor, J. C., *The Political Development of Tanganyika* (Stanford, 1963).

Tordoff, W., *Government and Politics in Tanzania: A Collection of Essays Covering the Period from September 1960 to July 1966* (Nairobi, 1967).

Twaib, F., *The Legal Profession in Tanzania* (Bayreuth, 1997).

Twining, W., *Law in Context: Enlarging a Discipline* (Oxford, 1997).

Twining, W., 'Legal Education Within East Africa', *British Institute of International and Comparative Law in East African Law Today*, Commonwealth Law Series No. 5 (1966).

Twining, W., *The Place of Customary Law in the National Legal Systems of East Africa: Lectures Delivered at the University of Chicago Law School in April–May 1963* (Chicago, 1964).

Twining, W., 'The Restatement of African Customary Law: A Comment', *Journal of Modern African Studies*, 1 (1963), pp. 221–228.

Weiner, M. J., *An Empire on Trial: Race, Murder, and Justice Under British Rule* (Cambridge, 2009).

Weston, A. B., 'Tanganyika', *Journal of African Law*, 6 (1962), pp. 150–155.

Who Was Who, 1971–1980: A Companion to Who's Who, Containing the Biographies of Those Who Died During the Decade 1971–1980 (New York, 1981).

Who Was Who, 1981–1990: A Companion to Who's Who Containing the Biographies of Those Who Died During the Decade 1981–1990 (London, 1991).

Who Was Who, 1991–1995: A Companion to Who's Who Containing the Biographies of Those Who Died During the Period 1991–1995 (London, 1996).
Who Was Who, 1920–2008; Online edn, Oxford University Press, 'MOSDELL, Lionel Patrick', [accessed 28 October 2011].
Widner, J. A., *Building the Rule of Law*, 1st edn (New York, 2001).

Unpublished Theses and Papers

Bates, M. L., 'Tanganyika Under British Administration, 1920–1955', D.Phil. thesis (University of Oxford, 1958).
Castelnuovo, S., 'Legal and Judicial Integration in Tanzania: A Study of Law and Political and Social Change', Ph.D. thesis (University of California – Los Angeles, 1969).
DuBow, F., 'Justice for People: Law and Politics in the Lower Courts of Tanzania', Ph.D. thesis (University of California – Berkeley, 1973).
Feingold, E. R., 'Power, Procedure, and Punishment: The Administration of Criminal Justice in East Africa c.1933', M.Sc. thesis (University of Oxford, 2007)
Mkenda, F., 'Building National Unity in Sub-Saharan Africa: The Impact of State Policies on the Chagga Community in Northern Tanzania', D.Phil. thesis (University of Oxford, 2009).
Mkenda, F., 'Tensions, Threats, and a Nation's Weakest Link: Muslim-Christian Relations and the Future of Peace in Tanzania', Unpublished paper (Campion Hall, Oxford, 2011).
Morris-Hale, W., 'British Administration in Tanganyika from 1920 to 1945: With Special References to the Preparation of Africans for Administrative Positions', Ph.D. thesis (University of Geneva, 1969).
Neville, R. R., 'Institutional Transfer and Change in Africa: The Introduction of British Court Structure in Tanganyika Territory, 1920–1946', Ph.D. thesis (Syracuse University, 1971).
Nicholson, M. E. R., 'Legal Change in Tanzania as Seen Among the Sukuma', Ph.D. thesis (University of Minnesota, 1968).
Onagoruwa, G. O., 'The History of the Judiciary in Commonwealth African Countries with Speical Reference to West Africa', Ph.D. thesis (University of London, 1969).
Swanepoel, P., 'Indifferent Justice? A History of the Judges of Kenya and Tanganyika, 1897–1963', Ph.D. thesis (University of Edinburgh, 2010).

Index[1]

A

Acculturation, 39, 40
Acting Chief Justice of Zanzibar, 219
Acting Judge of the High Court, 183, 185, 186
Acting Resident Magistrate for Iringa and Njombe, 149
Act of Settlement, 105
Administrative Secretary, 77
Administrators, 6, 7, 9, 26
  as magistrates, 27, 28, 65, 88, 91, 92, 147
  Native Authorities and, 66
  ten day courses, 74
  tensions with judiciary, 6, 26, 91, 94
  See also Colonial Administrative Service; Magistrates
Admiralty jurisdiction, 57
Advocates, 151
  Asian, 103, 187, 201, 202, 226
Advocates Ordinance of 1954, 144
African Administrative Assistants, 102
Africanisation, 166–172, 180, 188, 191n4, 193n32
  foreign judges and, 203, 211
Africanisation Committee, 169
African Regional Commissioners, 191n4
Africans
  associate judge post, 153, 219
  demands for voice in planning, 87, 98
  as judges, 101–103, 148, 149, 215–219
  justice for, 53, 58, 66–68, 91, 154
  Legal Probationership Scheme, 107, 129n135
  magistrates, 102, 154, 155
  as Regional Local Courts officers, 148–149
  training for judiciary, 166, 201–203, 215–225

[1] Note: Page numbers followed by 'n' refer to notes.

E.R. Feingold, *Colonial Justice and Decolonization in the High Court of Tanzania, 1920–1971*, Cambridge Imperial and Post-Colonial Studies Series, https://doi.org/10.1007/978-3-319-69691-1

Akidas, 55, 56
Alexander, Gilchrist G., 58, 64
Aligarh Muslim University, 217
American Consulate, 102–103
Aminzade, Ronald, 180
Anderson, David, 8
Appellate system, 57, 59, 66, 67, 77, 137, 174, 237, 239
  Local Courts Appeals Officer, 148
  See also Central Court of Appeal; Court of Appeal; Eastern African Court of Appeal
Arusha Declaration (1967), 212
Arusha High Court, 154
Asian advocates, 12, 15, 103, 187, 201, 202, 226
Asian community, 60, 75
Assessors, 62–64, 152
Assistant District Officers, 102
Associate judge, 153, 219
Attorneys General, 12, 77, 90, 142, 188

B

Backlog of cases, 58, 60, 70, 71, 92, 96, 154
The Bad Old Irish J's, 43–45
Bakari, Mdoe, 102, 127n105
Bannerman, E.A.L., 206
Bantu, Kasella, 213
Bantu patrilineal tribes, 140
Battershill Committee, 107
Battershill, William D., 107, 129n133
Bench of the Court of Appeal, 76
Berlin Conference of 1884–1885, 54
Biafra, Republic of, 206
Bill of Rights, 178, 196n87
Biron, Philip, 1, 15, 16, 166, 181, 182, 184–189, 204, 224, 225, 240
  as local, 189, 198n137
  as mentor, 188, 189
Bomani, Mark, 208, 218
Botswana (Bechuanaland Protectorate), 181
Bramble, Cecil, 210, 225
Brennan, James, 179
Brereton, Bridget, 45
British Central Africa (Nyasaland), 59
British Civil Administrator, 55
British High Commission, 176
British legal traditions, 4, 5, 56, 64, 68, 69, 72, 205
British Mandate for East Africa, 67
Brown, Roland, 142, 159n28, 176–179, 203, 205, 210
Building the Rule of Law: Francis Nylali and the Road to Judicial Independence in Africa (Widner), 12
Burma, 34
Burundi, 53
Bushe Commission, 88–96, 109, 239
Bushe, Henry G., 31, 35–37, 39, 40, 90
Bushe Report, 88–94, 120n10, 121n15, 150
Byatt, Horace, 55, 71

C

Cameron, Donald C., 53, 56, 69–73, 76, 77, 86n125, 88, 93, 137, 148
  Russell and, 70, 71, 85n104, 144
Career structure, 38–39
Carter, William M., 58, 71, 80n31, 81n44, 98
Castelnuovo, Shirley, 138, 140, 141
Central Court of Appeal, 100, 101, 103, 147, 148
  See also Court of Appeal
Central Line Railway, 60, 98
Chandrachud, Abhinav, 18n22

Chanock, Martin, 4, 18n27, 83n80, 130n155
Chief Justices, 11, 12, 22n47, 58, 90
  African, 12, 201, 217, 219, 222, 225, 226
  Eastern African Court of Appeal and, 104
  foreign, 202
  Judicial Service Commission and, 144
  post-war replacement, 94
  Puisne judges and, 143, 146
  under 1961 Constitution, 142
Chieftaincy, 56, 62, 149, 155
Christians, 215–216
Circuits (assizes), 60–62, 92, 95, 97
Citizenship, 170
Civil cases, 6, 55, 58, 60, 71, 75, 85n103
'Civilising mission', 4, 6, 38, 116, 238
Cluer, R.M., 94, 122n45
Colonial Administrative Service, 26, 28, 29, 35
  See also Administrators
Colonial Administrative Service course, 35
Colonial Development and Welfare Act of 1945, 87
'Colonial legal modernity', 6
Colonial Legal Service, 6–8, 10, 105–109, 175
  advertisements, 33
  after WWII, 105
  career structure, 39
  creation of, 1933, 25, 238
  development of, 13, 25–45
  incremental approach, 29–30
  language requirements, 36
  motivations for joining, 33–35, 45
  negotiation process, 37
  preparation and requirements, 35–38
  promotion, tenure, dismissal, and retirement, 38–42
  recruitment and appointments, 29–33
  as result of African expansion, 28
  transfer policy, 34–35
  unification scheme, 32, 35–37, 40, 43, 44
  See also Judiciary, colonial
Colonial legal systems, 4–6
  hierarchical system, 5
  policies and practices, 7
  racial bifurcation, 5, 36, 54, 58, 98–103, 135, 136, 138
Colonial Office, 7, 12–14, 31, 32, 87, 88, 93, 94, 106
  decolonisation and, 166, 167
  Dominions, barristers from, 33
  Her Majesty's Oversea[s] Civil Service, 108
  post-independence lack of recruitment, 173
  post-World War II, 106
  reconstruction and development, 14
  standardization, 25
  World War II, 94
  See also Colonial Administrative Service
Colony of the Straits Settlements, 89, 105
Colville, Margret 'Rita' Henderson, 186
Commerce, 6, 75, 139
Commissioner of Police, 170, 192n32
Commissions of inquiry, 89
  See also Bushe Commission
Common law, 3–5, 16n4, 25, 57, 223, 224
  TANU's political agenda and, 138–141
Conferences, early 1960s, 140
Conflicts of interest, 64

Conservative and Unionist Society of the Inns of Court, 105
Constitutional conferences, 141–143
Constitutions
1961, 137, 141–145, 166, 178
Bill of Rights, 178, 196n87
Interim Constitution, 1965, 178, 204, 212
Republican Constitution, 1962, 142, 145, 146, 214
'standard form', 142
Cory, Hans, 158n17
Court of Appeal, 66
East Africa, 104
Eastern African Court of Appeal, 59, 76, 100, 104, 145, 160n47, 181, 239, 240
See also Central Court of Appeal
Court of Appeal of Tanzania, 177
Courts Integration Officer, 151
Courts Ordinance of 1920, 57
Courts Ordinance of 1930, 77
Courts Ordinance of 1941, 77
Criminal cases, 6, 59, 90, 96, 97, 99, 175
Criminal Procedure Code (India), 57, 90
Criminal Procedure Code (Tanganyika), 57, 90, 154
Cross, Philip L.U. (Ulric), 209, 221, 224, 225
Customary courts, 5, 6
Customary law, 66, 67, 72, 99, 153
codification, 140–141
move toward independence and, 136
Customary Law (Declaration) Orders (1963), 140
Customary Law Codification and Unification Project, 140, 141, 158n17
Customs, local, 62

D
Dar es Salaam
Governor based in, 56
judiciary based in, 55, 58, 60–62, 91, 96–98, 154
Dar es Salaam Club, 110, 166, 175, 176, 179
Dar es Salaam Club (Dissolution) Act, 176
Davies, L.A., 113
Death penalty, 6, 8, 111, 125n79
Decolonisation, 3, 4, 8–11, 13–15
colonial judges asked to stay on, 165, 168, 190, 240
common law system used, 138
costs, 155
See also Empire, end of (1961–1965); Judiciary: restructuring and empowering High Court (1959–1964)
Denning Committee, 220, 221
Denning, Lord, 220, 221
Detention, preventive, 179, 213
Deutsch, Jan-Georg, 55
Development, rhetoric of, 95, 238
Devonshire courses, 129n137
Dismissal, 41, 42, 105, 128n130, 146
protections, 137, 145
District Commissioners, 56, 65, 100, 148, 149, 154, 170
Nyerere and, 112
District Courts, 77, 97, 100, 151
German East Africa, 54, 55
See also Magistrates
District Magistracy, 171
District Officers, 56, 57, 65, 68, 72
Dominions, barristers from, 30, 33
DuBow, Frederic, 150
Duff, Liam B., 182
Duignan, Peter, 7, 51n79
Duman, Daniel, 29

E
East Africa, 1, 34, 36–38
  increasing prestige of Bench, 103–104
  lack of access to legal education, 171
  See also Kenya; Nyasaland (Malawi); Tanganyika
East Africa Protectorate, 59
Eastern African Court of Appeal, 59, 76, 100, 104, 145, 181, 239
  See also Court of Appeal
Economy, 87, 104, 139, 141
Elites, 215, 216
El-Kindy, Z.N., 221
Ellis, Patrick, 149, 154
Emoluments, 30, 34
Empire, end of (1961–1965), 8, 165–190, 238–240
  from Africanisation to localisation, 166, 167
  colonial judges in fading Empire, 172–175
  from colonial magistrates to post-colonial High Court judges, 182–184
  See also Foreign and African judges
English, Irish, and Scottish barristers, 28, 33
Equity before the law, 4, 57
Ethnic groups, 62, 136, 140, 149
Europeans, cases involving, 5, 62, 64
Expatriate community, 60, 64, 167, 175, 176, 187

F
Faculty of Law (Dar es Salaam), 12, 15, 202, 219, 240
First Class courts, 57, 65
Foreign and African judges, 201–227
  Asian advocates, 12, 15, 103, 104, 187, 201–205, 226
  Chief Justice Georges, 202, 207, 212–214, 225
  dynamics of diverse Bench, 223–225
  first Tanganyikan African judges, 215
  from West Indies, 201, 207
  Nigerian experiment, 205
  position and responses to encroachment on judiciary, 211–214
  Saidi, appointment of, 225
  See also Empire, end of (1961–1965)
Foreign Compensation Commission, 181
'Formal' colonial states, 5, 17n16
Furse, Ralph D., 29, 44, 93, 108

G
Gandhi, Mohandas K., 171
Gann, Lewis H., 7, 45
Georges, Telford, 202, 207, 211, 224
  departure, 225, 230n48
German East Africa, 53–55
German justice system, 54, 239
Ghana, 241, 242
Global judiciary, 26
Gordon, Jay, 11
Gorrie, John, 45
Governor-General, 142–144
Governors, 28, 38, 43, 55–57, 70, 77
Governor's Appeal Board, 100
Guard of Honour, 42

H
Haile, P.H.W., 101
Halwenge, Edward, 102, 127n105
Hamlyn, O.T., 189
Her Majesty's Overseas Civil Service, 108, 168, 175, 182

Her Majesty's Overseas Judiciary, 108, 175
High Court building, 97, 115, 132n190
High Court of Tanganyika (High Court of Tanzania), 3, 4, 8, 45
  appeals from local Courts, 99, 100, 148, 150
  beginning of, 53, 54, 58, 238
  circuit courts (assizes), 60–62, 92, 95, 98
  functions, 58–64, 73
  hierarchical system, 5
  as hybrid institution, 58
  as legacy of British colonial rule, 114–118
  methods and sources, 11–13
  post-World War II, 11–13
  size of Bench, 144
  structure of system, 57–58
  as top tier of unified system, 137, 150, 151
  See also Indirect rule; Judiciary: restructuring and empowering High Court (1959–1964); Judiciary: resurgence and expansion (1945–1958)
His Majesty's Dinner for Judges, 43

I
Ibhawoh, Bonny, 6, 63, 82n63
Ideology, imperial, 54
Iliffe, John, 67, 87, 88
Imperial expansion, 3–4
Independence, 8, 9, 88, 106
  Africanisation and localisation, 166, 167
  customary law and, 136
  India, 171
  late 1950s, 135
  Nyerere and, 111–114
  staffing challenges, 153–155, 166, 168, 169
  transition to, Constitution and, 140–145
India, 27, 28, 171
  African students in, 217
Indian Association, 75
Indian Civil Service (ICS), 27, 28, 30
Indian Evidence Act, 57
Indian Penal and Criminal Procedure Codes, 57, 90
Indirect rule, 3, 5, 6, 8, 11, 88
  assessors and interpreters, 62–64
  backlog of cases, 58, 60, 92
  bifurcated legal system, 5, 6, 36, 54, 58, 139, 146
  customary law, 66–68
  District Officers, 56, 57
  marginalisation of the High Court under (1920–1944), 53–77
  Native Authorities, 56, 57, 66
  Native Courts Ordinance of 1929, 14, 53, 58, 69, 76
  rival ideologies, 70
  size of judiciary, 70
  subordinate courts, 57, 65, 66
Indirect Rule and the Search for Justice (Morris and Read), 11
Inns of Court, 32, 45, 218, 224
Interim Constitution of 1965, 204
Intermediaries, African, 62
Interpreters, 62, 63
Irish barristers, 44, 51n77
Islamic law, 66, 132n193, 140, 158n14

J
Jamaican Bench, 94
James, R.W., 212
Japan, 105
Jhaveri, Kantilal L., 113
Joint Committee for the Inns of Court, 31, 33, 108
Judges' and Magistrates' Conferences, 209

Judicial advisers, 100, 126n95
Judicial Advisers' Conferences, 100, 147
Judicial Committee of the Privy Council, *see* Privy Council
Judicial Service Commission, 143–145, 153
Judiciary, colonial, 1–3, 6–8, 88, 106
  administrators, tensions with, 26, 91, 94
  African, 101, 202, 205, 215
  age of entry, 41
  counterparts, interaction with, 76
  decolonization, judges asked to stay on, 165, 166, 168, 169, 190, 240
  in fading Empire, 172
  geographic flexibility, 26
  individual impact, 10, 167
  influence on administrators, 74
  limited prospects in Great Britain, post-independence, 172
  main role, 75
  motivations for remaining post-independence, 172, 181, 184, 185, 189, 190
  negative reputation, 26, 33
  in post-colonial state, 175–181
  salaries, 36, 70, 71, 85n104, 93, 124n65
  as second-rate barristers, 12, 13
  security of tenure, pre-1961, 41, 106, 137
  social interactions, 64, 110
  socio-economic class, 28, 29, 33–35, 42, 43
  subjects as, 28, 37, 38
  transfer between colonies, 25, 30, 32, 36, 37, 40, 41, 94
  See also Colonial Legal Service; Foreign and African judges; Judiciary, post-independence
Judiciary, post-independence
  professionalisation of, 137, 151–153
  security of tenure, 1961 provision, 137, 143, 144, 146, 156
  See also Foreign and African judges; Judiciary, colonial
Judiciary: restructuring and empowering High Court (1959–1964), 135–156, 173, 239
  British judges remaining, 153, 156
  common law and TANU's political agenda, 138
  constitutions and, 141–147
  costs, 155
  dismantling of 'parallel' court system, 135–137, 147–150
  expanded judiciary, 152–153
  peak of power: High Court and Magistrates' Courts Act, 151–153
  Privy Council and, 137, 143
  structural transformation, 136, 137, 147–150
  See also Unification
Judiciary: resurgence and expansion (1945–1958), 87–118
  Bushe Commission, 89, 95, 96, 109
  growing bench, 95–98
  High Court as legacy of British colonial rule, 114
  increasing prestige in East Africa, 103
  Legal Service after WWII, 105
  new crop of colonial legal officers, 109–111
  Nyerere and independence struggle, 111
  toward structural and racial integration, 98
Jury system, 62
Just' court systems rhetoric, 115
Justices of the Peace (Newfoundland), 26

K
Kalunga, Leopold, 208
Kambona, Oscar, 192n32
Kassam, F.M., 212
Kawawa, Rashidi, 168, 169
Kenya, 8, 37, 38, 59, 76, 89, 90, 92, 104, 126n94, 135, 241
  colleges, 219
  Mau Mau rebellion, 8, 111, 114, 175, 195n65
Kilimanjaro Native Cooperative Union, 217
Kimicha, Mark P.K., 218–219
Kings African Rifles, 109
Kirk-Greene, Anthony H.M., 28, 87
Kisanga, Robert H., 216, 222
Kiswahili language, 36, 63, 148, 152, 153, 209
Knighthood, 43
Kwikima, Musa H.H., 221

L
Language gaps, 62
Language qualifications, 36–37
Law, Charles E., 109
Law, Eric J.E., 34, 109, 175, 176, 178, 181, 195n65
Law Faculty, *see* Faculty of Law (Dar es Salaam)
League of Nations, 3, 11, 53, 55, 56, 88
Legal Advisers, 29, 31, 32, 35, 37, 75
  See also Bushe, Henry G.
Legal Probationership Scheme, 107, 129n135
Legal qualifications, 15, 30, 144, 156, 240
  fight for access to, 216
  first Tanganyikan African judges, 215
  post-independence challenges, 155, 168, 171
  training, post-independence, 201–203, 215–219
Legal Scholarship Scheme, 107
Legal Service, *see* Colonial Legal Service
Legislative Council, 102, 172
Lewis-Barned. John F., 148
Liberalism, 5
Lifestyle, 34, 42, 108
Local bar, 27
Local Courts, 99–101, 103, 135–137, 147–150, 238
Local Courts (Minister for Justice and Regional Local Courts Officers) Act, 149
Local Courts Adviser, 100, 101, 125n84, 125n90
Local Courts Appeals Officer, 148
Local Courts of Appeal, 148–149
Local Courts Ordinance (1951), 99–100
Local Government Training Centre (Mzumbe), 151
Localisation, 166, 167, 188
  Faculty of Law and, 219–223
Lord Advocate of Scotland, 32
Lord Chancellor of Britain, 115
Lord Chief Justice of Northern Ireland, 32
Lugard, Lord, 56, 73

M
Macleod, Norman, 182
Macmillan, Harold, 157n3
Magistrates, 12–14, 27, 28, 88, 147
  from colonial magistrates to post-colonial High Court judges, 182
  extended jurisdiction, 59–61, 91, 92
  first class, 57, 65
  professional, 65

resident magistrates, 1, 65, 75, 77, 79n24, 96, 217, 218
senior, 40
senior resident magistrates, 95
Tabora incident, 213
Third Class, 57, 65, 102
training, 74
See also Administrators; District Courts
Magistrates' Courts Act, 137, 151–153, 156, 219, 239
Majority rule, 141
Makame, Louis, 211, 216, 218, 224
Makerere College, Uganda, 215–217
Malecela, John, 217
Mandate system, 3, 17n17, 55, 56, 67, 78n12, 88
Manning, Julie, 222
Mau Mau rebellion (Kenya), 8, 111, 114, 175, 195n65
Mawalla, Juma, 218
McAuslan, Patrick, 203, 208, 220, 221, 223
McLaren, John, 27
Member of Local Government, 100
Minaki (St. Andrews College), 215
Minimum Sentences Act (1963), 166, 176–179
Minister for Legal Affairs, 148
Ministry of Lands, Settlemen and Water Development, 183
'Mixed-race' barristers, 38
Mkondya, Humphrey Noel Z., 218
Monarchy of Great Britain, 137, 142, 145
Morris, H. F., 11, 39, 101, 110
Mustafa, Abdulla, 204, 205, 224, 225
Mustafa, Sophia, 204–205
Mutiny and trial, 166, 178–180
Mwanza High Court, 97, 154, 209

N

Nairobi, Asian advocates in, 204
See also Eastern African Court of Appeal
National Assembly, 151
Native Authorities, 56, 57, 66
Native Courts, 10, 14, 18n18, 28, 57–59, 66, 91, 237
1925 ordinances, 66
1951 Local Courts ordinance, 99
customary law and, 66–68
See also Local Courts
Native Courts Ordinance of 1929, 14, 53, 58, 69, 76, 100, 150, 237
Natives, 54, 78n4
Natural law, 68
Newfoundland, 26
Nigeria, 56, 73, 86n125, 205, 242
judges from, 201
Non-Africans, 59, 60, 66, 139
civil servants, 168, 170, 171
'Non-natives', 54, 55
Nyalali, Francis L., 12, 222
Nyasaland (Malawi), 8, 59, 109, 111, 135
Nyerere, Julius K., 15, 111–114, 185
Africanisation and, 168–170, 172, 180, 188
Biron's views and, 184–187
Constitution and, 142, 159n28
Customary Law Codification and Unification Project, 140
dismantling of 'parallel' court systems and, 147
foreign judges and, 201–206, 213
Georges and, 209, 212, 224, 241
Minimum Sentences Act and, 176
mutiny and, 178–180
as President, 146, 170
as Prime Minister, 169
self-sufficiency as goal for Tanganyika, 219–220
trial of, 112

O

Onyiuke, G.C.M., 206, 207, 225
Order in Council, 1961, 160n47
Order in Council for Tanganyika (1920), 56, 57, 67, 79n13
Otto, A.E., 182
Overseas Aid Agreement, 169, 172
Overseas Civil Service, *see* Her Majesty's Overseas Civil Service
Overseas Service Resettlement Bureau, 174

P

Palestine, 175
'Parallel' court systems, 77, 98, 101, 115, 117, 139
  dismantling of, 136, 147, 239
Paris Peace Conference (1919), 55
Parkinson, Charles, 178
Parliament, 142–146
Parliamentary draftsman, 151
Patronage, 27
Paul, George G. (Graham), 94
Peripatetic model, 154
Personal ties and preferences, 167
Pfeiffer, Steven B., 106
Platt, Harold G., 176, 178, 179, 182–184, 224, 225, 240
Police, 167, 169, 170, 179, 214
Pre-colonial justice, 54
President, 145, 146
Presidential Commission on a One-Party State, 204
Preventive detention, 179, 213, 214
Preventive Detention Law, 179, 213
Primary Court magistrates, 151, 152, 154
Primary Courts, 151, 219
Prime Minister, 142–144, 169
Pritt, D.N., 113, 114
Privy Council, 6, 41, 59, 66, 100, 103
  Eastern African Court of Appeal and, 103, 146
  end of appeals to, 146
  restructuring and, 137, 143, 239
Promotion, 38–40
Provincial Commissioners, 56, 65, 72, 77, 96
  Local Courts and, 99
  post-World War II, 96
  removal from process (1962), 148, 170
Provincial Commissioners' Conference, 102
Provincial Local Courts officer, 148
Public Service Commission, 144
Public services, 171
Puisne judges, 58, 80n30, 143, 144, 146
Punishment and sentencing, 6, 90
  Minimum Sentences Act (1963), 166, 176–178
  revision, 57, 59, 72, 80n36

R

Racial issues, 10
  assessors and juries, 62
  Dar es Salaam Club, 110, 166, 176, 195n70
  German colonial legal system, 54–55
  judicial bifurcation, 5, 6, 54, 57, 58, 98, 136, 140, 147
  'mixed-race' barristers, 37–38
  move toward equality, 136, 137
Ranger, Terrance, 221
Rattansey, M.N., 113
Read, James S., 11, 39, 68, 178
Regional administration, 149
Regional Local Courts officers, 149, 154
Regional Secretaries, 170
Registrar to the High Court of Uganda, 90
Reide, Graham J.E., 182, 197n111
Religion, 215

Republican Constitution (1962), 137, 145, 146
'Repugnancy clause', 68, 72, 99
Resident magistrates, 1, 65, 75, 79n24, 96, 217, 218
  Tanganyikan Africans, 217
Resident Magistrates' Courts, 151, 152
Retirement, 40, 41, 143, 169, 173
  forced, 89, 105
Risley, J.S., 31
Roberts-Wray, Kenneth, 101, 173
Rule of law, 4, 6, 11, 12
Russell, William A. (Alison), 69, 74, 85n104, 108, 144, 150
Rwanda, 53

S

Saidi, Augustino B. (Augustine), 217–219, 222, 225, 226, 241
St. Francis School, Pugu, 215
St. Mary's Tabora Government School, 215
Salaries, 34, 71, 85n104, 93, 124n65
Samatta, Barnabas A., 222
Sauti ya TANU (newspaper), 112
Schools, 215–217
Scotland, barristers and judiciary, 28, 34, 182
Seaton, Earle E., 210, 211, 226
Second Class courts, 57, 66, 102
Secretary for Native Affairs of Tanganyika, 90
Secretary of State for the Colonies, 41, 90, 92, 101, 105
Senior resident magistrates, 95
Separation of powers, 11, 137, 143, 145, 149, 150, 153
Shauri councils, 55, 78n6
Sheridan, Joseph A., 72
Simmons, Ernest B., 172
Social interactions, 61, 64, 110
Societies Ordinance of 1954, 112
Solicitors, 28, 107
South Africa, 142
Southern Rhodesia, 142, 183
Special Tribunal, 57, 58
Special Tribunals Act, 179
Spry, John, 181
Staffing, 25–29
Standard form, 142
Standardisation, 25–26
Stipendiary Magistrates, 65
Stockwell, Sarah, 21n40
Subjects, colonial, 45, 62
  as judges, 28, 37
Subordinate courts (First, Second, and Third Class), 57, 65, 103
Sudan Political Service, 93
Summerfield, John, 113
Superior Judge, 55
Supervisory magistrates, 152
Supreme courts, 242
Swanepoel, Paul, 19n28

T

Tabora incident, 213
Tanganyika, 35, 38, 41, 44, 45
  beginning of British rule, 55–57
  constitution, 137, 141
  gains independence, 1961, 1–3, 135
  indirect rule, 53
  mutiny and trial, 166, 179
  peaceful transfer of power, 241, 242
  See also Tanzania
Tanganyika African National Union (TANU), 111–114, 136, 139, 204, 216
  Africanisation and, 168
  constitution and, 141, 146
  dismantling of 'parallel' court systems and, 147, 150
Tanganyika Law Society, 103, 174
Tanganyika Legislative Council, 204

Tanganyika Rifles, 170
The Tanganyika Territory, 55–56
Tanzania
  merger with Zanzibar, 1964, 16n3
  as one-party state, 204, 212
  as socialist state, 212, 240
Tenure, 41
Terrell, A.K. a'Beckett, 89, 105
Territorial governments
  incremental approach, 29–30
  language requirements, 36
  transfer policy, 25, 30, 32, 36, 40, 95
Territorial ordinances, orders, and proclamations, 57
Third Class courts, 57, 65, 102
Three-tier court system, 137, 151, 153, 162n87, 239
Traditional authorities and institutions, 3–5, 17n11, 56, 94
Tribes, 67, 140
Tribunals, 58, 146, 179
Trinidad, 208, 209, 225
Trusteeship Council (United Nations), 88, 102
Turnbull, Richard G., 113
Twining, Edward F., 112, 114
Twining, William, 220

U
Uganda, 38, 59, 76, 90, 92, 101, 215, 220
Ujamaa policies, 240
Unification, 32, 33, 35–37, 40, 43, 137, 138, 140, 141
  High Court as top tier of unified system, 138, 150
  tiers, 138, 151, 162n87, 239
United Nations, 87, 88, 102, 112
University of Dar es Salaam, 221
University of East Africa, 220
University of Khartoum, 171
University of London, 220–221

W
Walker, Robert, 58
Wa-Meru community, 211
'Water Court', 183
Webb, Henry, 94
Weiner, Martin, 4
West Africa, 57, 62, 107, 171, 190, 241, 242
  judges from, 201, 205–207, 240
West African Court of Appeal, 104
West Indies, 40
  judges from, 165, 190, 201, 207–211, 241
Weston, A.B., 220
Weston, Laurence, 181
Widner, Jennifer, 12, 139, 209, 212, 226
Wigs, 7, 227
Williams, David J., 173, 174, 197n111
Williams, J.K., 182
Wilson, Geoffrey, 192n32, 193n32
Wilson, Mark, 94
Windham, Ralph, 175, 179–181, 187, 189, 207, 208
Witnesses, 61, 91
Women judges, 222
Working Party on the Integration of the Court Systems, 151
World War I, 53, 55
World War II, 43

Z
Zanzibar, 16n3, 59, 219

Kolibri 360 GmbH
Ferdinand-Jühlke-Straße 7
99095 Erfurt, Deutschland
produktsicherheit@kolibri360.de